READER'S DIGEST

all-season guide to gardening

winter

READER'S DIGEST

all-season guide to gardening

winter

PUBLISHED BY
THE READER'S DIGEST ASSOCIATION LIMITED
LONDON • NEW YORK • SYDNEY • MONTREAL

plant selector 72

a photographic guide to the best plants in winter

garden projects 118

ideas and practical instructions on ways to improve your garden

contents

foreword

The *All-Season Guide to Gardening* provides a complete practical and inspirational guide to making the most of your garden season-by-season, with year-round detailed information to help you plan, plant and enjoy the garden of your dreams. Each of the volumes is presented in four key sections:

inspirations offers a source of design and planting ideas taken from contemporary and traditional gardens photographed during the season. The plants featured have been identified to enable you to re-create or adapt the ideas to your own garden scheme.

practical diary is a guide to the most important tasks to be done in the garden at this time of year. The information is divided into subject areas – such as Perennials, Climbers, or Patios & Containers – that reflect particular gardening interests. The headings appear in the same order in every volume in the series, so you can easily find the information you need. Under each heading is a list of the season's main tasks. The most important jobs are then explained in more detail, with step-by-step photographs and expert tips. The Healthy Garden, at the end of the section, is a full checklist of priority seasonal tasks for the whole garden. Since many jobs require follow-up attention in a later season, a 'Looking

useful terms

alpine Although this strictly refers to a mountain plant that grows naturally in free-draining soil at high altitude, the term is used by gardeners to mean any plant suitable for growing in a rock garden.
annual A plant that grows, flowers, sets seed and dies in one growing season.
anther The part of the flower that produces pollen.
aquatic plant In its widest sense, this can mean any water plant, but usually refers to plants such as water lilies that grow in deeper water, rooted in the bottom of the pond or in special baskets.
bareroot This refers to plants, usually trees and shrubs, that have been dug up and supplied to the customer without any soil on their roots. Roses are often supplied in this way.
bedding (plant) A plant used outdoors for temporary or seasonal display, often as part of a planned 'bedding scheme'.
biennial A plant that completes its life cycle in two growing seasons.
biological control The treatment or prevention of pests, diseases or weeds by natural, rather than chemical, methods, usually involving a naturally occurring parasite or predator.
cloche A glass or plastic cover used to shelter plants from cold or windy weather. Cloches are available as separate units or in tunnel form, often called 'continuous cloches'.
coldframe A low, unheated structure with a transparent top, in which plants can be grown in protected conditions.
cordon A plant restricted by pruning and training to a single, unbranching stem. Examples include apples, tomatoes and sweet peas grown on canes.
corm The swollen stem base of plants like crocuses and gladioli, where food is stored during winter. A new corm forms each year on top of the shrivelled remains of last year's.
cultivar A distinct, named plant variety that has originated in cultivation, rather than in the wild. Cultivars are often simply (but incorrectly) called 'varieties'.
deadhead To cut off the spent flowers.
die-back The result of attack by a fungal disease, which causes shoots or branches to die back from their tips.
direct sow To sow seeds in the ground where the plants are to grow, rather than starting them indoors or in a temporary seedbed for later transplanting.
drill A furrow or channel made in the soil at the correct depth for sowing seeds.
ericaceous Any plant belonging to the erica or heather family, for example pieris and rhododendrons. Also refers to the acid conditions these plants like and the special lime-free compost in which they are potted.
espalier A tree such as an apple or cotoneaster that is pruned and trained as a single upright trunk, with side branches extending horizontally to form symmetrical layers or 'tiers'.
foliar feed Liquid fertiliser sprayed or watered on the leaves of plants, usually applied for rapid results or when plants are not actively absorbing nutrients through their roots (after injury or in cold weather, for example).
glyphosate A chemical weedkiller that is absorbed through leaves and moves through the plant so that all parts, including roots, are killed (see systemic).
habitat The natural home of a plant growing in the wild. Not to be confused with habit, which is the typical form or shape of a plant.
harden off To gradually acclimatise a plant previously grown indoors to unprotected conditions outside in the garden.
hardwood cutting A piece of this year's shoot taken for propagation from a shrub, tree or climber during the autumn, when their stems are hard and ripe.
heel A small strip of bark torn from the main stem when a sideshoot is pulled off to make a (heel) cutting.
heel in To bury the roots of a plant in a temporary hole or trench when it is not to be planted immediately.
humus The dark, water-retentive component of soil that results from the decay of organic material.
in situ Literally, in position, or where plants are to grow permanently.
internodal cutting A cutting that is trimmed midway between two leaf-joints, rather than immediately below the leaves.
layering A method of propagation in which a shoot is rooted while still attached to the

ahead' feature indicates when you will find details of follow-up action in another volume.

plant selector is a directory of the plants which are at their best at this time of year, as selected by our gardening experts. Within each subject grouping the plants are arranged by colour, and within each colour sequence they are generally listed alphabetically by botanical name. Each plant is shown in a photograph, with information supplied including the plant's common name, size, site and soil preferences, best uses, general care and suggestions for good companions. Each plant is also given a 'hardiness' rating:

- 'Hardy' plants can be grown outdoors in all parts of the British Isles.
- Plants rated 'not fully hardy' can be grown outdoors in milder parts of the British Isles but elsewhere will need some protection in winter.
- 'Half-hardy' plants can withstand temperatures down to 0°C (32°F). They are often grown outdoors in summer displays, but propagated and kept under glass between autumn and late spring.
- 'Tender' plants require protection under glass for all or part of the year.

At the end of the section, there are lists of the plants best suited to different garden conditions and soil types.

garden projects offers ideas and instructions for garden improvements, ranging from building a patio, pergola or raised bed to designing and planting up a new border or pond. Major DIY projects are illustrated with step-by-step photographs and all the projects are within the capabilities of a fit, practical person. Although some projects are specific to a season, many of them can also be undertaken at other times of the year.

parent plant. Rooting a branch where it touches the ground is called simple layering, while serpentine layering involves rooting a long flexible stem in several places; long stems can be tip layered by burying their growing tips.
loam A type of soil that contains a balanced mixture of sand, clay and organic material.
marginal plant A waterside plant that is grown at the edge of the pond, either in shallow water or on the bank.
mulch Any material used to cover and protect the soil surface. Organic mulches include straw, manure and lawn mowings, while polythene sheet and stones are examples of inorganic mulches.
naturalise To deliberately plant, or allow plants to grow and spread, as in the wild.
node The place on a plant's stem where a leaf forms.
nursery bed A piece of ground specially reserved for raising young plants.
organic This literally refers to any material derived from decomposed animal or plant remains. It is also used to describe a gardening approach that uses little or no obviously chemical substances such as fertilisers and pesticides.
perlite A granular, absorbent soil or compost additive made from expanded volcanic rock.
perennial **(correctly herbaceous perennial)** A durable non-woody plant whose soft, leafy growth dies down in winter, but grows again the following year.
pinch out To remove a growing tip, using finger and thumb.
pot on To move a potted plant into a larger container.
pot (up) To transfer a plant from a seedtray or open ground into a pot.
prick out To transplant seedlings from where they have been sown to a container or piece of ground where they will have more space to grow.
rhizome An underground root (strictly, a stem) that behaves like a bulb by storing food from one season to the next. Also used to describe the buried creeping shoots by which some plants, especially grasses, spread underground.
rootballed This describes plants packaged for delivery by wrapping their mass of roots and soil or compost in a net bag.
rootstock (or stock) The rooted portion of a grafted tree. This usually influences the habit and ultimate size of the selected variety joined onto it (the scion).
seedbed A piece of ground for raising seeds, specially prepared by removing all weeds, stones and large lumps of soil.
semi-ripe cutting A section of this year's stem cut off for propagation, usually during summer while the tip is still soft but the base has become firm and woody.
softwood cutting A cutting prepared from a portion of a young new shoot that has not started to harden.
spit A measurement of depth equal to the length of a spade-blade (about 25cm/10in).
standard A trained form of woody plant with a single upright stem that is clear of all leaves and shoots. Full standard trees have trunks about 1.8m (6ft) high, half-standards 1.2m (4ft). Standard roses are about 1m (3ft) high, while half-standards have 75cm (2ft 6in) stems.
subsoil The lower layer of ground below the topsoil (see below). Often paler and relatively infertile, this is usually coarser in texture and hard to cultivate.
sucker A shoot growing from below ground and away from the main stem of a plant, sometimes from its rootstock.
systemic A type of pesticide, fungicide or weedkiller sprayed onto leaves and absorbed into all plant parts in its sap.
tender perennial A plant that can live for several years but cannot tolerate frost or very cold conditions.
thin out To reduce the number of plants, buds or fruit so that those remaining have enough room to develop fully.
tip cuttings Softwood cuttings (see above) formed from the outer ends of young shoots.
top-dressing An application of fertiliser, organic material or potting compost spread on the surface. Also refers to replacing the top layer of compost in a large container with a fresh supply.
topgrowth The upper, visible part of a plant above ground level.
topsoil The upper layer of soil, usually darker and more fertile than the layers below (see subsoil), and where plants develop most of their feeding roots.
tuber A fat, underground root (in dahlias, for example) or stem (begonias), constructed differently from a bulb or corm but used in the same way for storing food from one season to the next.
variety Botanically, a distinctly different variation of a plant that has developed in the wild, but commonly used to mean the same as cultivar (see left).

inspirations

The garden may appear to sleep in winter, but there is still much to enjoy, especially on those crystal clear mornings when the sun shines on frost or snow. Outside is a fascinating world of patterns and shapes, with the garden stripped bare to reveal its bones and structure. Delicate, often fragrant winter blossoms, handsome evergreens and the bewitching colours of stems and bark entice the gardener out to experience the crisp air and winter sun. In a well-planned garden, winter is foreshortened by the appearance of snowdrops or cheery yellow aconites, by fragrant winter honeysuckle and daphne, as well as early flowering rhododendrons. Spring is just around the corner.

winter wonderland

The redeeming joys of winter are crisp, Christmas-card scenes of frost and ice. Treading the first footprints in a garden blanketed with smooth clean snow and exploring the novelty of familiar landscapes clad in white will delight young and old alike.

The wildlife hedge and boundary trees of a country garden are spangled by glistening hoar frost (right). Having lost their leaves for winter, these deciduous plants are well adapted to withstand the cold.

The foliage and dead flower spikes of ornamental grasses persist until spring, providing valuable winter outlines. They appear ethereal when brought alive by frost, snow and swirling mist (above). Shear them back just before the new growth pushes through.

Minus their summer garb of foliage and flowers, gardens are pared back to their basic outlines. A good structure with well-shaped specimen trees and ornament pays off in this season (below).

Snow is an exciting and transforming phenomenon (below), changing not just the scenery, but altering familiar light patterns and muffling sound. Gently relieve evergreen branches of their heavy burden where necessary, to prevent permanent damage.

The flat planes of a contemporary garden are picked out in snow (left). The decking, boardwalks and water are simply edged with bamboo, but endless variation is provided by the play of light, reflection and shadows.

Garden features steal the scene in this snow-covered small town garden (below left). Snow accentuates every detail of the trellis work, the brick wall catches a coating along its top, and the box balls appear like puddings dusted with icing sugar.

Frosty weather is often welcome – especially when accompanied by sun and blue skies (below) – and it also helps to kill off overwintering bugs. Remember to put out food and, more importantly, water for the birds.

evergreen splendour

The outlines and foliage colours provided by evergreens add substance to a garden all year round, but their shapely domes, spires and mounds are most rewarding during winter.

Careful pruning and training to enhance and accentuate the natural shape of evergreens can turn them into living sculptures. Look at what nature delivers, then clear trunks and trim growth until plants like this *Juniperus* x *pfitzeriana* really stand out in the winter garden (left).

A good mix of evergreen and deciduous shrubs provides variety in a winter border, their twiggy outlines complemented by bolder evergreen shapes (below). Frost highlights the shoot tips and leaflets of *Choisya ternata* and, behind, the pale, dangling flower tassels of *Garrya elliptica*.

In winter, the bones of a garden shine through (left), and hard materials like shingle, gravel and brick are almost as important as the tufted sisyrinchium and medusa-like *Euphorbia myrsinites*. Sage and ornamental grasses are left unpruned until spring.

Box clipped into rounded shapes adds valuable substance to a winter garden (above). Maintain topiary by one or two clips between mid-spring and summer. Russet beech and dark green cypress provide walls of contrasting foliage.

Against a backdrop of natural, informal evergreens, the lines of clipped hedges and topiary add drama to the garden. The larger leaves of the variegated holly contrast beautifully with the tight foliage of a yew hedge (below).

Conifers offer endless variety of shapes, colours and textures, creating magical winter scenes. This selection is set off by the russet beech hedge (left).

A dramatic evergreen, *Helleborus foetidus* has lobed leaves and pale green winter flowers that contrast well with box and purple-tinged *Viola labradorica* (right).

shapes & outlines

Stripped to its bones by winter weather, the beauty of a garden falls back on sound basic structure, rather than relying on its summer finery. This framework depends on well-shaped plants, the silhouette of trees and the flow of lawns, paths and boundaries.

Ivy leaves drape this low wall, hiding its hard, angular outlines and complementing the box spirals (above). Ivy is a fast, easy plant to grow and will need keeping in check. Cut back invading stems when necessary.

The angular shape of timber structures is reflected by the box pyramids punctuating a low hedge of looser foliage (right). Formal repetition makes pleasing patterns and is worth the effort spent in planning, shaping and clipping.

A dusting of snow highlights the theatrical elements in this whimsical town garden (left). Crinkled ornamental cabbages, container rims and clipped box are all outlined in powdery white.

Relying entirely on deciduous plants, this juxtaposition of tree trunks at varying heights creates a cathedral-like garden 'room' (right). A line of pleached trees rises higher than the glowing beech enclosure, framing still taller trees beyond.

The strong shapes of yew and solid, spherical cardoon heads provide focal points among the frosted stems of shrub roses and perennials (left). Without these 'pegs', the wispy remains of last season's borders are in danger of looking messy.

The contorted hazel (*Corylus avellana* 'Contorta') makes fantastic patterns against landscape and sky (right). If you cannot find room in a bed or border for this sculptural plant, it will thrive in a large container, perhaps underplanted with *Euphorbia amygdaloides* var. *robbiae* and dwarf narcissi.

A crisp frost hardens the shapeliness of this dynamic winter garden (below). Packed borders and vertical conifers are offset by the sweeping curve of lawn and hedge. Arcs etched in the lawn are a clever detail. Set deep, they will not interfere with mowing.

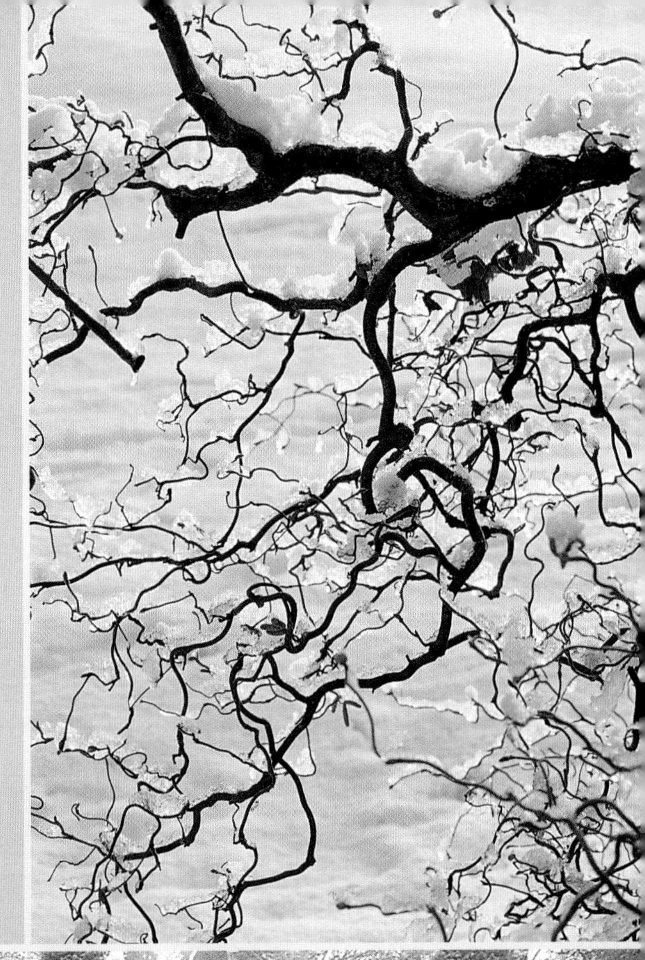

bark, berries & flowering shrubs

Plants whose chief display is timed for the colder months provide the gilding of the winter garden. Shrubs with colourful stems, bark and twiggy outlines lend a permanent beauty, while those with berries and flowers give a succession of surprises.

Massed plantings of burgundy-leaved *Cotoneaster horizontalis* and the grass *Stipa arundinacea* look most effective during winter (left). Snowy birch stems complete the scene.

Plants chosen for their dramatic stem colours work well in bold groups (below). The ghostly wands of *Rubus thibetanus* rise from winter-flowering heathers behind the rounded leaves of *Bergenia* 'Sunningdale'. Prune this rubus by cutting all stems back hard, almost to the base, in spring.

Iris foetidissima

The Himalayan birch (*Betula utilis* var. *jacquemontii*) has brilliant white bark (below).

Of all the dogwoods grown for their winter stems, *Cornus sanguinea* 'Winter Beauty' (left) is probably the best for smaller gardens as it grows slowly and to less stature than some of its cousins. The frost-covered, shrimp-pink stems associate well with the *Juniperus virginiana* behind.

If considering a small tree for the garden, bear in mind the witch hazels (*Hamamelis*). These slow-growing plants (below) have abundant spidery, scented flowers of yellow, orange or red that open against bare branches in late winter. They enjoy sheltered woodland conditions.

Some evergreen shrubs present lively and often scented winter flowers as well as colourful foliage. *Mahonia* x *wagneri* 'Moseri' (left) will reach 1.5m (5ft). It will grow in shade, but its leaves colour best in sun.

Plants whose fruit persists well into winter breathe colour and life into gardens sleeping under winter's mantle. *Cotoneaster frigidus* 'Cornubia' makes a large shrub liberally strung with shiny red fruit (right).

walls & fences

Walls and fences look best when they blend with the landscape and harmonise with the style of house and garden. Their structure, material, proportion and position are all made more prominent by the sparsity of winter, highlighting the tone of mellow brick or the lines of shapely woodwork.

Strong boundaries serve a practical purpose, but also play an aesthetic role, adding beauty and proportion on wintry days (above). When snow settles on the horizontals, it brings a simple beech hedge and rustic fence alive.

Old walls are a bonus to gardens, offering a sympathetic and protective backdrop for most plants. A cherub ornament complements weathered bricks, and in winter has gained an attractive cap of snow (top right).

Bleak, snowy landscapes and pale winter skies encourage dramatic silhouettes. Full advantage is taken here, with a topiarised yew flanking the post of a 'Lutyens-style' oak gate (right).

Criss-crossed by leafless stems, a close-boarded fence forms a natural backdrop to the skeletons of winter (left). The bleached grasses, gaunt sea holly and supports for dead or dormant climbers and perennials are enhanced by frost and sun.

A trelliswork screen (above) adds an instant vertical surface for climbers in summer, while in winter the low sun creates interesting shadow patterns from the bare structure. Vistas appear in the openings, giving possibilities for siting ornaments, seats or key plants.

A walled garden is the ultimate retreat (below), especially when the walls are of natural stone. Expertly placed in the landscape, this wall and doorway are perfectly proportioned. Note the paired topiary and grey-green *Garrya elliptica*, accentuating a simple formal design.

cold-weather containers

Use containers to bring colour right up to the house, even in winter. A microcosm of all that is good in the garden can be admired, whatever the weather, just outside the door or window. Use mixtures of evergreens and seasonal flowers.

Containers provide the opportunity to grow hardy shrubs that may not suit the soil of your garden. Acid-loving pieris (far left) are lime-haters, but can be potted into ericaceous compost and watered with rain collected in a butt.

Garden centres offer a good choice of seasonal plants to fill a large pot for late winter. Here, *Helleborus hybridus* takes centre stage, surrounded by *Narcissus* 'February Gold' and *Euonymus fortunei* Blondy. *Chamaecyparis pisifera* 'Sungold' adds a touch of brilliance (left).

A stone trough filled with ivy, *Iris reticulata* and snowdrops.

A late winter container display of snowdrops and *Iris reticulata* can be enjoyed close to the house. Here, the plants are simply arranged in an old metal bucket and clay pots (left). Plant the bulbs in autumn, or cheat and buy plants in bud.

Plants in pots can be a moveable feast. These heavy terracotta pots filled with tufts of evergreen sedges (below) are sitting on neat platforms fitted with castors, which keep the pots raised off the ground for good drainage as well as making them more mobile.

Planted up in autumn, this combination of hebes, heathers, winter-flowering pansies, conifer and ivies (left) is a fine example of a collection that will take over from summer-flowering plants for the autumn, winter and spring period.

Winter hanging baskets need to be brim-full right from the start, as they will not grow much until spring. This clever mixture of hardy cyclamen, hellebore, marble-leaved arum, ivies and white-flowered heather (above) relies chiefly on foliage shape and colour. Hang in a sheltered place, safe from cold winds.

The winter cherry (*Solanum capsicastrum*) is surprisingly hardy as long as there isn't a prolonged freeze. Here, it forms the centrepiece for a mixture of hardy, silvery *Brachyglottis* 'Sunshine' and variegated *Euonymus fortunei* 'Silver Queen' (above). The solanum can be replaced if it succumbs to the weather.

For a tall narrow space, a standard *Viburnum tinus* is potted into a slender galvanised container (left). This winter-flowering evergreen is hardy, but its blooms will benefit from some shelter.

A winter window box of red-berried skimmia and glossy ivies (below) is festive, and ideally suited to a town house. In spring, the skimmias can be transplanted to the garden, making space in the box for summer flowers.

winter borders

Bright stems, fresh winter flowers, evergreens, and the seed heads and skeletal remains of last season's growth – winter borders allow us to enjoy plants at every stage, and give us cause to celebrate all the different seasons of the garden.

Many gardeners now leave the cutting back and clearing until late winter or spring, letting their gardens drift into sleep as autumn turns to winter. This approach favours wildlife, while dying growth insulates the plants and frosted outlines remain to be enjoyed (right).

This double herbaceous border of classic proportions (above) is enhanced by a dramatic silvering of frost. The dead stems and decaying flower and seed heads create a scene that is all the more magical for being so fleeting.

The bareness of winter draws attention to minute details of leaf and form. Frost outlines the toothed divisions of silvery cotton lavender (*Santolina*), while the dry flowerheads make interesting shapes against the sword-like leaves of new zealand flax (right).

The spidery, fragrant burnt-sugar blossoms of witch hazel (*Hamamelis* x *intermedia* 'Jelena') lead the way in this cheerful late winter border (left). Ghostly backing is provided by *Rubus biflorus* and the ivy-clad ground is studded with winter aconite (*Eranthis hyemalis*) and pink-flowered heaths.

Winter borders need never be dull. Here, the red stems of *Cornus alba* back the deep green leaves and pale flowers of *Helleborus foetidus*, with ivy and winter-flowering heaths (below).

An inspired mix of *Iris sibirica*, asters and other herbaceous perennials creates ribbons of texture and shape long after the flowers have faded (above).

The dainty purple *Crocus tommasinianus* (right) is one of the delights of late winter. Crocus naturalises well, spreading its horizons annually. By the time perennials begin to stir in spring, its foliage has died back and it disappears until the following year.

practical diary

Winter gives both garden and gardener time to draw breath after the busy growing season. There are still important jobs to be done, but these need not be tackled with the urgency of spring and summer work, and they often deserve more thought. The siting of new trees and shrubs, and the pruning and training of existing ones, requires a degree of artistry and consideration. Other tasks, like winter digging and clearing the vegetable plot, ensure that, bit by bit, the garden is brought back under control. This is a good time for cleaning tools and pots, for tidying sheds and repairing fences. And as the days lengthen in late winter, the new year's early sowings can be made under glass.

perennials

Most perennials become dormant in winter, which makes the few that flower or hold their leaves an especially welcome sight. Lift your spirits in winter by bringing on new plants for the year ahead, from plug plants or root cuttings.

now is the season to . . .

- **plant bare-rooted perennials** such as lily of the valley, which are sold dormant, usually by mail order, at this time of year. (You can also plant container-grown plants, though with less urgency as they are available year-round.)
- **in late winter buy and pot up young plants,** or 'plugs', available by mail order. Grow them on in a coldframe or an unheated greenhouse.
- **in cold or exposed gardens,** protect perennials on the borderline of hardiness if not done in autumn.
- **group pot-grown plants** together in a sheltered spot to reduce the risk of their rootballs freezing.
- **check new plants** put in during autumn and refirm any lifted by frost.
- **look for vine weevil larvae** in the compost of container-grown perennials if you suspect damage (see Autumn).
- **pick off old and tattered foliage** of early flowering evergreen perennials, such as bergenias, Lenten rose (*Helleborus orientalis*) and epimediums in late winter.
- **protect flowers for cutting** of Christmas rose and *Iris unguicularis* from severe weather and bird damage, using cloches, or sheets of glass or rigid plastic balanced on bricks.
- **in fair weather, prepare new borders** for spring planting. Dig them over to two spades' depth (see Autumn, double digging), incorporating plenty of well-rotted organic matter, but be sure to bury annual weeds and remove the roots of perennial weeds.
- **remove and clean plant supports,** and store ready for spring. Paint metal supports if necessary.
- **in late winter, divide** any summer-flowering perennials and herbaceous climbers that have formed large clumps, so long as the ground is not frozen or waterlogged (see Autumn).

perennials and grasses for winter interest

Evergreen and winter-flowering perennials may be few in number, but they create welcome colour in the garden through the darkest months of the year. The pure white blooms of the Christmas rose (*Helleborus niger*) and the wonderful blue, honey-scented flowers of *Iris unguicularis* are also both good for cutting. Other plants offer double value: bergenias bloom white, purple or pink in late winter while their rounded leathery leaves develop red and bronze tints; the daintier Lenten rose (*Helleborus orientalis*) bears its beautiful flowers above jagged dark green leaves.

Most ornamental grasses die back in winter, but their parchment-coloured foliage gives an ethereal beauty to the garden, particularly when each fragile leaf is silvered with frost. A few evergreen grasses bring more substantial foliage interest, notably the golden-leaved *Carex oshimensis* 'Evergold', and the dramatic black lilyturf (*Ophiopogon planiscapus* 'Nigrescens').

Ornamental grasses and phormiums enhanced by a dusting of frost.

taking root cuttings

1 **Dig up** a strong, healthy plant and wash the soil off the roots.

2 **Select young,** vigorous roots of pencil thickness and cut them from the parent plant near the crown.

■ **divide container-grown perennials** that have outgrown their pots, but delay dividing pot-grown grasses until early spring.
■ **take root cuttings** of selected perennials (see below).
■ **occasionally water tender perennials** that are overwintering under glass, to keep the compost just moist. Check plants once a week, and remove dead leaves and flowers that could become infected with grey mould (botrytis).
■ **water evergreen perennials** in containers or very sheltered spots if no rain has fallen for several days.

and if you have time . . .

■ **top-dress perennials** and grasses in containers.
■ **weed, tidy and mulch** borders when soil conditions permit in late winter, cutting dead stems to ground level.

root cuttings

This type of cutting is a useful way to propagate perennials with thick fleshy roots (see below). No special equipment is needed and the cuttings can be left outdoors during winter, although standing them in a coldframe is preferable. In spring or early summer, when leaves appear, pot up the cuttings individually and grow them on for planting outside in autumn or the following spring.

After taking the cuttings, replant the parent plant immediately into soil that you have improved by forking in some well-rotted organic matter and a little slow-release fertiliser.

The Lenten rose (*Helleborus orientalis*) is one of the earliest hellebores to come into bloom.

looking ahead . . .

☑ EARLY SPRING Divide grasses and late flowering perennials.
☑ LATE SPRING Pot up root cuttings when leaves appear.

perennials **to raise from root cuttings**

• acanthus • *Anchusa azurea* • japanese anemone (*Anemone* x *hybrida*) • echinops • gypsophila • oriental poppy (*Papaver orientale*) • romneya • verbascum

3 **Cut each root** into 7–10cm (3–4in) lengths, cutting straight across the top and slanting at the bottom (so you know which way up to plant them).

4 **Fill a deep** 13cm (5in) pot with moist cuttings compost. Insert six to eight cuttings round the rim, 2–5cm (1–2in) apart, their tops level with the surface.

5 **Cover the compost** with a fine layer of grit and place the pots in a coldframe, a sheltered place outdoors, or on the windowsill of a cool room.

annuals & biennials

Enjoy taking time out to scan catalogues for new varieties, and make your preparations for spring sowings. Check biennials are still in good condition after hard weather and start sowing half-hardy annuals under glass.

now is the season to . . .

- **clear beds where late annual displays** have finished. Weed, then cover the ground with a layer of garden compost ready to be forked in early in spring.
- **check biennials after bad weather** and firm in plants loosened by winds and frost. Remove any that are severely frosted, but do not replace them until early spring.
- **thin autumn-sown seedlings** to leave young plants at least 5cm (2in) apart as a precaution against damping-off disease, which is often encouraged by overcrowding.
- **in very cold weather, cover seedlings** and young plants with

Universal pansies are one of the few annuals to bloom in the depths of winter. If planted in a hanging basket or container, they will need to be watered sparingly in dry weather.

choosing annuals

Besides the many popular annuals, such as marigolds, tagetes, ageratums and salvias, that are happy in a sunny position in most garden soils, the following plants will suit particular requirements:

FOR CUTTING • antirrhinum • calendula • china aster • chrysanthemum • gypsophila • larkspur • molucella • nigella • scabious • sunflower • sweet peas • verbena

FOR FRAGRANCE • alyssum (*Lobularia*) • evening primrose • heliotrope • mignonette • mirabilis • nicotiana • petunia • stocks • sweet peas

FOR FOLIAGE • amaranthus • atriplex • *Begonia semperflorens* (bronze-leaved varieties) • castor oil plant (*Ricinus*) • coleus • kochia • nasturtiums (*Tropaeolum* Alaska Series) • variegated pelargoniums • perilla

FOR SHADE • alyssum (*Lobularia*) • begonias • cleome • coleus • impatiens • lobelia • mimulus • nicotiana • pansies • schizanthus

FOR MEADOWS • borage • candytuft • clarkia • corncockle • cornflower • cosmos • eschscholzia • larkspur • nasturtiums • pansies • poppies • sunflowers

FOR CLIMBING • *Cobaea scandens* • *Eccremocarpus scaber* • morning glory • sweet peas • *Thunbergia alata* • trailing nasturtiums

QUICK FILLERS • candytuft • chrysanthemums • linaria • nigella • night-scented stocks

Eschscholzia californica

cloches, fleece, polythene tunnels or newspaper.

■ **plan next year's display** by exploring catalogues. Order seeds early to ensure a wide selection of varieties.

■ **start cultivating sites** for annuals towards the end of winter when the weather is fair (see Early Spring). Prepare a small area of ground as a nursery bed in which to sow hardy annuals for transplanting. Delay this until early spring in a wet season or if your soil is heavy clay.

■ **sow half-hardy annuals** under glass from January onwards, and prick them out when they are large enough to handle (see below).

■ **in February, place your orders** for seedlings and plug plants for spring delivery; this is often an easier and less expensive alternative to raising your own in a heated greenhouse.

and if you have time . . .

■ **pot up some of the seedlings** sown in autumn under glass, and grow them on in a greenhouse or coldframe for early flowers indoors.

looking ahead . . .

☑ EARLY SPRING Finish preparing beds and start sowing outdoors.

☑ Plant out sweet peas and spring biennials raised under cover.

☑ Direct sow sweet peas in warmed soil.

☑ Continue sowing half-hardy annuals under glass.

sowing half-hardy annuals

Pelargoniums benefit from early sowing, in January or even late December, but most other half-hardy annuals that need a long growing season can wait until the first week of February. These early sowings will germinate reliably in a propagator kept at a steady temperature of 13–15°C (55–60°F).

Use clean seed trays and fresh seed compost, pre-warmed by keeping it in the greenhouse for a week. Many seeds will germinate in a few days, but some, such as *Begonia semperflorens*, can take several weeks. Protect seedlings against damping-off disease (see Early Spring), and as soon as they are large enough to handle, prick them out into trays or small pots. Bushy and trailing lobelia are small and slender when young, and are usually pricked out in clusters of six to eight seedlings, rather than singly. This is made easier by sowing in rows (see below), rather than evenly across the seed tray.

there is still time to . . .

• **sow sweet peas during January** in pots under glass. Alternatively, cover an outdoor bed with polythene to warm the soil, and sow direct early in March.

***timetable* for sowing half-hardy annuals**

JANUARY • antirrhinums • *Begonia semperflorens* • pelargoniums

FEBRUARY • anagallis • brachyscome • impatiens • kochia • lobelia • nemesia • nicotiana • petunia • *Phlox drummondii* • scarlet salvia • verbena

MARCH • ageratum • cosmos • bedding dahlias • tagetes (including french and african marigolds) • zinnia

raising lobelia

1 **Fill a seed tray** with moist seed compost and lightly firm and level. Use a pencil or thin cane to press parallel grooves about 1cm (½in) deep in the compost. Sow seeds sparingly along these channels, but do not cover with compost, as light is essential for germination. Cover the tray with polythene or a clear lid and stand in a warm place.

2 **When the seedlings** are about 1cm (½in) high, fill another tray with moist potting compost, and make holes about 5cm (2in) apart. Lift small clumps of seedlings with a dibber and transfer to the holes in the new tray.

3 **Lightly firm** with your fingers, water through a fine rose, then put the tray in a propagator or cover it with a clear lid.

bulbs

In pots and outdoors, the first flowers will be opening before the turn of the season. While you are enjoying these harbingers of the new year, get ahead with sprouting summer bulbs and preparing their ground, for the longest possible display.

now is the season to . . .

- **clear leaves and other debris** from around the shoots of snowdrops, scillas, muscari and other early bulbs, but do not fork or hoe the surface as this can cause damage.
- **protect buried bulbs,** especially tulips, from mice and squirrels. Lay panels of chicken wire on the ground and secure at the corners with large stones or bent wires.
- **move or divide snowdrops** while they are in flower or have green leaves (see opposite).
- **cover spring bulbs with cloches** or a low polythene tunnel to advance flowering if you planted them in rows for cutting. Remember to ventilate plants on mild days to keep them free from rot.
- **start moving forced bulbs** into light and gentle warmth in December, no more than 10°C (50°F); hyacinths should have plump shoots with buds visible, and narcissi should be about 10cm (4in) high, with visible flower buds. Tulips and crocuses are often not ready until late January or February, when they show flower colour.
- **remove dead blooms** after flowering, then feed with a high-potash fertiliser. Move plants to a coldframe or sheltered position outside to continue growing and storing food to fuel next year's display.
- **buy lilies** for growing in pots or outdoors. Refresh any that look dry and shrivelled by burying them in a tray of leaf-mould or moist compost for a week or two before planting.
- **pot up amaryllis,** a few at a time for a succession of blooms (see opposite).
- **carefully empty pans of lilies** propagated two years ago from seed or bulbils. These are usually large enough to separate and pot up individually in small pots. Leave one-year-old bulbs for another year.

If your lily bulbs look dry and shrivelled, place them in a pot or tray and cover with moist compost to plump them up.

- **prepare sites during February** for summer-flowering bulbs such as gladioli, alliums, lilies and tigridias. Fork the ground thoroughly, removing perennial weeds and mixing in plenty of leaf-mould or garden compost. Delay this work until spring on frosted, wet or heavy soils.

Low-growing winter aconites (*Eranthis hyemalis*) push up through the leaf litter, their golden yellow flowers a cheering sight in late winter.

planting amaryllis

1 Choose a pot a little larger than the bulb, and part fill with moist potting compost so the bulb sits with its tip above the rim. Fill round the bulb with compost to within 2–3cm (1in) of the rim, then water.

2 Do not water again until the flower bud shows, then keep just moist.

3 When in flower, water plants regularly and feed every 7–14 days with liquid fertiliser.

■ **sprout begonias and dahlias** in boxes under glass, either for taking cuttings in early spring or for planting out in late spring (see right).

moving snowdrops

1 Lift large clumps of snowdrops carefully with a fork while they are still in flower ('in the green').

2 Tease into smaller clumps and replant immediately in ground you have already forked over and enriched with leaf-mould or compost.

growing amaryllis

These popular bulbs, correctly called *Hippeastrum*, are easy to grow indoors and often flower six to eight weeks after potting. Although they are evergreen, the bulbs flower best if rested annually, so start to reduce watering in August and allow the leaves to die down. Keep the bulbs dry for two to three months, then force into growth in early winter at a temperature of 13–15°C (55–60°F). Amaryllis will also grow well in cooler surroundings and start to flower in February or March. Repot the bulbs every two to three years (see above).

sprouting dahlias and begonias

If you want to multiply your stocks from cuttings or division, start tubers into growth in January or February in a warm greenhouse (see page 68) or on a windowsill. By April, the shoots should be about 10–15cm (4–6in), long enough to remove and root as soft-tip cuttings (see Late Spring).

there is still time to . . .

- **plant tulips, hyacinths** and early flowering *Gladiolus nanus*.
- **clean dried gladiolus corms** after autumn lifting by removing the old withered corm from the base, together with any loose skins. Check corms in store, and remove and destroy any that are spongy or shrivelled. Dust others with an insecticide if you notice any grubs present.

looking ahead . . .

- ☑ EARLY SPRING Start planting gladioli.
- ☑ Take cuttings from sprouted dahlias and begonias.
- ☑ LATE SPRING Plant or pot up sprouted begonias and dahlias.
- ☑ Plant summer bulbs.

roses

Although apparently lifeless, roses are merely resting during their winter dormancy. You can plant or move them now and, as winter draws to an end, prune them to concentrate their energy for the coming season.

The large hips of the sweet briar (*Rosa rubiginosa*), shine out in the winter garden, their shapes enhanced by a riming of frost.

now is the season to . . .

- **continue tidying rose beds.** Cut back any ground-covering herbaceous perennials and edging plants around the roses, clear weeds and pick up all fallen rose leaves.
- **give plants a final spray of fungicide** if black spot, rust or mildew have been serious that year. Choose a mild December day, drenching all stems to the point of run-off.
- **check recently planted roses** after frost and tread firm any that have lifted from the ground. If it gets very cold, cover young plants with straw (see Autumn).
- **continue preparing** the ground for new roses. In January break down with a fork heavy soil roughly dug in autumn, ready for planting in late winter.
- **plant new roses** as they arrive, or heel them into some vacant ground until you are ready. Plant only when the soil breaks up easily and is not frozen or waterlogged.
- **protect roses** of borderline hardiness with two or three layers of fleece. Varieties sensitive to frost include the banksian roses (*R. banksiae* cultivars), *R.* x *odorata* 'Mutabilis' and, in exposed positions, the yellow climber 'Mermaid'.
- **inspect supports and ties,** especially after high winds, and readjust where necessary (see page 37).
- **start pruning climbing roses** during February, but delay the work until March in a cold or frosty season (see opposite).
- **move potted roses** into the greenhouse during January for forcing early blooms (see below).

and if you have time . . .

- **in February increase the resistance** of roses that have been badly affected by black spot by spreading 35g per m^2 (1oz per sq yd) sulphate of potash over soil shaded by the branches.
- **in mild areas, begin pruning** shrub roses (see Early Spring).

replacing rose-sick soil

1 Dig out an area roughly 60cm (2ft) square around where the old rose grew, removing the top 38–45cm (15–18in) of soil. This soil is fine for growing other plants, so exchange it for the same amount dug from an area where roses have not been grown before.

2 Work plenty of compost or rotted manure into the replacement soil.

3 Leave the soil to settle for a few weeks before planting a new rose or one moved from another part of the garden.

dealing with rose-sick soil

Where a rose has been grown for eight years or more, a replacement planted in the same spot is likely to grow sickly, with stems dying back. This is due to specific replant disease, or 'rose sickness', a combination of soil exhaustion and a build up of diseases. It is better to plant a new rose somewhere fresh, but you can replant successfully in the same spot if you either replace the soil (see left) or use a soil-sterilising concentrate, following the manufacturer's instructions.

forcing roses

Roses that were pruned back to 15cm (6in) and potted up in autumn for early forcing can be brought inside from late December onwards.

- **wash the outsides** of the pots, and weed and loosen the surface of the compost, then stand the plants in a well-lit greenhouse or conservatory, maintained at a minimum temperature of 5°C (40°F).

- **ventilate well** in mild weather, and water so the compost is evenly moist but not saturated.

pruning climbing roses

Healthy climbers will have produced several new shoots during the summer. Retain the best and strongest of these when pruning to replace some of the older framework stems being cut out, or to fill in gaps (see right).

raising roses from seed

Rose seeds need exposure to frost before they will germinate. This process is called stratification. After a hard winter, you may notice rose seedlings growing under parent plants and you can move these to a nursery bed to grow on for a year or two until they are large enough to plant out. If you want to raise your own plants from a special variety or one you have deliberately cross-pollinated, you can do this using seed from hips (see below).

there is still time to . . .

- **gather hips** for sowing your own seeds (see below).
- **pot up new roses** for forcing early flowers under glass.
- **cut back tall stems** on climbing and shrub roses to safeguard the plants against wind damage.

looking ahead . . .

- ☑ EARLY SPRING Continue pruning bush, shrub and climbing roses.
- ☑ Finish planting bare-rooted roses.
- ☑ LATE SPRING Plant out and feed roses forced in pots.
- ☑ Start spraying against pests and diseases if necessary.

pruning climbing roses

1 Prune out all dead stems and ends of stems, cutting back to healthy wood, then cut out two or three of the oldest branches, either to ground level or to where a strong replacement stem originates.

2 Stimulate flowering by shortening all sideshoots to leave two to four buds.

3 Tie new stems to their supports to make an even spread of branches; some may need re-tying to avoid overcrowding or crossing growth.

raising roses from seed

1 Gather hips when they are almost fully coloured but before they start to shrivel. Bury them whole in a potful of moist sharp sand or grit and keep in a warm place for three to four weeks. Then stand the pot outdoors, protected from mice and birds but not from frost.

2 In late winter bring the pot indoors and squeeze the seeds out of the hips into a bowl of water; discard any that float. Sow the remaining seeds in pots on the surface of seed compost and cover them with a layer of grit. Keep under glass, unheated or heated.

3 The seedlings will come through erratically. Carefully prick them out individually into final pots when the first true leaves appear, and leave the rest to germinate.

climbers

Winter is the time to get to grips with deciduous climbers, for while they are dormant you can see what lies beneath their cloaks of growth. This is the best season to prune certain climbers and service their supports. During very cold spells, evergreen and slightly frost-tender climbers will benefit from protection.

now is the season to . . .

- **protect climbers** on the borderline of hardiness during cold, frosty periods (see opposite). If any leaves or shoots become damaged by frost, leave them in place until early spring because, although unsightly, they give protection to undamaged shoots below.
- **continue to plant hardy** climbers when the soil is workable, and not frozen or sodden (see Autumn).
- **lift and divide herbaceous** climbers that have formed well-established clumps (see page 36).
- **propagate selected climbers** by layering or taking hardwood cuttings (see page 36).
- **prune ornamental vines,** winter jasmine, wisteria and any overgrown deciduous climbers (see opposite).
- **check trellis** and other supports before growth begins, and repair or treat if necessary (see page 37).
- **tie in climber stems firmly** to avoid wind damage, and loosen existing ties if they threaten to cut into stems.
- **trim self-clinging climbers** away from woodwork and guttering.
- **occasionally water climbers** that are growing in sites sheltered from rain, such as beneath the overhanging eaves of a roof, if necessary.

and if you have time . . .

- **weed and mulch** around established plants.

pruning deciduous climbers

Early winter is the time to prune ornamental vines (*Vitis*), when the pruning cuts are least likely to 'bleed' sap. Shorten shoots as necessary. Prune back weak or thin stems hard, to encourage more vigorous growth, but prune strong growing stems lightly.

Prune winter jasmine (*Jasminum nudiflorum*) as soon as flowering has finished because next winter's flowers open on new shoots produced during the coming year (see opposite).

Hard pruning ornamental vines while they are still dormant will stimulate vigorous new growth in spring.

The star-shaped flowers of winter jasmine brighten a wooden fence. Once flowering is finished, prune to promote the growth of new shoots that will carry flowers the following winter.

You can also prune overgrown deciduous climbers that will bloom on new wood produced in the coming year, such as trumpet vine (*Campsis*), summer jasmine (*Jasminum officinale*) and honeysuckle (*Lonicera periclymenum*). Late flowering clematis are better left until early spring unless February is particularly mild.

winter-pruning wisteria

Wisteria is pruned twice a year: initially around midsummer, then again in winter to stimulate the formation of short sideshoots that will bear summer flowers. Plants left unpruned tend to put their energy into producing leafy growth, not flowers.

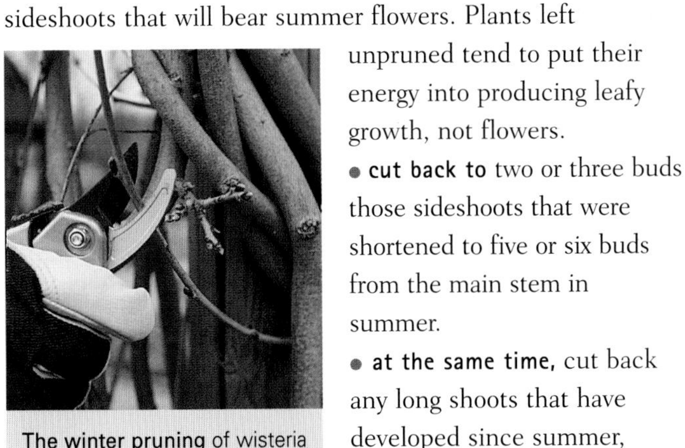

The winter pruning of wisteria is intended to encourage the formation of short flower-bearing sideshoots.

- **cut back to** two or three buds those sideshoots that were shortened to five or six buds from the main stem in summer.
- **at the same time,** cut back any long shoots that have developed since summer, pruning them to 15cm (6in).
- **if your plant is shy** to flower, feed it with sulphate of potash towards the end of winter.

protecting plants of borderline hardiness

You can increase the chances of these plants surviving by growing them against a sunny south-facing wall in a site sheltered from winds, as the wall will hold some warmth and create a 'storage-heater' effect. However, plants such as ceanothus, evergreen clematis (*C. armandii* and *C. cirrhosa*), and trachelospermum, need additional protection during very cold weather or in cold and exposed gardens.

A protective screen is simple to make and quick to install when frost threatens:

- **you will need two long wooden battens** and a large piece of fine windbreak netting or thick horticultural fleece of a size that is sufficient to cover the whole plant.
- **secure the battens** along the top and bottom of the netting or fleece using a staple gun or other means.
- **fix two or more** large hooks along the top of the wall or fence. Hang one batten from the hooks and let the other rest on the ground, close to the base of the plant.
- **insulate tender plants** or those in very exposed sites by packing straw or dry bracken behind the netting or fleece and around the plant.
- **for the blue passionflower** (*Passiflora caerulea*) it is usually sufficient to pack straw around the base of the stems and over the root area, as it tends to regrow from the base even if the top growth is killed by frost.

pruning winter jasmine

1 **Cut back all sideshoots** that have borne flowers to around three buds from the main stem.

2 **Shorten the main framework** shoots if necessary to restrict growth.

3 **On well-established plants,** take out several of the older, more woody stems close to ground level.

climbers/2

planting and propagation

Winter is the time not only to propagate more climbers and check their supports, but also to plant them. One of the most beautiful combinations of all is a climber growing through the branches of an established tree to give an extra season of colourful flowers or foliage.

climbers for trees

The golden rule is to match the vigour of the climber to the size of the tree, as a rampant climbing plant would overwhelm a small specimen. For the climber to grow successfully you need to pay particular attention to soil preparation, planting and aftercare, because it will have to compete with the roots of the tree for water and nourishment (see opposite). The planting position should not be close to the trunk but towards the edge of the branch canopy, where the soil should have fewer roots and more moisture.

climbers for trees

FOR SMALL TREES • annual climbers such as morning glory and canary creeper (*Tropaeolum peregrinum*) • *Clematis alpina* • *C. macropetala* • *C. tangutica* • *C. viticella* • large-flowered clematis hybrids • golden hop (*Humulus lupulus* 'Aureus') • rambler roses 'Emily Gray' and 'Phyllis Bide'

FOR LARGE TREES • *Clematis flammula* • *Clematis montana* • parthenocissus • vigorous rambler roses such as 'Bobbie James', 'Paul's Himalayan Musk', 'Rambling Rector' and 'Seagull' • ornamental vines (*Vitis*) • wisteria

propagation

There are various methods of propagating climbers at this time of year. Mature herbaceous climbers, such as golden hop, perennial pea (*Lathyrus latifolius*) and flame flower (*Tropaeolum speciosum*), are divided in the same way as herbaceous perennials (see Autumn) when soil conditions are suitable.

Many deciduous climbers and wall shrubs, including *Actinidia kolomikta*, honeysuckles, parthenocissus and vines (*Vitis*), are simple to propagate by hardwood cuttings once their leaves have dropped. Take cuttings 15cm (6in) long and root them outdoors in well-drained soil (see Autumn). They should be ready for planting by next autumn or the following early spring.

layering

The chocolate vine (*Akebia*), trumpet vine (*Campsis*) and ornamental vines (*Vitis*) are liable to 'bleed' sap if cut when in leaf, so they are best layered in late winter when dormant.

- **select a long, pliable,** healthy shoot that can be bent down to touch the ground. About 30cm (12in) from the end of the stem, use a sharp knife to remove a sliver of bark from the underside, close to a leaf joint, to stimulate rooting.
- **peg the wounded stem** to the ground with loops of wire, cover with a layer of soil and tie the tip of the shoot to a short stake to keep it upright. Leave for at least six months before severing, after checking that it has rooted.

The cream-centred leaves of *Hedera helix* 'Goldheart' brighten even the dullest of vertical structures in winter.

Use a stiff brush to clean dirt and algal growth off wooden trellis and supports, then check for signs of decay.

Renew ties where necessary on wall shrubs such as this early flowering *Chaenomeles* x *superba* growing against trellis.

looking after supports

Keep trellis and other wooden plant supports in good condition by treating them with a preservative every few years. An annual inspection of the wood during winter will show when the coating begins to deteriorate and you can take advantage of a spell of dry weather to make it good.

- **first clean the wood** using a wire brush to remove algal growth and stubborn patches of dirt. Then scrub it well with a stiff brush and clean water, and allow to dry. Treat any small areas of rotting wood with wood hardener.
- **choose a preservative paint or stain,** making sure it is non-toxic if plants are growing close by. Follow the instructions for application, and wear protective gloves and safety glasses if necessary.
- **check support posts,** particularly where they go into the ground as this part is the most prone to rot. If rotting has occurred, you can often repair the post by bolting the sound part to a metal spike or a concrete spur, rather than putting in a new one.
- **remove rust and flaking paint** from metal supports with a wire brush. Then wash the structure and allow to dry before painting.

looking ahead . . .

☑ EARLY SPRING Plant evergreen climbers and wall shrubs, and any plants of borderline hardiness.
☑ Prune late flowering clematis.
☑ SUMMER Summer-prune wisteria.
☑ AUTUMN Plant or pot up rooted cuttings and layers.

training a climber into a tree

1 **At the edge** of the tree's canopy of branches dig a planting hole about 60cm (2ft) wide and 45cm (18in) deep. Incorporate plenty of well-rotted organic matter and some slow-release fertiliser or, if the soil is very poor, replace it with good-quality topsoil mixed with organic matter and fertiliser.

2 **Plant the climber** at the same depth as it was growing previously, with the exception of clematis, which benefit from deep planting with 10cm (4in) of soil covering the top of the rootball.

3 **Set up one or several** training canes or lines of string to lead the climber into the branches and attach the climber to these using soft string.

4 **Water and mulch** the new climber and make sure that it does not dry out during its first year.

shrubs & trees

Apart from routine matters such as planting and protection, winter is pruning time for many shrubs and trees and an opportunity for you to use your artistic skills to shape and train them to suit your garden.

now is the season to . . .

- **check recently planted shrubs** and trees after any high winds or hard frost. Make sure their supports and ties are secure, and refirm any plants that have lifted.
- **brush snow off** hedges and shrubs, as the weight can damage the dense growth of evergreens in particular.
- **continue planting** deciduous shrubs and trees in prepared sites if the ground is not frozen or waterlogged (see Autumn).
- **move misplaced shrubs and trees** to more suitable sites if the soil is workable (see page 40).
- **repair damaged hedging** and fill gaps (see page 41).
- **prune established shrubs and trees,** and shape young specimens (see page 44).
- **protect flowering cherry buds** from birds in late winter with fleece, or use harmless deterrent sprays and bird scarers.

Wintersweet (*Chimonanthus praecox*) often opens its sweetly fragrant blooms during December. It should be pruned once it has finished flowering.

Cover early rhododendrons with fleece to protect flower buds against frost damage.

- **protect early rhododendron flower buds** against frost with fleece, and pull up any suckers that you see.
- **clear hedge bases** (see opposite).
- **trim back invasive roots** where hedges grow next to borders, by plunging a spade full depth along a line about 45cm (18in) away from the hedge.
- **tidy shrubs** such as *Buddleja globosa* and tree peonies, which do not need regular pruning. Remove dead or diseased wood, and any live branches that spoil the shape of the plant.
- **prune** wintersweet and witch hazel (see opposite).
- **prepare planting sites** for rhododendrons (see below).
- **take hardwood cuttings** of deciduous plants while they are leafless (see Autumn).
- **transplant suckers** to propagate new plants (see opposite).

and if you have time . . .

- **pot up small specimens** of early flowering shrubs like deutzia, hydrangea and viburnum. Stand them in a cool greenhouse for early blooms.
- **cut spindly flowering stems** from ribes, cornus, prunus, willows and viburnums, and bring indoors to flower.
- **paint or spray deciduous trees** that have a history of pest and disease attack while leafless, using winter wash to kill moss and overwintering insect eggs, but first spread plastic sheeting to protect surrounding plants (see page 59).

preparing for new rhododendrons

Rhododendrons and azaleas are acid-loving plants so it is important to test the soil on the proposed site before you do any work or buy plants. If the pH is higher than 5.5 these shrubs will not survive, so plant them in containers or raised beds filled with lime-free (ericaceous) compost instead. In addition to an acid soil, rhododendrons also need a very well-drained spot in light shade, shielded from early morning sun.

About six weeks before planting, dig over an area 1m^2 (10sq ft) and 45cm (18in) deep, working in at least one large bucketful of leaf-mould or garden compost per plant. Level the soil, rake in a granular fertiliser formulated for acid-loving plants, and leave to settle until planting time in mid-spring.

transplanting suckers

Some trees and shrubs produce suckers from their own roots – these are separate shoots, growing from shallow roots or close to the base of the parent plant. You can lift these and grow them on, ready for planting out in a year's time.

The spidery blooms of witch hazel (*Hamamelis mollis*).

pruning winter-flowering shrubs

Wintersweet (*Chimonanthus praecox*) can take many years to reach flowering size, and is best left unpruned until then. After flowering, cut out one stem in three to encourage vigorous new growth from the base of the plant.

Winter-flowering witch hazels (*Hamamelis*) are similarly slow growing and should not be pruned until mature. Then, as soon as the flowers fade, shorten or remove surplus branches, and tidy or lightly trim the rest of the shrub to maintain shape and size.

transplanting a lilac sucker

1 Identify the sucker and dig down to its base to make sure the sucker has plenty of roots of its own.

2 Cut the sucker off where it joins a main root and pot it up in a 15–20cm (6–8in) pot of soil-based potting compost (lime-free for acid-loving gaultherias). Alternatively, space several suckers 45cm (18in) apart in a nursery bed. Leave tree suckers unpruned, but cut back shrub suckers by half.

Gather up and dispose of the debris at the foot of a hedge as it can harbour disease.

clearing the base of hedges

Fallen leaves and other wind-blown debris collects in large quantities at the bottom of hedges. Although this may provide winter shelter for wildlife, it also harbours pests and diseases.

- **rake out loose material** to expose overwintering pest eggs and grubs for birds. Add leaves and rotting vegetation to the compost heap, but burn woody material as a precaution against diseases.
- **clear weeds** and use a fork to prick over the soil.

plants to raise from suckers

- dogwoods (*Cornus*) • gaultheria • kerria • lilacs • quince
- snowberry (*Symphoricarpos*)
- sumachs (*Rhus*)

there is still time to . . .

- **screen recently planted shrubs** and trees against cold winds and mulch well to prevent frost heave (see Autumn).
- **cut back overgrown** deciduous hedges (see Autumn).

looking ahead . . .

☑ EARLY TO LATE SPRING
☑ Prune late flowering shrubs.
☑ Renovate overgrown shrubs and evergreen hedges.
☑ Plant evergreens.
☑ Start pruning conifers, topiary and most hedges.
☑ Move evergreens.
☑ SUMMER Prune spring shrubs after flowering.

shrubs & trees/2

moving misplaced plants

Despite careful planning, it sometimes happens that a tree or shrub is obviously in the wrong place. If it is well established, consider first whether it might be easier to move neighbouring plants or even sacrifice them for the sake of a prized specimen that might not survive transplanting. Do not attempt to move magnolias or other plants with fleshy roots.

In general, the younger the plant the greater the chances of it surviving the move, but all plants, even small ones, need special care before, during and for two or three years after transplanting. Bear in mind also the weight of a heavy rootball and get some help if the plant is fairly large.

Prepare the new site in advance in the same way as you would for planting a tree (see Autumn). Move deciduous plants while they are dormant, between late November and late February, but leave evergreens until spring or autumn on heavy soils. Larger plants will need some root preparation a year or two in advance, and after transplanting they will need staking or guying with thin rope attached to short stakes to keep them upright. Younger plants should not need root preparation.

root preparation for larger shrubs and trees

To reduce the shock of transplanting trees and shrubs larger than 1m (3ft) across, prepare the rootball in late autumn or early winter a year in advance, as follows:

- Mark a circle round the plant just within the area shaded by its branches.
- Dig a trench as described below, but continue downward until you meet the thicker roots. Cut through these.
- Refill the trench with the excavated soil mixed with plenty of garden compost or a proprietary tree-planting mixture; firm and water well. Make sure the area of refilled soil does not dry out during summer.
- When you come to move the plant the following winter, you will find the rootball already defined and showing signs of healthy new fibrous roots.
- You could extend the preparation over two years: cut and refill one half of the trench in the first year, complete the circle the second year and move the tree in the third.

repairing a damaged hedge

Bare or damaged areas are often more noticeable when the hedge is dormant during winter, which is the best time to assess hedges for repair.

large gaps caused by plants dying

Open these up by pruning the healthy growth on either side so you can remove the remains of the dead plant and its roots. Then fork over the soil, adding compost and fertiliser, and replant with young specimens. Keep the adjacent growth tied back through the year so the new plants get as much light as possible.

moving young trees and shrubs

1 **Excavate a hole** about 1m (3ft) across and 45cm (18in) deep in the new site. Then use a spade to mark a circle 60–75cm (2–2ft 6in) in diameter around the plant to be moved. Tie up arching branches with string.

2 **Dig a trench** one spade blade deep outside the circle. With a fork loosen some of the soil from the fibrous roots to reduce the weight of the rootball.

3 **Undercut the rootball** by digging down at an angle, slicing through woody roots. Work round until the rootball is free. Check that the new hole you have dug is big enough, and adjust if necessary.

4 **Tilt the plant to one side** and ease a piece of strong sacking or plastic sheet underneath. Lean the plant the opposite way and pull the sheet through.

5 **Tie up the sheet securely** to keep the rootball intact, and lift or drag the plant on the sheet to its new home. Plant at the same depth as before, firm in, water well and mulch.

To avoid specific replant disease, which can affect young plants growing where closely related species grew previously, dig out the soil to a depth of 30–38cm (12–15in) and replace with soil from elsewhere in the garden (see 'replacing rose-sick soil', page 32).

small gaps

You can 'patch' smaller holes in a healthy hedge by training neighbouring branches across the gap (see right). Alternatively, insert a cane vertically in the middle of the gap and tie branches from each side to this. Another solution is to layer plants with pliable growth by bending some of the lower branches across the gap and pegging them down in the soil in one or more places. Tie back any growth that heavily shades the layers until they have rooted, then either sever them from the parent plants or leave attached.

tall conifer hedges

If the weight of snow or high winds force branches out of place, clip back slender sideshoots to the face of the hedge, then push larger branches that may have moved back into the foliage. To keep the large branches in place, tie them with plastic string or soft wire to strong upright stems deep within the hedge.

patching gaps in a hedge

1 **First cut out** all the dead or damaged growth using sharp secateurs.

2 **Tie healthy shoots** together across the gap with soft string. Snip off their tips to encourage bushy side growth.

The dormant winter season is the best time to transplant misplaced trees and shrubs to a more suitable place in the garden, but avoid doing this in frosty conditions (right).

shrubs & trees/3

pruning essentials

Many people find pruning intimidating, or feel that cutting off healthy growth must be counter-productive. On the contrary, however, judicious pruning at the right time can do much to improve the shape, flowering and fruitfulness of plants compared to those left to grow naturally.

why prune?

Pruning entails the selective removal of parts of a plant for a particular reason. The main purposes of pruning are:

- **maintaining health** Controlling disease is an important part of keeping plants vigorous and attractive. Cutting out dead and diseased portions of branches, as well as removing rubbing branches, prevents further spread and disfigurement and, in the case of trees, ensures that they are safe.
- **early training** Young trees and shrubs flower or fruit sooner, and develop into more attractive specimens, if they are pruned in ways that emphasise a well-spaced framework of branches. Early formative pruning aims to correct misshapen or excessive growth.
- **keeping a balance** Strongly growing plants can make a lot of leaf and stem growth at the expense of flowers, while mature specimens may stop producing new growth and only flower erratically or at the branch tips. Routine annual pruning encourages a regular supply of young productive shoots while controlling more mature growth.
- **improving quality** Sometimes less is more; pruning can divert energy from heavy yields of small flowers and fruits into fewer, but higher quality, blooms. Similarly, some shrubs and trees with handsome foliage or bark are pruned to ensure plenty of young growth with enhanced colour or shape.
- **limiting size** All healthy plants continue growing until they reach maximum size, which in many cases is too big for their allotted space. Hedges must be clipped to keep them in shape and the growth of shrubs and trees restricted to keep them in balance with a garden.

how pruning works

Several different hormones regulate plant activity. Those responsible for producing new growth tend to be concentrated in the top few buds of shoot tips, where they encourage stems to lengthen while suppressing the growth of buds lower down.

If you cut off these active areas of growth, the plant redirects its energies elsewhere, usually into the buds just below the pruning cut. In this way, pruning is not just the removal of excess, misplaced or unwanted growth, but also the creative and predictable redirection of new growth.

pruning equipment

- **garden knife** Use a garden knife to trim young, thin growth, to tidy round large cuts, and to take cuttings.
- **secateurs** A pair of secateurs is the essential pruning tool to cut stems up to 1cm (½in) thick. Check out the various types to find the one you prefer (see Early Spring).
- **long-handled pruners, or loppers** Secateurs with long handles give greater reach and more leverage when cutting stems up to 2cm (¾in) thick.

A valuable winter-flowering evergreen shrub, *Mahonia* x *media* 'Winter Sun' needs little pruning, other than to cut out dead branches and maintain its overall shape.

the correct pruning cut

Pruning cuts through the bark, which is what protects a plant from disease. The cleaner the cut, the faster the wound will dry and heal, so it is important to keep tools sharp, and avoid ragged cuts and torn bark. Plants have natural defences against injury concentrated in certain places, such as in the joint where a bud or leaf grows. Cutting close to this point helps the wound to heal quickly.

Always prune just above a bud, sloping the cut to direct water away from the bud.

Where buds are in pairs on opposite sides of the stem, cut straight across, no more than 5mm (¼in) above the buds.

A correctly pruned cut (below) will heal quickly, whereas using blunt secateurs produces a ragged cut and torn bark, which will take longer to heal.

- **tree pruners** Ideal for removing high branches up to 2–3cm (1in) thick, tree pruners are basically a pole, sometimes telescopic, topped with a secateur-like cutting blade.
- **pruning saw** A narrow-bladed saw deals with branches up to 8cm (3in) thick. Straight, curved and folding models are available, with large teeth for cutting sappy wood or smaller teeth for dry material.
- **bow saw** This has a bent metal frame and a slim detachable blade; use a bow saw to cut through large tree branches.

pruning buddleia

1 **At winter's end,** prune buddleias by cutting shoots back to a strong pair of buds or shoots at the preferred height.

2 **To rejuvenate older plants** and improve flower size, use loppers or a saw to shorten some stems just above the trunk or main framework branches.

when to prune

EARLY FLOWERING DECIDUOUS SHRUBS

Plants that flower during the first half of the growing season – for example forsythia, philadelphus and weigela – generally do so on stems that grew the previous year. Prune immediately after flowering to allow plenty of time for new growth in the second half of the growing season.

LATE FLOWERING DECIDUOUS SHRUBS

Plants that flower late in the year do so on shoots developed earlier in the same year; for example, *Buddleja davidii* (see left), caryopteris and perovskia. Prune during winter, or wait until March or April as this helps to avoid frost damage to new growth.

BROAD-LEAVED EVERGREENS

Most evergreens need little pruning except to remove dead material and maintain shape. Regardless of whether they are flowering species, such as skimmia, or foliage plants, such as spotted laurel, prune if necessary in April or May, since their new growth can easily be damaged by frost.

CONIFERS

Apart from removing dead material, you can trim ornamental specimens occasionally to encourage bushy growth and cut back the main shoot if it is growing too tall. Prune if necessary during autumn or early winter, to avoid the excessive gumming that occurs when the sap is rising.
Do not prune in frosty weather. Trim coniferous hedges in late summer.

shrubs & trees/4

routine pruning

Before you prune make sure your tools are sharp and clean, and that you have plenty of time. Choose a pleasant day when you will enjoy doing the job well and the plants will not be under stress due to severe weather.

the basic routine

Never prune without a good reason and always cut off less rather than too much, because you can always remove more later. It is better not to prune at all rather than do the wrong kind of pruning in the wrong season or in unsuitable conditions, such as frost or drought.

The deciduous *Viburnum farreri* bears clusters of pinkish white scented flowers throughout winter and into early spring; it needs minimal pruning.

pruning young shrubs

Early training and formative pruning determine the future shape of a young plant and, if done correctly, will avoid pruning problems later on.

- **immediately after planting** select the strongest three or four shoots as main branches and shorten them by half their length, cutting just above an outward-facing bud. Remove completely any weak and badly placed shoots.
- **after one year,** cut out weak and misplaced shoots, and any that cross the centre. Shorten the longest main branches to establish a shapely outline.
- **in the following years,** start a regular routine of pruning the established shrub according to its type and flowering season (see page 43).

pruning young trees

A one or two-year-old tree is supplied either as a single stem with few or no sideshoots (a whip, or maiden), or as a stem with several strong sideshoots (a feathered whip, or feathered maiden). After planting, keep the main stem supported by a sturdy

pruning an overgrown deciduous shrub

1 **Take a close look** at your overgrown shrub in winter: even with evergreens it is easier to see its structure then, especially at the end of winter when frost injuries should be apparent.

2 **First cut out** all dead, damaged and diseased wood, then remove any weak, spindly stems.

3 **Using loppers** or a puning saw, cut out any stems that interfere with the growth of a more important branch, or that cross the centre of the shrub. Then thin out any overcrowded stems.

4 **Only then prune** the main flowering or structural branches, according to variety.

5 **In many cases** you need to cut back almost to the base of shoots that have recently flowered to restrict size, but prune less severely if you want a large shrub.

6 **The newly pruned shrub** admits more light and air to the centre of the plant, promoting healthy growth.

stake and protected by a guard around the base if rabbits are a problem. (For what to do if the main stem is damaged, see page 47; for special effects, see page 48.)

- **three or four years** after planting, remove the stake and cut off any low shoots growing from near the base of the tree.

for standard trees

The presence of sideshoots supports a tree's early growth and also helps to thicken the main stem. But if a standard tree with a clear stem about 1.5–2m (5–6ft) high is required, remove the sideshoots while they are small to avoid large pruning scars later.

Newly planted trees benefit from protection by plastic spiral tree guards for the first few years. A mulch of plastic sheeting will suppress weeds.

shrubs and trees that need little or no pruning

• amelanchier • *Buddleja globosa* • caragana • chimonanthus • corylopsis • daphne (deciduous) • enkianthus • eucryphia (deciduous) • fothergilla • hoheria (deciduous) • japanese maples (*Acer palmatum*) • magnolia • poncirus • rhamnus (deciduous) • viburnum (deciduous)

PRUNING PRUNUS TIP Do not prune ornamental cherries, plums, peaches and apricots in winter. Wait until late spring or early summer to avoid infection from disease.

raising the crown of an established tree

The branches of a maturing tree often bend under the weight of foliage, casting excessive shade and even becoming a hazard to anyone passing underneath. Raising the crown improves the situation by removing the lowest branches (see below); this can involve taking off one or more sizable boughs (see page 47). Where several large branches are involved, it is a good idea to spread the work over two to three years, re-assessing the shape of the tree each summer.

thinning the crown

Trees such as malus or sorbus develop a cluttered head of twiggy growth that may eventually cast unwanted shade and offer high resistance to wind, sometimes resulting in wind damage and disease. Removing some smaller branches and sideshoots during winter can improve the air circulation. Carry out any further thinning the following midsummer, when you can assess how much reduction in shade you have already achieved.

PRUNING MATURE TREES TIP Any pruning should retain the characteristic shape of the tree, and it is advisable to have the job done by a qualified tree surgeon, especially if much of the work needs to be done off the ground.

pruning a young tree

1 **The autumn** after planting, cut out the sideshoots (or feathers) on the lowest third of the stem to clean the trunk. This is sometimes known as 'feathering'.

2 **Shorten sideshoots** on the next third of the trunk by half, and leave the top third unpruned. Repeat this each year until the clean trunk is the required height, above which natural branching can be allowed to develop.

raising the crown

1 **When the tree is dormant,** work your way up the trunk, removing enough of the lowest branches to raise the tree's crown, or head, of branches.

2 **While the tree retains** its distinct profile, the crown is then carried on a taller trunk.

shrubs & trees/5

pruning out problems

Frost, wind and shade as well as age, pests and diseases all modify growth in various ways. Remedial pruning can often restore good health and shapeliness.

pruning for health

Although easily overlooked in a busy garden, pruning for health is an important part of the annual routine, and if done in time will often prevent a condition from spreading.

Make a point of inspecting all shrubs and trees during the dormant season, and prune back any dead or damaged shoots to live, healthy wood, cutting just above an outward-facing bud to encourage bushy regrowth away from the plant's centre. Check again in spring, after the worst frosts, to cut out frost-damaged shoots, especially on evergreens and conifers.

Pruning can be the quickest and most effective treatment for disease, and it is worth inspecting all woody plants every month in the growing season for initial signs. Shoots affected by mildew, canker and die-back, for example, should be cut back to healthy wood before starting other remedial treatments and this may even be sufficient to control the problem. Before and after cutting diseased wood, dip your pruning tools in horticultural disinfectant; this is essential for serious diseases such as fireblight, which disfigures and even kills cotoneasters and pyracanthas.

The variegated *Euonymus japonicus* is a valuable shrub in winter. It should only need pruning if it outgrows its allotted space.

Some variegated shrubs, such as euonymus and hollies, produce plain yellow or white shoots, and these should be removed.

preventing reversion

Many variegated shrubs and trees show an occasional tendency to revert to their original all-green form, by producing more vigorous green shoots. Left untreated these can eventually crowd out the variegated foliage. Cut out reverted shoots at their point of origin, removing a whole stem or branch if necessary. Do this in winter for evergreens, and deciduous shrubs as you see them.

removing suckers

Suckers are shoots produced from the base or the roots of a tree or shrub, especially if the variety has been grafted on a different rootstock. They often look distinctive and grow vigorously, spoiling the shape of the plant, and if derived from a rootstock can come to dominate the rest of the shrub – so they must be cut out while young (see below).

Thin stems, known as water shoots, often grow on a trunk, especially around the edge of a wound left after the removal of a branch. Although these are not, strictly speaking, suckers, they too spoil the look of a plant and should also be removed.

removing suckers

1 **Suckers grow** vigorously and must be removed.

2 **Cut off larger suckers** as close to the stem or roots as possible. For the best results, scrape back the soil and pull them off at source. You can use suckers from ungrafted plants as a method of propagation (see page 39).

If a tree has competing main shoots (leaders), select the strongest shoot and cleanly cut out its rivals at their base. Check in a year or two that no shoots are growing from the pruning wounds.

Remove an over-vigorous leading shoot with loppers before it is too large, cutting at or just below the main outline. Trim the tips of other main shoots to check their growth and encourage them to branch.

keeping a tree symmetrical

Sometimes the growing tip of a tree splits to produce two or more competing main shoots (leaders). As well as spoiling the overall symmetry of the tree, these usually branch at a narrow angle, creating a weak point that can later be damaged by strong winds. Some trees and shrubs, such as holly, produce vigorous new leading shoots that spoil the shape of the bush or tree if they are left to grow and these need to be cut out so a more balanced profile can develop (see above).

weeping trees

Encourage a young weeping tree to gain height by tying the topmost shoot vertically to a strong cane. Once this shoot develops sideshoots, you can trim off some of the lower branches to raise the crown (see page 45).

- **if the main shoot** gets broken or damaged, train the nearest branch vertically to a cane, or to the broken shoot, provided it is healthy. The replacement will later take over, then you can remove the damaged shoot at its base.
- **some weeping trees**, especially standards, are grafted, or joined, onto a straight, clear stem of a different variety, which may suddenly produce upright shoots. These should be cut right out before they spoil the shape of the tree's head.

The weeping pear looks just as beautiful when pruned to a mophead as when it trails down.

pruning large branches

Before cutting off a large tree branch, make sure you feel able to do the work safely. If in doubt, or if the branch is more than 20cm (8in) in diameter, consider hiring a qualified tree surgeon, especially if the branch is well above ground level. Make the final cut flush not with the trunk but with the branch collar, the swollen area where branch and trunk join.

removing a large branch

1 To prevent the branch splitting and tearing the bark, use a sharp pruning saw to make a preliminary upward cut, about a quarter of the way through the branch and 30–45cm (12–18in) away from the trunk.

2 Saw through the branch from above, cutting 2–3cm (1in) outside the first cut, which will close and absorb the weight of the branch, making it easier for you to saw.

3 Saw off the stub by making a small cut on the underside, close to the trunk but not quite flush with it, and finish by sawing from above to meet this cut.

shrubs & trees/6

pruning for special effects

You can enhance the ornamental value of some trees and shrubs using special pruning techniques that emphasise the colour or shape of leaves and bark.

coppicing and pollarding

Woody plants react to pruning by producing fresh growth. The harder they are pruned, the more vigorous is their response, and this predictable behaviour is often exploited in hard pruning shrubs and trees whose young stems and foliage are more colourful or shapely than those of mature plants. Two traditional methods of hard pruning are coppicing (or stooling), and pollarding. Both styles are useful but they produce dramatically different effects.

- **coppicing shrubs** produces a large crop of new shoots of medium height and allows a number of plants to be grown in a relatively small space. All growth is cut back regularly, usually annually, close to ground level.
- **pollarding** is like coppicing, but leaves permanent main stems of manageable size. It allows plants to retain single or multiple main stems of a certain height, above which all growth is hard pruned.

HEAVY PRUNING TIP Frequent heavy pruning can weaken plants unless they are fed and well mulched afterwards.

for colourful stems

Hard prune coloured willows, red, green and yellow-stemmed dogwoods and the white-stemmed bramble, *Rubus cockburnianus*, in spring to stimulate plenty of young regrowth with the brightest winter colouring (see opposite).

- Immediately after planting, cut all stems down almost to ground level. This helps shrubs like dogwoods to form a low woody base, while the bramble responds by producing numerous young canes.
- Thereafter, cut stems back hard in late winter to mid-spring.
- To enjoy the flowers of dogwoods in combination with the bright young stems, coppice half the stems and leave others untouched. This also helps the shrub to build up strength, and is a useful compromise if new growth has been poor.

for improved foliage

Some trees produce their most handsome leaves on young stems, and coppicing is a useful technique for displaying these to advantage. Tree of heaven (*Ailanthus*), paulownia and many ornamental elders such as the golden cut-leaved *Sambucus racemosa* 'Plumosa Aurea', all produce luxuriant foliage, often brightly coloured or of enormous size, when coppiced in spring. The smoke bush, *Cotinus coggygria*, has fine foliage if coppiced, or attractive wispy flowers when left unpruned. Young *Eucalyptus gunnii* has rounded, blue-green juvenile leaves that are more attractive than the grey-green adult foliage. This and other eucalyptus can be coppiced or pollarded to 1–1.2m (3–4ft) high in March or April, with all growth trimmed annually to 5–8cm (2–3in) from its base.

Young green-stemmed dogwoods (*Cornus stolonifera* 'Flaviramea') need to be coppiced in spring in order to produce brightly coloured stems.

coppicing hazel

1 **Purple hazel** produces more vividly coloured foliage and also useful crops of peasticks if coppiced when two to three years old.

2 **Cut off all growth** to ground level, leaving cuts that slope away from the centre of the plant; feed afterwards for maximum regrowth.

training standard trees

Standard trees with a single stem 1.5–2m (5–6ft) high are rewarding tree forms in gardens because the clear trunk allows easy access all round, and other plants can be grown beneath without competition for light. There are two kinds.

- **central-leader standard** retains a central main stem for the tree's full height and is the shape favoured for forest and woodland trees, such as oak and beech. Cut out any competing main shoots (see page 47) and prune sideshoots off the trunk as the tree develops (see page 45).
- **branched-head standard** is the preferred shape for most small ornamental trees like crab apples, cherries and rowans. Trained like this, they achieve a symmetrical arrangement of similar-sized main branches radiating from the top of the trunk. To create a branched-head standard tree:
- For the first three to four years prune as described on page 45.
- When four or five strong branches have developed above the required height of the main stem, prune back the central upright or 'leading' branch to a strong bud.
- Afterwards, thin out resulting sideshoots to help develop an open, symmetrical crown; remove strong vertical branches.

training shrubs against a wall

Hardy shrubs such as cotoneaster, chaenomeles, ceanothus and ornamental prunus varieties occupy less space, yet cover a large area to good effect, if trained against a wall as fans and espaliers. Start training early for the most complete coverage and provide support in the form of trellis or wires (see Autumn).

Chaenomeles trained against a wall on horizontal wires will display its flowers to best effect.

- After planting, tie the main shoot and branches in a well-spaced arrangement. Prune out weak and surplus shoots, shorten outward-growing sideshoots to two or three buds or leaves, and remove any growing towards the wall.
- Keep tying in developing growth to create a framework of branches; prune out redundant shoots to define the shape.
- Once a framework is established, prune annually according to the shrub's flowering season (see page 43). In midsummer remove inward-growing shoots and cut back those growing out from the wall to keep the shrub neat and densely leaved.

tiered shrubs

Shrubs with a naturally tiered structure, such as *Viburnum plicatum* 'Mariesii' and some japanese maples, need careful pruning to retain this habit. The removal of dead and diseased wood is often all that is needed, but you may need to cut out a crossing branch or uncharacteristic upright shoot. On mature plants, be prepared to cut out one or two older branches for replacement by younger shoots, and to shorten some sideshoots.

hard pruning dogwoods

1 **Shrubs such as dogwoods** (*Cornus*) can be coppiced (see opposite) or pollarded annually to leave taller main stems. Either method will stimulate plenty of regrowth with the brightest bark.

2 **Once the coloured stems** begin to bud, in late winter, cut the stems back hard, in stages, until the shrub is reduced to its framework of permanent branches.

3 **After pruning,** feed the shrub with a balanced fertiliser and mulch.

alpine gardens

Now that there is little likelihood of damaging plant growth, you can spruce up alpine plantings in rockeries, raised beds and containers. So pick off dead foliage, clear weeds, add more top-dressing, if necessary, and protect susceptible plants from the worst of the winter wet.

now is the season to . . .

- **ensure good drainage** for alpines growing in containers as they dislike wet soil. Raise the containers just off the ground so water drains away freely.
- **remove dead leaves** and flowers to prevent the spread of fungal diseases.
- **pull up weeds,** taking care to remove all the roots of perennial weeds. If any weeds are growing through plants, dig up the clump and tease out the roots. Otherwise make a note to treat the weeds with systemic weedkiller in spring. Lift up the foliage of carpeting plants where weeds may grow undetected.
- **protect alpines with fleshy or woolly leaves** from excess wet with cloches or panes of glass, unless already done in the autumn. Susceptible plants growing in containers should be moved to an unheated greenhouse or coldframe.
- **top up mulches** of stone chippings or fine gravel to keep a thickness of at least 2–3cm (1in). These materials prevent rotting by creating a 'collar' of good drainage around plants, where moisture could otherwise collect.
- **propagate more alpines** from seed, by scooping out rosettes, or by taking root cuttings (see below and opposite).

The fleshy-leaved *Saxifraga spathularis* will survive a dusting of frost, but it is important that this succulent is not allowed to get too wet.

A pane of glass supported on upturned pots can protect fleshy-leaved alpines from wet winter weather.

propagation

Winter is the time to sow seeds of alpines as many require a period of cold, known as stratification, in order to germinate. There are exceptions, and these include anemone, corydalis, primula and pulsatilla, all of which need sowing when the seed is freshly collected.

A few alpines, such as *Anacyclus depressus*, erodiums and *Primula denticulata*, are propagated from root cuttings in autumn and winter. Follow the method described on page 27 for perennials, but take smaller cuttings about 5cm (2in) long.

Plants that form rosettes, such as many saxifrages and *Primula denticulata*, can be propagated by scooping out rosettes to encourage new, young plants to develop. Select healthy, strong-growing rosettes and cut them off using a sharp knife to expose the top of the root, then discard. Brush the exposed area with fungicide powder to prevent disease. Soon, a cluster of shoots should develop all round the edge of the cut area and, when 2–5cm (1–2in) tall, these can be separated from the parent. Pot up individually, using the compost mix described opposite for sowing, to give the sharp drainage required.

alpines to sow now

- campanula
- chiastophyllum
- dianthus
- dodecatheon
- draba
- saxifraga
- scutellaria
- sedum

Sedum spurium

sowing seeds

To give alpines the sharp drainage they need, mix a special potting compost of equal parts by volume of seed and cuttings compost and perlite or sharp sand. Water the compost before sowing to avoid washing the seeds down deeply where they would not germinate.

After sowing stand the pots in a coldframe. The seedlings may take several months to show. Prick them out carefully once two true leaves have formed, then put the pot back in the coldframe. It can take up to a year for some seeds to germinate.

SOWING TIP Large seeds with hard coats will germinate more readily if chipped with a sharp knife or soaked overnight in tepid water before sowing.

sowing seeds

1 Fill pots with compost, firm gently and water using a can fitted with a fine rose. Spread the seeds thinly and evenly over the surface.

2 Cover the seeds to their own depth with sieved compost, unless the seeds are very fine, and top with a 1cm (½in) layer of grit to protect the seeds and prevent moss from growing. For fine seeds cover only with grit.

3 Once the seedlings start to show through, prick out those that have two true leaves, then return the pot to the coldframe to encourage others to germinate.

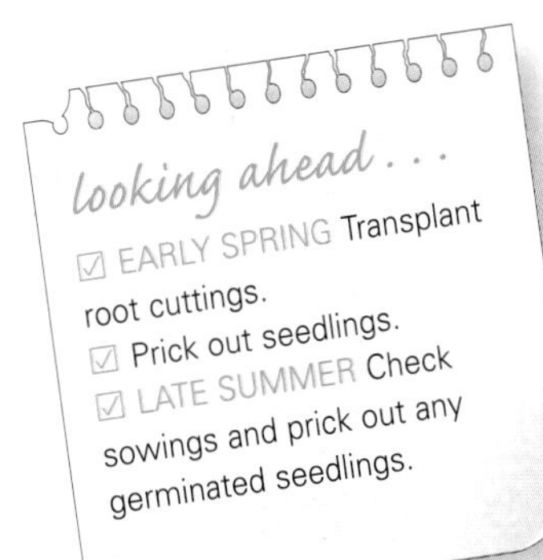

looking ahead . . .

☑ EARLY SPRING Transplant root cuttings.
☑ Prick out seedlings.
☑ LATE SUMMER Check sowings and prick out any germinated seedlings.

water gardens

Once you have cleared the pond of leaves and plant remains, and taken care of the pump, there is little to do until the frosts arrive. Then it is essential to keep an area of water ice-free, so that fish and other pond creatures can survive the sub-zero conditions.

now is the season to . . .

- **remove dead plant growth** if not done earlier (see Autumn), or it will rot down and pollute the water. Cut back the stems of marginal aquatic plants to just above the water level.
- **always keep** a small area of water ice-free in freezing weather (see below).
- **plan new planting** for the spring (see opposite).
- **sweep off snow** lying on the ice after a couple of days, so that light can penetrate to the depths.
- **scoop out leaves** that have blown into the pond and are starting to sink using a child's fishing net or an old kitchen sieve. Take care not to dredge the bottom where frogs and toads are likely to be hibernating.
- **do not feed fish** in winter as they live off their reserves during cold weather.
- **run pumps** that remain in water, insulate external pumps and service those that have been removed (see right).

keeping the pond ice-free

A solid layer of ice on the pond is potentially lethal to fish, and to frogs and toads that may be hibernating at the bottom, as it prevents vital oxygen from entering the water and toxic gases from escaping. It is essential, therefore, to keep a small area of open water. One solution is to install a pond heater, which can replace a pump removed for the winter. Otherwise, you can buy an ice-guard device and float it on the surface of the water; this will also provide a hibernation place for frogs and toads. If a thick layer of ice does form, never break it with a sharp blow as the shock waves can kill fish and other pond-dwellers. Instead, set a pan of boiling water on the surface of the ice to gently melt a hole in it.

If your pond is ice-bound, stand a saucepan of boiling water on it to melt a hole. Never break it with a sharp blow.

winter pump care

If you have not already done so, remove submersible pumps from the water. Clean them thoroughly in fresh water, drain and allow to dry before storing over winter. If necessary, send the pump for servicing while it is not needed. Any pumps that remain in water over winter should be at least 45cm (18in) deep to prevent them from freezing. Run the pump for a short time once a fortnight to prevent the build-up of scale or silt. Drain external pumps and insulate them with bubble plastic.

Once the edges of a pond start to freeze, take steps to keep at least part of the water ice-free for the sake of the wildlife within it.

storing a pump

Lift the submersible pump out of the water, with the brick on which it is mounted.

Carefully remove the filter in order to clean the pump before putting it away for winter.

plants for ponds

SMALL PONDS (*minimum size 1 x 1.5m/3 x 5ft*)

1 water lily (*Nymphaea*) such as: 'Aurora', 'Froebelii', 'Hermine', 'James Brydon', 'Laydekeri' varieties and 'Sioux'. Plant in water 30–45cm (12–18in) deep.

4–5 marginal plants such as: • marsh marigold (*Caltha palustris*) • *Iris laevigata* 'Variegata' • corkscrew rush (*Juncus effusus* f. *spiralis*) • american water mint (*Mentha cervina*) • water forget-me-not (*Myosotis scorpioides* 'Mermaid') • arum lily (*Zantedeschia*)

MEDIUM-SIZED PONDS (*minimum size 1.8 x 2.4m/6 x 8ft*)

1 water lily (*Nymphaea*) such as: 'Conqueror', 'Marliacea Albida', 'Marliacea Chromatella', 'Paul Hariot', 'Rosennymphe'. Plant in water 45–75cm (18–30in) deep.

6–8 marginal plants such as: • *Acorus calamus* 'Variegatus' • flowering rush (*Butomus umbellatus*) • manna grass (*Glyceria maxima* var. *variegatus*) • *Houttuynia cordata* 'Chameleon' • *Iris pseudacorus* 'Variegata' • water mint (*Mentha aquatica*) • water forget-me-not (*Myosotis scorpioides*) • pickerel weed (*Pontederia cordata*)

All plants listed for small ponds are also suitable.

choosing plants for your pond

While pond planting should be done in spring or early summer, now is a good time to plan new planting and to order aquatic and marginal plants for delivery as soon as the weather warms up. The most important aspect is to choose plants of a suitable size to match that of your pond, because marginal plants and water lilies vary considerably in spread and vigour. This is crucial for small to medium ponds as plants that are too large will produce profuse quantities of foliage that needs regular trimming, but comparatively few flowers.

Ensure that your pond looks good from spring to autumn by choosing a mixture of foliage plants that provide long-lasting interest and flowering plants for each season. Always have oxygenating plants to help keep the water clear, planting three small bunches to each square metre of pond surface area (one bunch per square foot).

looking ahead . . .

☑ SPRING Remove pond heater.
☑ Start feeding fish, sparingly at first.
☑ Install submersible pumps.

A pond in winter, devoid of all planting, takes on an ethereal beauty.

patios & containers

Hardy shrubs and seasonal flowers in tubs and window boxes keep the patio cheerful throughout the winter, but in all but the mildest areas containers will need protection from frost. Towards the end of winter, take time to tidy up and clean patios and any other hard surfaces to prevent them from becoming slippery.

now is the season to . . .

- **move containers** that are not frost-proof under cover, to a greenhouse, conservatory or coldframe.
- **clean paved paths,** patios and decking (see Early Spring).
- **empty out containers** of frost-tender plants that are dead. Scrub the containers using hot water and a mild detergent, rinse and leave to dry, then store under cover.
- **protect container-grown plants** against frost (see right). The extent of the protection required depends on the hardiness of the plant.
- **top-dress pot-grown lilies** while the bulbs are dormant by replacing the top 10cm (4in) of old soil with fresh loam-based potting compost.
- **water occasionally** if the compost begins to dry out. Regularly check containers that are standing close to a wall and so may not receive any rainfall.

frost protection

All container-grown plants need some degree of protection from frost, because both rootball and topgrowth are above the ground. Evergreens are particularly vulnerable, as they continue to lose water through their leaves and are unable to replenish their stocks if their roots are in frozen compost. The ideal solution is to move any susceptible plants into an unheated greenhouse, porch or conservatory, but if there is no such structure available plants have to be protected outside.

ensuring good drainage

It is vital to provide good drainage as soggy compost that freezes can result in severe damage to plants. When planting up pots, first put in a 5cm (2in) layer of drainage material, such as pieces of broken pot or chunks of polystyrene. Make

Stalwarts of winter containers, evergreen *Skimmia japonica* 'Rubella', *Heuchera micrantha* var. *diversifolia* 'Palace Purple' and ivy (left), are brightened by the cheerful 'faces' of universal pansies (*Viola* 'Ultima Scarlet').

protecting plants

Tall plants, such as standard evergreens and tree ferns, benefit from individual protection. Remove coverings during the day unless very low temperatures persist.

Tie up the leaves of cordylines, then wrap the whole plant in fleece or bubble plastic.

sure that surplus water can drain away by raising all containers just off the ground, either on 'pot feet' or pieces of tile, or by standing them on gravel.

grouping containers

If severe weather threatens, move all containers against a wall, standing them shoulder to shoulder; this will raise the temperature around the pots by a valuable few degrees.

- **wrap insulating material,** such as bubble plastic, sacking or thick wads of straw around the pots.
- **cover the plants** with thick horticultural fleece during very cold spells, but remove this during the day or as soon as the weather improves, otherwise fungal disease may become a problem.
- **remember that** well-protected plants may need watering.

A window box planting for winter relies on colourful foliage. This one includes silver-leaved cineraria, grey-leaved senecio, variegated ivy and the winter cherry (*Solanum capsicastrum*).

Insulate container-grown plants that are not fully hardy with an 'overcoat' of sacking and straw in severe weather (above).

Wrap the stems of standard evergreens in pipe insulation (top left), then cover the pot and the head of the plant with fleece (left).

Fold the dead fronds of tree ferns over the top of the crown (below), before encasing the whole plant in a 'jacket' of bubble plastic (bottom).

lawns

Although we think of winter as a time when the lawn takes a rest, this really only applies when conditions are very cold. During mild spells the grass will often grow and you can mow, repair turf or even make a new lawn.

now is the season to . . .

- **rake up any leaves,** which if left will block out light, hold moisture and encourage moss to establish.
- **scatter worm casts** with a stiff broom or besom to prevent the mounds of soil being smeared by feet or by the mower and killing the grass.
- **make a final winter cut** with the mower blades on a high setting (see opposite). Rake off any clippings to prevent them from killing the grass beneath. In mild winters you may need to cut the grass more than once if it continues to grow.
- **avoid walking over a frosted lawn** as the pressure damages the grass, causing it to turn brown and, possibly, to die.
- **'top' newly established lawns** with the mower blades on their highest setting to encourage more shoots from the base of the plants. If the new grass is quite low, roll it lightly to encourage branching and a denser lawn (not in frosty conditions).
- **apply lime** to lawns on acid soil if moss has been a particular problem.
- **improve drainage** by spiking or slitting (see right).
- **in mild conditions carry out minor repairs,** such as mending damaged lawn edges, and even out bumps and hollows that have formed as parts of the lawn settle (see Autumn).
- **prepare the soil for new grass** in mild weather. You can lay turf or sow seed in winter, but growth will be slow if the soil temperature drops below 5°C (40°F). In early winter, seed is the better option, as turf may dry out along its edges if there are any hard frosts within the first weeks after laying.

improving drainage

The problem that causes most damage in winter is wet, rather than cold, as long periods of mild wet weather starve the roots of air as they are trying to grow. During the summer lawns often develop a compacted, impervious layer just below the surface from regular foot traffic, and this impedes drainage unless it is opened up by spiking or slitting.

- **spike** with a garden fork, or preferably, a hollow-tine lawn spiker, to help air get to the grass roots. Drive in the tines 15cm (6in) deep every 15–20cm (6–8in).

This specimen cherry tree in the middle of a contoured lawn is a striking centrepiece even in winter, with its tracery of bare branches outlined against the frosted grass.

Stepping stones set into a lawn prevent people having to walk on the grass in frosty weather, which can damage the grass blades and make them turn brown.

- **slitting** with a powered scarifying machine is an easier and quicker way to deal with a large lawn and also gathers surface debris, such as dead grass and moss. Blades cut into the top 2–3cm (1in) of soil. As well as improving drainage, scarifiers prune the grass roots, encouraging them to branch.
- **after spiking or slitting,** top-dress lawns on heavier soils with a mixture of equal parts of sand and loam, brushing it into the holes. This will help to improve drainage.
- **for areas that get very wet,** you can lay land drains (see Autumn); do this early in winter before the ground is too wet.

CLEANING TIP Use a plastic scraper to clean off any caked grass stuck to the mower. This not only makes it easier to examine, but also protects your mower, as grass sap stains plastic and corrodes metal. Where grass is lodged in places that are difficult to clean, blow it out with a few blasts from a bicycle pump.

equipment overhaul

In late autumn and winter, when the grass hardly grows, take the opportunity to check over your mower and other lawn equipment. Clean electrically powered machinery such as mowers and scarifiers. Check and oil all moving parts, and sharpen blades with a file to regain a sharp edge, or replace them if necessary.

- **petrol-driven mowers** can be washed clean with a power hose and left to dry, but this is not recommended for machinery powered by battery or electricity.
- **cylinder mowers** need to be serviced by a specialist, who will sharpen the blades on a grinding lathe.

raising the blades of a rotary mower

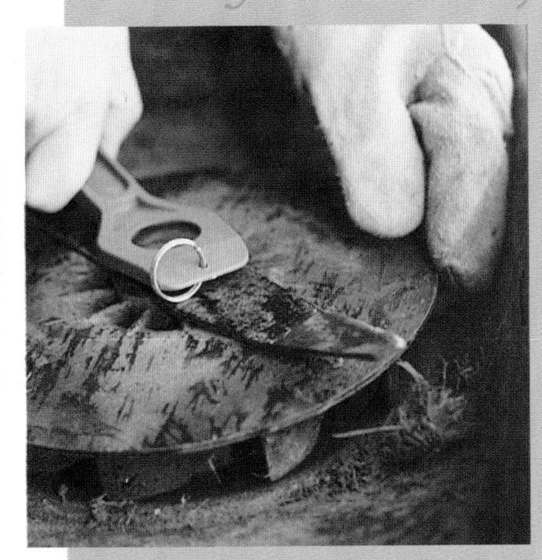

1 **Using the spanner** provided, slacken the spindle nut that holds the cutting blade onto the underside of the mower. Always wear a thick leather glove to grip the blade as it may be sharp.

2 **Carefully remove** the spindle nut, the cutting blade and the spacer washer from the mower.

3 **Now re-attach** the blade and spindle nut (but not the spacer washer – keep this safe); tighten the spindle nut. Without the spacer washer, the blade is raised and the mower will cut at a higher setting.

fruit

With all fruit crops harvested and safely stored, winter is mainly a time for maintenance, pruning and taking precautions against pests and diseases, but even now some fruits are nearly ready for forcing into early life.

now is the season to . . .

- **inspect stored fruit** every two to three weeks. Use any that is showing signs of deterioration, and discard rotting fruits before decay can spread.
- **continue planting** new fruit whenever conditions are suitable.
- **check ties and supports:** secure, adjust or repair if needed.
- **clear weeds** for a distance of 60cm (2ft) around fruit plants and hoe the surface, to expose pest eggs and larvae to foraging birds.
- **prune gooseberries and autumn-fruiting raspberries** by cutting all canes down to 5–8cm (2–3in).
- **finish taking hardwood cuttings** of bush fruits while plants are dormant.
- **carry out essential winter pruning** before the end of January (see right).
- **look over blackcurrant bushes** for big bud (see opposite).
- **check grease bands** on fruit trees; reapply grease if needed.
- **deal with canker** on apple and pear trees (see opposite).
- **apply a winter wash** to dormant fruit trees (see opposite).
- **protect fruit buds** from birds.
- **guard peaches** and nectarines from peach leaf curl with screens of polythene as described for climbers on page 35, and spray with copper-based fungicide.
- **grass down** established fruit trees if yields are low (see opposite).
- **start fruits under glass** into growth (see page 67–68).

and if you have time . . .

- **place cloches** over strawberry plants to force early crops.
- **cover rhubarb** with boxes or forcing pots for an early harvest (see page 67).

winter pruning guide

A simple winter pruning routine applies to all tree and bush fruits except plums, cherries, peaches and other stone fruits (see Early Spring). These are pruned in spring after the buds have opened, to reduce the chance of disease.

Prune apple trees in winter, when they are completely dormant.

- **cut back any dead,** damaged and diseased stems to healthy live wood.
- **remove branches that cross** others or grow towards the centre of the plant; bushes, in particular, should be kept open-centred in a goblet shape.
- **further shorten sideshoots** on cordons, espaliers and fans, which were summer-pruned to four or five leaves, to just one or two buds. For gooseberries and red and white currants, prune back the tips of main branches at the same time.
- **thin out congested spurs** on mature trained forms of apple and pear; shorten long spurs by half, and remove completely some that are growing closely together.
- **encourage sideshoots** and spurs to develop on young espalier and fan-trained fruit by shortening main branches by half. Cut to a downward-facing bud.
- **on overgrown or neglected trees,** cut out completely one or two main branches to admit more light and air and encourage new growth.

Snow settles on a row of neatly trained raspberry canes, forming a ghostly structure in the garden.

treating pests and diseases

There are measures you can take now to protect plants from pests and counteract several serious diseases.

blackcurrant big bud

Blackcurrant gall mites overwinter inside buds, causing them to swell and fail to develop. The mites also spread reversion virus, a serious and incurable disease. Check bushes in winter and early spring for the characteristic fat, rounded buds. Pick off any you find, and burn or otherwise destroy them.

apple and pear canker

This fungal disease can be serious if allowed to spread unchecked. Cracks and lesions develop on branches and at the base of spurs and sideshoots, often causing them to die back altogether if infection rings the stem. The disease is most prevalent on wet soils and is often controlled by improving drainage. Some apple varieties, such as 'Cox's Orange Pippin', are particularly vulnerable, whereas 'Bramley's Seedling', 'Lane's Prince Albert' and 'Newton Wonder' are more resistant.

Canker is a potentially serious fungal disease of apple and pear trees, most often caused by wet conditions.

- **remove diseased** and mummified fruits.
- **prune back affected shoots** and cut out lesions on main stems; paint the cuts with fungicidal wound paint.
- **grass down** older trees to prevent rain splashes, which spread the spores (see below).
- **remove and destroy** badly infected trees.

winter washing fruit

Painting or spraying fruit trees with a tar-oil winter wash is a traditional way of killing overwintering pest larvae and eggs, disease spores, moss and lichen. This wash is a very toxic substance so the whole area under the trees should be covered with plastic sheeting or thick layers of newspaper before treatment to keep splashes off neighbouring plants. It is also indiscriminate in its treatment, killing eggs and the larvae of beneficial insects as well as fruit pests.

grassing down to improve yields

If fruiting on mature trees is in decline, sow grass seed or turf right up to their trunks to help restore the balance of nutrients in the soil. Don't feed the trees for two or three years, or use a high-potash, low-nitrogen fertiliser.

there is still time to . . .

- **prune blackberries** and summer-fruiting raspberries (see Autumn).

looking ahead . . .

☑ LATE SUMMER Summer-prune trained fruit.
☑ AUTUMN Spray against peach leaf curl just before the leaves fall.

pruning gooseberries

1 Shorten to two buds all sideshoots that were summer-pruned to five leaves, and completely remove any thin or spindly shoots.

2 Cut out one or two of the old, dark branches where young shoots are growing and tie these in, as replacements.

3 Remove any surplus shoots growing from the base, clear weeds and mulch with straw, bracken or well-rotted manure.

vegetables

Take advantage of mild spells to get ahead in the vegetable garden by digging and preparing seedbeds. There are still some fresh crops to pick to supplement those stored away in late summer and autumn. On dark, chilly days draw up plans for next year, so you can get your orders for seeds, young plants and potatoes in early.

now is the season to . . .

■ **plan next year's crop rotation** (see pages 142–3) and order seeds and potatoes for the coming season.

■ **create a seedbed** early in winter. Cover the area with plastic sheeting to warm the soil for early crops (see opposite).

■ **hoe off weed seedlings.**

■ **watch for pest and diseases** in mild periods. Look for aphids hiding in the outer leaves of cabbages, cauliflowers and other overwintering vegetables.

■ **be prepared to control slugs** with baits or chemicals. Young slugs start feeding on plants almost immediately the eggs hatch in warm spells.

■ **watch for bird damage:** crops will be attacked as food supplies become scarce, and hungry wood pigeons can devastate a crop of cauliflowers. Protect vegetables with netting or use bird scarers. A length of twine or old video tape stretched just above the crop deters many birds but not wood pigeons, which tend to walk in to feed, rather than fly direct.

■ **use stored vegetables** and check those that remain; discard any with signs of mould or rot. Watch for vermin damage, as mice may nest and feed in your store during cold periods.

harvesting now

• brussels sprouts • celeriac • jerusalem artichokes • kale • leeks • parsnips • swedes • winter cabbage • winter cauliflower • winter radish • winter spinach

Celeriac ready for lifting

■ **check storage temperatures:** if stored vegetables start to sprout, this indicates the store is too warm, and produce will deteriorate rapidly.

■ **put in place cloches** or low polythene tunnels to warm the soil and help it to dry out after wet weather.

■ **make early sowings** of beetroot, broad beans, carrots, lettuce, peas, radishes, spinach or turnips when the soil has warmed sufficiently and spring is approaching.

In a colourful winter vegetable bed, leeks 'Longbow' grow with two varieties of brussels sprout ('Rubine Red' and 'Icarus'). Pick the sprout tops for eating as greens, and to reduce the plants' exposure to wind.

winter cultivation

Complete winter digging when conditions allow. The heavier the soil, the earlier it should be dug to let frost break it down; lighter, free-draining soils can be left until later. The depth of cultivation depends on your soil and the plants you grow.

single digging

Single digging is ideal for shallow-rooted salad crops and small round-rooted vegetables. It entails digging trenches to a depth of about 30cm (12in), or one spade blade deep and wide. Work systematically across the plot; bury any plant debris and old mulch from the surface in the base of the previously opened trench, and cover it with soil as you dig the next (see Autumn).

double digging

Double digging improves poor drainage and is good preparation for deep-rooted crops, such as carrots and parsnips, and long-term crops like asparagus and rhubarb. It is similar to single digging but more strenuous, as you cultivate to approximately 60cm (2ft) or the depth of two spade blades. Well-rotted manure or garden compost is forked into the base of each trench. It is vital not to mix the darker topsoil with the paler, infertile subsoil as you work (see Autumn).

Double digging incorporates manure or garden compost, giving root crops a good start.

preparing a seedbed

Dig over the soil in autumn or early winter, especially if it is heavy. Roughly level the surface and leave for a month or two so the frost can break up the clods and make final preparation easier. This time lag also allows weeds to germinate, for easy removal later on.

Two or three weeks before sowing, when the weather is fair and the soil is not so wet it clings to your tools, lightly fork over the surface to break up any remaining clods and rake the surface level (see below). After the seedbed is prepared, warm the soil by covering it with cloches, low polythene tunnels, or black or clear plastic sheeting. Black plastic excludes light and heats up the soil more quickly, whereas the advantage of clear plastic is that it provides ideal conditions for weed seeds to germinate, for easier removal before sowing.

EARLY SOWING TIP Don't be tempted to sow seeds in periods of mild weather without first checking the soil temperature, as many seeds need the soil to be between 5–7°C (40–45°F) before they will germinate. Insert a thermometer into the top 8–10cm (3–4in) of soil regularly.

making a seedbed

1 **Break up any lumps of soil** on the prepared bed with the back of a fork, then rake the surface until it is fine and level.

2 **To warm the soil** for early sowings, cover the seedbed with plastic sheeting. Spread the plastic over upturned plant pots so that condensation drains to the edges rather than dripping on the prepared surface.

3 **Hoe off any seedling weeds** after two or three weeks, disturbing the soil as little as possible, or treat with weedkiller for a clean start.

vegetables/2

winter crops

Early winter is the time to browse through catalogues and order seeds and young plants. By late winter you can begin to sow for the year ahead in pots or cellular trays under cover and outside, if conditions are suitable. The success of your vegetable garden hinges on careful planning, both in terms of what you grow (see page 146) and how you operate your crop rotations (see page 142).

Winter cabbages can stay in the ground until you need them. This variety, with its distinctive crinkled leaves, is 'Winter Savoy'.

peas and beans

- **inspect autumn-sown broad beans** in spells of very cold weather and protect the plants with cloches or a covering of horticultural fleece.

Young broad beans may need to be protected with fleece.

- **sow broad beans** into 8–10cm (3–4in) pots, one or two per pot, in a cool greenhouse, ready to transplant in early spring.
- **check autumn-sown peas** under cloches and insulate with thick fleece or a layer of loose straw if very cold days and nights are anticipated.
- **sow early varieties of peas** in 8–10cm (3–4in) pots, two or three seeds per pot, in a cool greenhouse. These will be large enough for transplanting in mid-March and should crop in May.
- **sow early peas outdoors** under cloches to follow on the batches you have raised under glass.

cabbage family

- **harvest brussels sprouts:** pick the largest first from the base and work up the stem. Support the plants with short canes and string ties to prevent them from blowing over in exposed areas. Pick the leafy tops for eating and to reduce their vulnerability to wind rock.
- **when harvesting kale,** remove and compost larger outer leaves each time the young shoots are picked over.
- **cut winter cabbages** as required. Cut off the head, leaving 8–10cm (3–4in) of stalk protruding from the ground. Cross-cut these stalks to encourage a secondary crop of leafy greens in mid-spring.
- **in cold spells,** protect spring cabbages from pigeons by covering the crop with nets or by using bird scarers.

Pests may strip the leaves of brussels sprouts, but this will have no detrimental effect on the sprouts themselves.

Jumbo garlic cloves can be planted in cellular trays under glass, to plant outdoors once they have sprouted.

onion family

- **use stored onions,** shallots and garlic. Check bulbs and remove immediately any that show signs of rot or mould, before the infection can spread.
- **the last chance to plant garlic** is in February. Plant cloves 2–3cm (1in) deep and spaced 15–20cm (6–8in) apart, on a ridge if your soil is heavy.
- **plant shallots early,** from December to March. Plant the small bulbs, or sets, setting them 1cm (½in) deep and 10–15cm (4–6in) apart.
- **lift mature leeks** as required during mild spells; lifting them when the ground is frozen will cause bruising and stem rot.
- **during late winter, sow leeks** and onions in cellular trays or small pots and place in a cool greenhouse; sow four or five onion seeds per pot for transplanting in mid-spring.

salad crops

- **protect overwintering lettuce** with cloches or low polythene tunnels, allowing some ventilation to reduce the risk of fungal rots.
- **sow short rows of lettuce,** radish and spinach in late winter under cloches on previously warmed soil.

other crops

- **lift jerusalem artichoke** tubers as required. If cold weather is forecast, lift and temporarily store some for immediate use.
- **order asparagus crowns** for planting in early spring. Prepare planting trenches for the new beds by double digging (see Autumn).

Rows of lettuce seedlings are protected in a coldframe. Pick alternate plants and allow the others to develop a heart.

looking ahead . . .

☑ EARLY SPRING Plant early potatoes and asparagus crowns.

☑ Begin to plant out hardy crops started off under glass.

potatoes and root crops

- **use carrots and beetroot** in store, discarding any that are showing signs of rot.
- **lift celeriac, parsnip and winter radish** as required when the weather is mild and the soil is not frozen or waterlogged. If a cold spell is forecast, lift and store some roots in a shed so they are ready for use.
- **sow early varieties** of beetroot, carrot and turnip in open ground if the soil conditions are suitable. Pre-warming the soil and cloche protection will be necessary for the earliest sowings in all but the mildest gardens.
- **sow celeriac** in late winter in cellular trays in a cool greenhouse for transplanting in late spring.
- **order seed potatoes early** and sprout, or chit, early varieties indoors from February.

Early potatoes are sprouted, or 'chitted', in late winter or early spring. Lay them in seed trays or egg trays, rose end up (this is the end with most buds, or 'eyes'), in a cool, light frost-free place. About six weeks later, in early spring, each potato will have formed four to five shoots 2–3cm (1in) long. When conditions are suitable the tubers can then be planted (see Early Spring).

herbs

Fresh pickings come mostly from herbs in pots now that all but a few evergreens have died down in the garden. Most herb care is confined under glass, but outside you can rejuvenate leggy sage and thyme, and prepare to make early sowings.

Salad burnet is one of the few herbs to keep growing through winter, and makes a tasty salad crop.

now is the season to . . .

- **ventilate herbs under glass** in mild weather as a precaution against fungal disease.
- **water sparingly** lemon verbena and other overwintering tender herbs.
- **lay hard paths** in a new herb garden and start constructing new beds (see Late Summer).
- **protect containerised herbs** outdoors. In severe weather, bring the most vulnerable indoors or gather pots together and cover with fleece or bubble plastic (see page 54).
- **in early winter, pot up roots** of mint and tarragon for fresh early supplies.
- **order seeds of annual herbs** in good time (see opposite).
- **clear annual crops** and tidy beds. Mulch with garden compost or well-rotted manure, which can be forked in just before sowing in early spring.
- **cultivate new beds** for annual herbs (see opposite).
- **prepare a mint bed** where the roots will not invade other plants. Buy mint plants in late winter or lift and divide existing healthy roots for replanting 30cm (12in) apart.
- **propagate old leggy plants** of sage, thyme and other woody herbs by mound layering or dropping (see opposite).
- **protect bay trees** from cold and remedy any frost damage in late winter (see below).
- **cover a few parsley** and chive plants with cloches to revive growth for early pickings.

Pot up root cuttings of mint in a box of compost to force under glass.

protecting bay trees in winter

The shallow roots of bay trees less than three or four years old are vulnerable to frost, and severe cold weather can scorch the foliage of even mature trees. To guard against injury, plant bay in a sunny sheltered position, and screen from cold winds. In winter bring potted bay plants indoors, or protect both plant and container with fleece or bubble plastic and clad bare stems in foam pipe insulation (see page 55). A thick mulch of leaf-mould or straw over the roots helps to prevent freezing in pots or open ground.

Bay trees are susceptible to frost, which can scorch their leaves in winter.

- **if a few leaves turn brown,** remove them, but leave shoots intact in case fresh growth appears later in the year.
- **extensive leaf browning** usually indicates the death of the top growth, but provided the roots have been kept frost-free, new shoots may sprout from the base. So cut down the tree at the end of winter, leaving stumps about 10cm (4in) long, and apply a balanced fertiliser.

growing annual herbs

Annual or biennial herbs such as parsley, chervil and dill are usually sown in rows or in a special bed within the kitchen garden. Every two or three years it is advisable to prepare a new bed in a different position.

- **dig clay soil in autumn,** leave it rough and break it up finely with a fork in late winter. Add plenty of leaf-mould or garden compost to improve the texture and drainage.
- **dig light soils in late winter,** adding plenty of garden compost or well-rotted manure to improve water retention. Many annual herbs are leafy and grow fast, so need moister conditions than many aromatic perennials.
- **just before sowing** or planting, fork a balanced fertiliser into the top 8cm (3in) of soil. Then rake to leave a fine, level seedbed.

Sow parsley *in situ* in late winter; once germinated, and with cloche cover, it will rapidly put on leafy growth.

dropping a rosemary

1 Dig up the leggy plant in late winter or early spring and excavate the hole 30cm (12in) deeper than it was.

2 Replant in the same hole, spreading out the branches. Return the soil to cover the centre of the plant and the bare portions of the branches.

3 Keep moist in dry weather and transplant any rooted layers in autumn, or leave them to form a wider clump.

annual & biennial herbs

to raise from seed

- basil (tender) • borage
- caraway • chervil
- coriander • dill • parsley
- summer savory

Dill (*Anethum graveolens*)

propagating leggy herbs

Some woody herbs get very bare at the base if they are not clipped back regularly to keep them compact. If your herbs have become leggy you can take cuttings or layer some of the lower branches, and then discard the old plants. The alternative methods of 'dropping' (see left) or mound layering in late winter will give you numerous new plants while improving the appearance of the parent shrub until it is superseded. Dropping is best suited to sage, rosemary and lavender.

mound layering

This works well for thymes as well as other small woody herbs.

- Mix together equal parts of soil-based compost and grit and heap it over the bare centre of the plant, working it well in between the branches.
- Keep the plant moist in dry weather during the summer months.
- In early autumn, carefully explore around the branches, most of which will have formed roots. These layers can now be detached for transplanting.

Heap a mixture of compost and grit over the middle of a leggy thyme and keep it moist in dry weather to encourage layers to develop roots.

there is still time to . . .

- **plant new perennial herbs** and hedges when the ground is in a workable condition.

looking ahead . . .

- ☑ EARLY SPRING Sow annual and biennial herbs.
- ☑ Continue dividing perennials.
- ☑ AUTUMN Detach and pot up layers from mounded or dropped plants.

the greenhouse

A greenhouse is a comfortable sanctuary for gardeners as well as for tender plants. Visit it regularly to sow, prune and check that all is well; air it on fine days and water growing plants occasionally. Forced bulbs and early strawberries will be coming into flower if you have provided a little warmth.

now is the season to . . .

- **water plants sparingly** in cold weather, and avoid wetting foliage (see opposite).
- **open ventilators** for a short period on frost-free and fog-free days to prevent the air from stagnating.
- **make sure heaters are working** properly, and monitor temperature levels with a maximum-minimum thermometer.
- **keep insulation materials** securely in place, and have newspapers, blankets or fleece handy for covering plants in extreme weather, especially in unheated greenhouses.
- **remove dead flowers** and leaves, diseased plants and mildewed cuttings to keep healthy plants free from infection.
- **check for vine weevils** if any of your plants suddenly collapse (see page 69).
- **inspect stored bulbs** and tubers to make sure that they are still sound.
- **continue to bring potted bulbs** in from outdoors as they show signs of growth and flower buds (see page 30).
- **pot up amaryllis** and restart older bulbs (see page 31).
- **continue potting up lilies** for early flowers.
- **prune indoor grape vines,** and lower their stems (see page 68).
- **prune greenhouse climbers** and tie in any new stems (see page 68).
- **start under glass fruit trees** such as apricots for early fruit; hand-pollinate once flowers appear (see page 68).
- **bring in potted strawberries** and rhubarb crowns for forcing (see opposite).
- **from midwinter, sow greenhouse flowers** such as begonias and gloxinias, and the first half-hardy annuals.
- **start begonia and gloxinia tubers** in trays for a supply of cuttings (see page 68).
- **sow half-hardy annuals and early vegetables** in pots or trays.
- **sow lettuce and radish** in the greenhouse border if you have one. Sow tomato seeds in pots in mid-February for planting under glass in early April.
- **cut down greenhouse chrysanthemums** and encourage new growth for cuttings (see page 68).

Strawberries that were potted up last autumn and left outside should be brought into the greenhouse to force early fruits.

forcing early fruits

Strawberries and rhubarb (see below) are two fruits you can enjoy early with a frost-free greenhouse.

strawberries

Bring in batches of strawberry plants potted up in late summer or autumn and left outside to stimulate the production of flower buds. Clean the pots and remove any dead leaves, then stand the plants on a high shelf in the light.

- Water lightly at first, but increase as growth revives. Feed with a balanced liquid fertiliser every 14 days once in flower.
- Pollinate the flowers by gently brushing their centres with a soft paintbrush.
- Support developing fruit trusses with twigs. After harvest, harden the plants off and transplant into the garden.

On fine days open top ventilators slightly for an hour or two in the morning.

Use a maximum-minimum thermometer to check temperatures as these are critical in winter.

winter greenhouse management

Special care is essential in winter to keep plants healthy. Temperature and light levels are low, and knowing how much water and air to give plants can be tricky.

watering

Only plants in active growth will need much water. To keep these evenly moist, stand pots and trays in water until the surface starts to look damp; watering from above may just moisten the surface and leave the roots dry. Take care to avoid overwatering sensitive plants such as calceolarias and cinerarias, which can collapse suddenly if too wet. Most other plants need just enough to prevent the compost from drying out. Try to water in the mornings, so that surplus dries before nightfall, and avoid wetting the foliage.

ventilation

A dry atmosphere with a gentle circulation of air without cold draughts is the ideal, so open one or two top ventilators for an hour or so during the day, unless it is foggy or frosty. If possible, open vents on the side away from the wind, and close them by midday so that warmth has time to build up before sunset.

heat

Most plants benefit from temperatures above 5–7°C (40–45°F) (see page 139); use a thermometer to check. You can economise by gathering tender plants in a well-insulated area and heating only this. Germinate seeds on a windowsill or in a warm cupboard in the house, or invest in a heated propagator.

forcing rhubarb

1 **Bring in the strong crowns** you dug up and left exposed to frost in autumn, from December onwards. Place them under the greenhouse staging, blacking out the light with plastic or blankets. Pack straw, dry leaves or used potting compost between the plants, water well and drape another blanket from the front of the staging to ensure total darkness.

2 **Check weekly for watering** and to monitor growth. Pull sticks when they are a useable length. Discard the crowns once picking is over.

the greenhouse/2

plant care

Fruit trees growing under glass, such as peaches, nectarines and apricots, can be started into growth during January for fruits from June, if you provide a minimum temperature of 7°C (45°F). Keep ventilators closed until buds break, and mist the branches and sideshoots with warm water every other morning to stimulate growth. When flowers open, fertilise them by brushing the centres with a soft brush, or open the ventilators on a warm day to admit bees and other pollinating insects.

pruning climbers

In midwinter, clear all dead flowers and leaves from climbers, and then prune them according to size and variety. Strong-growing plants such as passionflower and bougainvillea can take over a small greenhouse unless pruned hard annually.

- Thin the congested growth, aiming for a balanced arrangement of main branches. Remove any weak or spindly stems, then shorten sideshoots almost to their base.
- You may need to cut out one or two older branches to allow replacement with young, more vigorous shoots. Sort the prunings for potential cuttings before discarding them.
- Finally, check the plant is symmetrical and well shaped, with plenty of light reaching all the stems.
- Clean the glass or wall behind the climber, prick over and weed the soil, and mulch plants growing in the ground.

pruning vines in winter

Prune greenhouse grape vines as soon as they have lost all their leaves. They are usually grown with a system of parallel main branches, or rods, from which fruiting sideshoots grow each year.

- Cut back sideshoots to one or two buds.
- Rub or pull any loose bark from the rods to expose and eliminate hiding places for pests.
- After pruning, untie the rods and lower them until they are horizontal or a little lower. This encourages all buds to start growing together, after which the rods can be retied in place. Do this in December, January or February: it depends on whether the variety is early, mid-season or late.

starting begonias, dahlias and gloxinias

Encourage tuberous-rooted begonias, dahlias and gloxinias into growth now to make large flowering plants and also to supply early shoots for cuttings (see below).

chrysanthemums from cuttings

When greenhouse and slightly tender border chrysanthemums finish flowering, cut down their topgrowth to 5–8cm (2–3in) high. Overwinter them in a cool frost-free place: indoor varieties in their pots, border kinds dug up and packed in soil in a coldframe or under the greenhouse staging. Keep watering to a minimum, just enough to prevent the plants from drying out. New shoots appear from late December onwards,

starting begonias into growth

1 Fill a tray with moist potting compost and press tubers into this, 5cm (2in) apart, so their tops are just above surface level. Make sure they are the right way up, with the rounded base downwards and the hollowed area uppermost, then water.

2 Cut very large tubers in half with a sharp knife to increase the number of plants, but dust the cut edges with yellow sulphur powder as a precaution against rotting. Use a propagator or cover the tray with a clear lid and keep moist at 13–15°C (55–60°F). In a cooler greenhouse, delay planting until early spring.

3 When growth appears, pot up the tubers individually.

Even in the coldest winter weather, plants inside the sheltered environment of the greenhouse will be safe and warm.

depending on the variety. Use these for cuttings when they are about 8cm (3in) long.

- Cut off all the lower leaves and trim each cutting just below a leaf joint.
- Insert them 2–3cm (1in) deep in pots of cuttings compost mixed with added sharp sand; five will fit comfortably in a 15cm (6in) pot.
- Water, cover with a clear plastic bag and keep in a light, warm position until rooted.

vine weevils

The damaging effects of this troublesome weevil whose grubs feed on roots can be obvious in winter. If plants start to look sick and then suddenly collapse, tip them out carefully and explore the compost for the curved larvae, creamy white with brown heads.

- **inspect plants** in the evening for irregular holes round the edges of leaves, typical evidence of adults feeding, and crush any you find.
- **during summer,** when the temperature is at least 12°C (54°F), use a biological control: water plants with a parasitic nematode (*Heterorhabditis*) to kill the grubs.
- **throughout the year,** tip out plants occasionally to check for grubs and inspect new plants before introducing them to the greenhouse.
- **surround the rims** of precious plants with double-sided sticky tape to trap adults before they can lay eggs.
- **try using** an insecticidal compost containing imidocloprid.

looking ahead . . .

☑ LATE SPRING Plant forced strawberries in the garden.
☑ Start hardening off young plants.
☑ SUMMER Introduce biological pest controls.

there is still time to . . .

- **clean out the greenhouse,** and wash the glass and all equipment (see Autumn).

Yellow-flowered *Lachenalia* enjoys the protection of a greenhouse, along with *Pelargonium graveolens* cuttings and a tray of developing seedlings.

the healthy garden

While plants are dormant or just biding their time in the cold weather, take the opportunity to stand back and reassess your garden. On fine days, clean tools and other equipment, so they are ready for use in spring.

winter checklist

Use this checklist to make sure you have not overlooked any important seasonal jobs.

- **clear fallen leaves,** especially from hedge bottoms, ponds and alpines that might rot, and stack to decay into leaf-mould. Don't clear leaves from wildlife hedges as they provide useful winter habitats for a range of animals and insects.

Give wooden fences and other timber structures a coat of preservative every few years.

- **inspect fences,** trellis and supports. Make necessary repairs, and in dry weather treat wooden structures with preservative.
- **clean and store pots,** trays, canes and labels for spring.
- **empty hosepipes,** roll them up and store under cover. Wash watering cans and hang them up to drain and prevent algae growing inside.
- **continue planting** new trees, shrubs and perennials, except in frosty or wet conditions. Re-firm recent plantings after frost or high winds.
- **shake settled snow off** evergreen hedges and shrubs.
- **keep fleece** and bubble plastic handy to protect outdoor containers, coldframes and plants in unheated greenhouses.
- **empty compost heaps** when the contents have decayed sufficiently, and spread on bare ground as a mulch or for digging in. Spread rotted manure in the same way.

Lag or insulate taps in a hard winter and clean out water butts in case the water freezes.

- **continue cultivating heavy soil,** but leave light soils until spring before digging; cover with compost or manure to protect the surface.
- **clean paths, patios** and other hard surfaces if necessary, pressure washing or scrubbing them with an algicide to prevent surfaces becoming green and slippery.
- **keep off the lawn** whenever it is wet or frosted. Clean and store mowers for winter, or send for service.
- **in ponds, keep an area** of water ice-free for fish and other wildlife (see page 52). Small concrete ponds can crack under pressure, so melt ice even if no fish are present.
- **walk around the garden,** noting which plants make a winter contribution, and see if there is room for improvements.
- **read seed and plant catalogues,** and order while there is still plenty of choice. Try something new as well as old favourites.

cleaning and maintaining tools

Take the opportunity to clean and maintain pruning and other tools at this quiet time of year.

- **scrape off accumulated soil** with a paint scraper or offcut of wood, and finish off with a wire brush.
- **repair broken handles** and paint all wooden parts with linseed oil; spray metal parts with oil or rub them over with an oily cloth before hanging them up.
- **sharpen the blades** of spades and hoes with a file, and hammer out dents on a flat surface.
- **clean secateurs,** loppers and shears with a wire brush and, in extreme cases, dismantle the parts and clean individually. Sharpen the cutting edge with a file before storing.
- **rinse out sprayers** with warm soapy water; dismantle and clean all parts. Smear a little petroleum jelly on all sealing rings before you reassemble.

cleaning secateurs

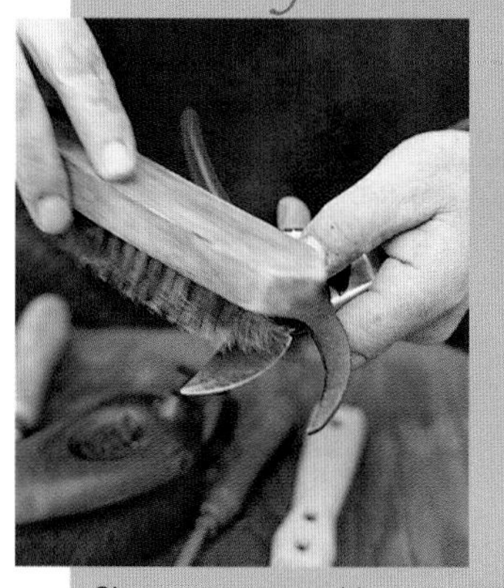

Clean secateurs with a wire brush to remove any accumulation of sap.

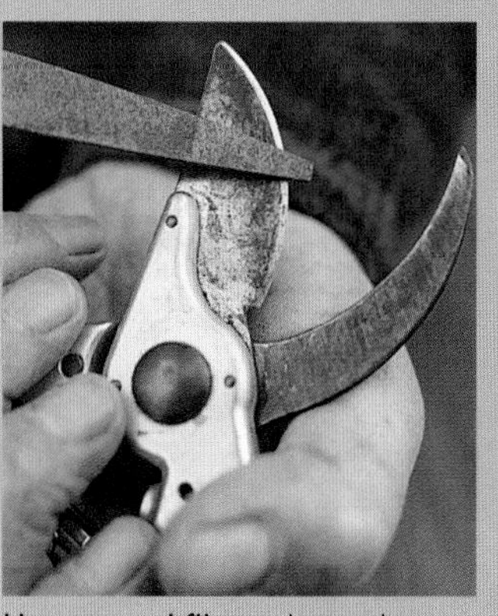

Use a metal file or sharpening stone to sharpen the blades; hold it at the angle of the blade edge.

using windbreaks

Gardeners rightly regard frost as a serious threat to many plants, but high winds can be just as damaging, breaking stems and shoots, disturbing roots and causing uneven growth. A solid fence or wall aggravates this effect, whereas a hedge or line of shrubs or trees filters wind and shields plants for a distance of about five times its height.

Shelter new plants in exposed gardens with a temporary screen of windbreak netting, wattle hurdles or open fencing until they are established (see Early Spring). Check after gales that the screen is secure and undamaged. For a more permanent windbreak, plant a boundary hedge or shorter hedges within the garden.

Winter is a good time to clean, sharpen and oil all pruning and cultivating tools, before they are in constant use.

making birdcake

1 **Soften a block of lard** to a creamy consistency, then stir in an equal volume of rolled oats and add any of the following: sunflower seeds, finely chopped nuts, sesame seeds, linseed or leftover seeds from your herb store. Quantities can vary – no need to measure.

2 **Split a narrow log** in half and chisel out several holes on the rounded side. Pack in the mixture firmly, finishing flush with the surface.

3 **Hang the split log** against a wall to feed birds such as nuthatches and woodpeckers.

looking after birds

Garden birds appreciate extra food in winter, especially if you encourage them into the garden at other seasons. Mould some birdcake into balls or hang birdcake logs (see above). Keep bird feeders full of concentrated foods, such as black sunflower seeds, peanuts and nigella seeds. Hang several feeders around the garden, and move them occasionally to encourage shy birds. A regular supply of fresh water is also vital, especially when usual supplies may be frozen.

plant selector

There is a surprising variety of star turns and solid garden performers to lift the spirits during the darker months. Evergreens are the stalwarts of the season, and their myriad forms and leaf shapes will weave a tapestry of greens. Tightly clipped box, walls of deep green yew and jazzy variegated hollies lend themselves to hedges and topiary, and provide the backbone that knits a garden together. There can be flowers in winter, too – scented viburnums and daphnes, spidery witch hazels and yellow mahonias. Berries can last well into winter on malus, cotoneasters and holly, while hellebores, marbled-leaved arums and the earliest of bulbs beautify beds and borders.

Hamamelis x *intermedia* 'Pallida'

perennials

Although most perennials are herbaceous, a few are evergreen and some flower in winter. Most are best planted in late autumn or early spring.

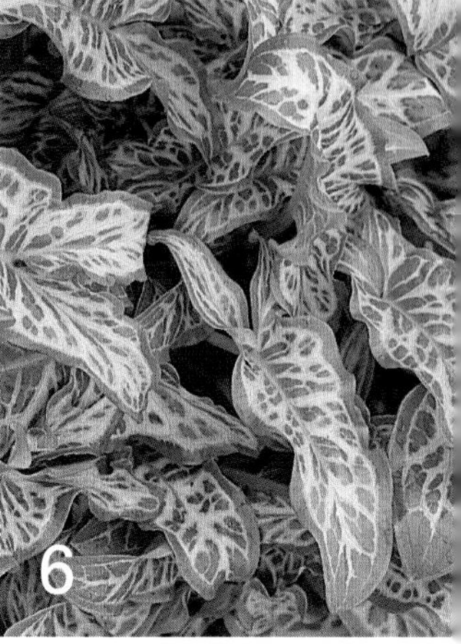

blue, violet and purple

1 Pulmonaria angustifolia 'Munstead Blue'

Blue cowslip, Lungwort

Unlike most lungworts, this is not evergreen nor is the foliage spotted. The bristly lance-shaped leaves appear with the first flowers in late winter. The clear blue, funnel-shaped blooms are carried on erect stems well into spring. Hardy.

Height: 20cm (8in) **Spread:** 45cm (18in)

Site: Partial shade, shade. Moist but well-drained soil

Use: Border, underplanting for shrubs

Good companions: *Aquilegia* 'Hensol Harebell', *Dicentra* 'Langtrees', *Geranium sylvaticum* 'Mayflower'

2 Viola odorata

English violet, Garden violet, Sweet violet

Semi-evergreen perennial that spreads by underground runners to form dark green mats of almost heart-shaped leaves. Scented violet to white flowers emerge through the foliage from late winter to mid-spring. Hardy.

Height: 15cm (6in) **Spread:** 30cm (12in)

Site: Sun, partial shade. Moist but well-drained soil

Use: Wild garden, woodland garden

Good companions: *Ajuga reptans* 'Purple Torch', *Galanthus nivalis, Primula vulgaris*

pink and mauve

3 Bergenia x schmidtii

Evergreen hybrid with rounded leaves on long stalks. Against the rich green sprays of pink flowers stand out in late winter and early spring. Hardy.

Height: 30cm (12in) **Spread:** 60cm (2ft)

Site: Sun, partial shade. Well-drained soil

Use: Border, ground cover, woodland garden

Good companions: *Epimedium* x *youngianum* 'Niveum', *Prunus* x *subhirtella* 'Autumnalis', *Sarcococca hookeriana* var. *digyna*

bronze and red

4 Bergenia 'Ballawley'

This evergreen hybrid makes a substantial green clump in summer, but takes on rich purple and bronze tones when touched by frost. In spring it produces sprays of bright red-pink flowers. Hardy.

Height: 60cm (2ft) **Spread:** 50cm (20in)

Site: Sun, partial shade. Well-drained soil

Use: Border, gravel garden, ground cover

Good companions: *Allium hollandicum* 'Purple Sensation', *Euphorbia* x *martinii, Gladiolus communis* subsp. *byzantinus*

5 Pulmonaria rubra 'Redstart'

Lungwort

Evergreen lungwort that bears small clusters of coral-red flowers from midwinter, but often peaks in late winter or early spring. Hardy.

Height: 30cm (12in) **Spread:** 75cm (2ft 6in)

Site: Partial shade, shade. Moist but well-drained soil

Use: Border, underplanting for shrubs, woodland garden

Good companions: *Asplenium scolopendrium, Dicentra* 'Luxuriant', *Viola riviniana* Purpurea Group

cream and white

6 Arum italicum subsp. italicum 'Marmoratum'

Clusters of red berries on erect stems are eye-catching in autumn, but in winter it is the glossy foliage that counts. The spear-shaped leaves are rich green with ivory veining; they emerge in winter and attain their full size in early to mid-spring. Toxic if ingested and contact can cause allergic reactions. Hardy.

Height: 40cm (16in) **Spread:** 45cm (18in)

Site: Sun, partial shade. Humus-rich and well-drained soil

Use: Border, underplanting for shrubs

Good companions: *Galanthus* 'Atkinsii', *Helleborus argutifolius, Rubus* 'Benenden'

7 Helleborus niger

Christmas rose, Hellebore

Evergreen hellebore valued for the glistening white flowers that stand on purplish stems above dark evergreen fingered leaves. It often starts to bloom in early winter and continues until early spring, the petals usually taking on a pink flush as they age. Harmful if ingested and the sap can cause allergic skin reactions. Hardy.

Height: 30cm (12in) **Spread:** 45cm (18in)
Site: Partial shade. Humus-rich and moist but well-drained soil. Good on lime
Use: Lightly shaded border, woodland garden
Good companions: *Cyclamen purpurascens, Dryopteris erythrosora, Tiarella wherryi*

8 Helleborus x nigercors

Hellebore

The leathery evergreen leaves of this hybrid have three to five toothed lobes and the flowers, borne in clusters on short stems from midwinter to early spring, resemble white or pale pink saucers. Harmful if ingested and the sap can cause allergic skin reactions. Hardy.

Height: 30cm (12in) **Spread:** 75cm (2ft 6in)
Site: Partial shade. Humus-rich and moist but well-drained soil. Good on lime
Use: Lightly shaded border, woodland garden
Good companions: *Helleborus hybridus, Hosta lancifolia, Polygonatum* x *hybridum*

green

9 Helleborus argutifolius

Corsican hellebore

Stiff-stemmed bushy evergreen plant with deep green leathery leaves that are lighter underneath and divided into three conspicuously toothed and veined leaflets. Clusters of yellow-green flowers first open in late winter, but last for many weeks. Harmful if ingested and the sap can cause allergic skin reactions. Hardy.

Height: 1m (3ft) **Spread:** 1.2m (4ft)
Site: Sun, partial shade. Moist but well-drained soil
Use: Border, underplanting for shrubs
Good companions: *Epimedium* x *rubrum, Euphorbia amygdaloides* 'Purpurea', *Tricyrtis formosana*

10 Helleborus foetidus Wester Flisk Group

Bear's foot, Dungwort, Stinking hellebore, Stinkwort

Evergreen hellebore with deep to grey-green, divided fan-shaped leaves that smell unpleasant if bruised. The drooping thimble-like flowers, which are green with a maroon rim, are borne in large clusters from midwinter to mid-spring. The stems, stalks and leaf bases are all tinted red. Harmful if ingested and the sap can cause allergic skin reactions. Hardy.

Height: 60cm (2ft)
Spread: 45cm (18in)
Site: Partial shade, shade, sun. Moist but well-drained soil
Use: Border, underplanting for shrubs and trees, woodland garden
Good companions: *Anemone sylvestris, Galanthus nivalis, Iris foetidissima*

11 Helleborus x sternii Blackthorn Group

Hellebore

The grey-green leaves of this evergreen hybrid are composed of three conspicuously veined leaflets and carried on purple stems. The nodding green flowers, borne from late winter to mid-spring, are overlaid with purple or pink. Harmful if ingested and the sap can cause skin reactions. Not fully hardy.

Height and spread: 40cm (16in)
Site: Sun, partial shade. Moist but well-drained soil. Good on lime
Use: Border, underplanting for shrubs
Good companions: *Cyclamen hederifolium, Disporum sessile* 'Variegatum', *Lilium martagon* var. *album*

12 Polystichum munitum

Sword fern

Clump-forming evergreen fern with glossy, dark green arching fronds. Each one is composed of numerous paired narrow segments that are spiny toothed. Hardy.

Height and spread: 1m (3ft)
Site: Shade, partial shade. Humus-rich and moist but well-drained soil
Compost: Soil-based (John Innes No. 2) with added leaf-mould
Use: Container, shady border, woodland garden
Good companions: *Anemone nemorosa, Galanthus elwesii, Helleborus foetidus* Wester Flisk Group

annuals & biennials

A few perennials that are usually grown as annuals or biennials are particularly valued in the winter garden because they produce colourful flowers with gay abandon. They are suitable for bedding and containers.

lilac, pink and mauve

1 Viola x wittrockiana Mello Series

Winter-flowering pansy

Mello Series is sufficiently hardy for winter and spring displays and the upward-facing flowers come in a wide range of simple colours. Hardy.

General care: Sow seed in early to midsummer and plant out in autumn. Deadhead regularly.

Height: 15cm (6in) **Spread:** 20cm (8in)

Site: Sun, partial shade. Humus-rich and moist but well-drained soil

Compost: Soil-based (John Innes No. 2) or soil-less

Use: Container, formal bedding, front of border

Good companions: *Hyacinthus orientalis* 'Ostara', *Primula* Cowichan Garnet Group, *Tulipa* 'Couleur Cardinal'

2 Viola x wittrockiana Ultima Series

Winter-flowering pansy

The rich green, almost heart-shaped leaves form a spreading tuft. The flowers are available in a wide range of single and mixed colours. Hardy.

General care: Sow seed in early to midsummer and plant out in autumn. Deadhead regularly.

Height: 15cm (6in) **Spread:** 20cm (8in)

Site: Sun, partial shade. Humus-rich and moist but well-drained soil

Compost: Soil-based (John Innes No. 2) or soil-less

Use: Container, formal bedding, front of border

Good companions: *Narcissus* 'Dove Wings', *Scilla siberica* 'Spring Beauty', *Tulipa* 'Madame Lefeber'

red and russet

3 Primula Pacific Giant Series

From late winter to mid-spring these polyanthus bear scented, usually yellow-eyed flowers in a range of vivid colours above an evergreen or semi-evergreen rosette of crinkled leaves. Hardy.

General care: Sow seed in summer and plant out in autumn.

Height and spread: 20cm (8in)

Site: Sun, partial shade. Moist but well-drained soil

Compost: Soil-based (John Innes No. 2) or soil-less

Use: Container, formal bedding, front of border

Good companions: *Hyacinthus orientalis* 'Carnegie', *Narcissus* 'Dove Wings', *Viola* x *wittrockiana* Universal Series

4 Viola x wittrockiana Universal Series

Winter-flowering pansy

Flowers reliably in mild weather from late autumn to late spring. Some single colours are available, but the seed is usually sold as mixtures. Hardy.

General care: Sow seed in early to midsummer and plant out in autumn. Deadhead regularly.

Height: 15cm (6in) **Spread:** 20cm (8in)

Site: Sun, partial shade. Humus-rich and moist but well-drained soil

Compost: Soil-based (John Innes No. 2) or soil-less

Use: Container, formal bedding, front of border

Good companions: *Bellis perennis*, *Puschkinia scilloides* var. *libanotica*, *Tulipa* 'Heart's Delight'

yellow and orange

5 Primula Crescendo Series

These evergreen perennial polyanthus are grown as biennials for their scented yellow-centred flowers in late winter and early spring. Seed is available as mixtures or as separate colours. Hardy.

General care: Sow seed in summer and plant out in autumn.

Height and spread: 20cm (8in)

Site: Sun, partial shade. Moist, well-drained soil

Compost: Soil-based (John Innes No. 2) or soil-less

Use: Container, formal bedding, front of border

Good companions: *Anemone coronaria* De Caen Group, *Crocus vernus* 'Remembrance', *Narcissus* 'Jack Snipe'

bulbs

Perennials with underground food-storage organs – bulbs, corms, tubers and rhizomes – are a very varied group. Early flowering species give a strong foretaste of the riches that will follow in spring.

purple, blue and violet

1 Anemone blanda
Wood anemone

In late winter or early spring flowers are borne freely over prettily divided foliage. Colours include shades of blue, white and pink. Hardy.
General care: Plant in autumn with the top of the tuber about 8cm (3in) deep.
Height and spread: 15cm (6in)
Site: Sun or partial shade. Well-drained soil
Compost: Soil-based (John Innes No. 2) with added leaf-mould
Use: Container, planting in grass, raised bed, rock garden, underplanting for shrubs and trees
Good companions: *Colchicum* 'Rosy Dawn', *Eranthis hyemalis, Narcissus* 'February Gold'

2 Crocus chrysanthus 'Ladykiller'
In late winter or early spring each corm produces honey-scented, white globular flowers with rich purple outer markings and scarlet styles. Hardy.
General care: Plant in autumn with the top of the corm about 8cm (3in) deep.
Height: 8cm (3in) **Spread:** 5cm (2in)
Site: Sun. Gritty, well-drained soil
Compost: Soil-based (John Innes No. 1) with added grit
Use: Container, raised bed, rock garden, sunny bed
Good companions: *Campanula carpatica, Iris* 'Natascha', *Rhodanthemum hosmariense*

3 Crocus tommasinianus 'Whitewell Purple'
In late winter or early spring red-purple flowers, which teeter on white tubes, open in sun to reveal a silvery mauve inside. The leaves appear with the flowers and have a white midrib. Hardy.
General care: Plant in autumn with the top of the corm about 8cm (3in) deep.
Height: 8cm (3in) **Spread:** 5cm (2in)
Site: Sun. Gritty, well-drained soil
Compost: Soil-based (John Innes No. 1) with added grit
Use: Container, front of sunny border, raised bed, rock garden, planting in grass
Good companions: *Aubrieta* 'Doctor Mules', *Colchicum speciosum, Crocus speciosus*

4 Scilla mischtschenkoana
In late winter produces up to four very pale blue starry flowers marked with darker stripes. Hardy.
General care: Plant in late summer or autumn with the top of the bulb about 8cm (3in) deep.
Height: 10cm (4in) **Spread:** 8cm (3in)
Site: Sun or partial shade. Moist, well-drained soil
Compost: Soil-based (John Innes No. 2) with added leaf-mould
Use: Container, front of border, rock garden, planting in grass, underplanting for shrubs and trees
Good companions: *Eranthis hyemalis, Galanthus* 'S. Arnott', *Scilla siberica* 'Spring Beauty'

pink and mauve

5 Crocus imperati subsp. imperati 'De Jager'
The flowers produced with the dark green leaves in late winter or early spring are mauve inside and buff outside with purple lines. Hardy.
General care: Plant in autumn with the top of the corm about 8cm (3in) deep.
Height: 10cm (4in) **Spread:** 5cm (2in)
Site: Sun. Gritty, well-drained soil
Compost: Soil-based (John Innes No. 1) with added grit
Use: Container, raised bed, rock garden
Good companions: *Chionodoxa sardensis, Hypericum olympicum, Tulipa humilis* Violacea Group

6 Crocus laevigatus 'Fontenayi'
The white to mauve-blue flowers are feathered on the outside with mauve-purple and the feathery stigma is orange. Hardy.
General care: Plant in autumn with the top of the corm about 8cm (3in) deep.
Height: 5cm (2in) **Spread:** 2–3cm (1in)
Site: Sun. Gritty, well-drained soil
Compost: Soil-based (John Innes No. 1) with added grit
Use: Container, raised bed, rock garden
Good companions: *Crocus chrysanthus* 'Ladykiller', *Muscari botryoides* 'Album', *Tulipa turkestanica*

pink and mauve
(continued)

1 Cyclamen coum
From early or midwinter this tuber produces glossy foliage and 'shuttlecock' flowers. These are white, pink or carmine-red with dark stains above the white mouth. The rounded leaves are plain deep green or patterned in silver. Hardy.
General care: Plant in early summer, just after the leaves have died down, with the top of the corm just below the surface of the soil and cover with leaf-mould. Mulch with leaf-mould annually in summer.
Height: 8cm (3in) **Spread:** 10cm (4in)
Site: Partial shade. Well-drained soil
Compost: Soil-based (John Innes No. 1) with added leaf-mould
Use: Container, raised bed, rock garden, underplanting for shrubs, woodland garden
Good companions: *Cyclamen hederifolium, Galanthus nivalis, Helleborus hybridus*

2 Tulipa humilis Violacea Group
In late winter or early spring the egg-like bud opens to form a pink to violet-purple star with yellow or blue-black markings. The leaves develop fully after the flowers and often lie flat. Hardy.
General care: Plant in late autumn with the top of the bulb about 15cm (6in) deep. Plants usually persist for several years without lifting.
Height and spread: 15cm (6in)
Site: Sun. Well-drained soil
Compost: Soil-based (John Innes No. 1)
Use: Container, front of sunny border, raised bed, rock garden
Good companions: *Erodium* 'County Park', *Geranium cinereum* 'County Park', *Oxalis adenophylla*

yellow and orange

3 Crocus chrysanthus 'Zwanenburg Bronze'
The honey-scented globular flowers appear in late winter or early spring with the grass-like leaves. They are bronzed tan outside and open wide in sun to reveal a deep gold interior and orange style. Hardy.
General care: Plant in autumn with the top of the corm about 8cm (3in) deep.
Height: 8cm (3in) **Spread:** 5cm (2in)
Site: Sun. Gritty, well-drained soil
Compost: Soil-based (John Innes No. 1) with added grit
Use: Container, raised bed, rock garden, sunny bed
Good companions: *Crocus chrysanthus* 'Cream Beauty', *Euphorbia myrsinites, Iris reticulata*

4 Crocus korokolwii
The deep yellow flowers have brown or bronze markings on the outside. They appear in the second half of winter with the leaves. Hardy.
General care: Plant in autumn with the top of the corm about 8cm (3in) deep.
Height: 10cm (4in) **Spread:** 5cm (2in)
Site: Sun. Gritty, well-drained soil
Compost: Soil-based (John Innes No. 1) with added grit
Use: Container, raised bed, rock garden
Good companions: *Crocus imperati* subsp. *imperati* 'De Jager', *Festuca glauca* 'Seeigel', *Iris* 'George'

5 Eranthis hyemalis
Winter aconite
Each pale yellow flower is set off by a ruff of bright green leaves in winter and early spring. Best naturalised in large drifts. Hardy.
General care: Plant in early spring before growth dies down or in autumn with the top of the tuber about 5cm (2in) deep.
Height: 8cm (3in) **Spread:** 5cm (2in)
Site: Sun or partial shade. Humus-rich, well-drained soil
Use: Planting in grass, underplanting for shrubs
Good companions: *Anemone blanda, Galanthus nivalis, Muscari aucheri*

6 Narcissus 'Cedric Morris'
Trumpet daffodil
Short-growing bulb with prettily frilled 'trumpets' that often flowers throughout winter. Hardy.
General care: Plant in early autumn with the top of the bulb about 8cm (3in) deep.
Height: 20cm (8in) **Spread:** 8cm (3in)
Site: Sun or partial shade. Moist, well-drained soil
Compost: Soil-based (John Innes No. 2)
Use: Border, container, planting in grass, rock garden, underplanting for shrubs and trees
Good companions: *Chionodoxa luciliae* Gigantea Group, *Primula* 'Miss Indigo', *Scilla siberica* 'Spring Beauty'

7 Narcissus 'Rijnveld's Early Sensation'

Trumpet daffodil

Produces long-lasting yellow trumpet-shaped flowers in late winter with the leaves. Hardy.

General care: Plant in early autumn with the top of the bulb about 8cm (3in) deep.

Height: 30cm (12in) **Spread:** 10cm (4in)

Site: Sun or partial shade. Moist, well-drained soil

Compost: Soil-based (John Innes No. 2)

Use: Border, container, planting in grass, underplanting for shrubs and trees

Good companions: *Narcissus* 'Jack Snipe', *Puschkinia scilloides* var. *libanotica, Tulipa sprengeri*

8

9

10

cream and white

8 Crocus chrysanthus 'Cream Beauty'

In late winter or early spring each corm produces scented, rich cream globular flowers with a pale bronze-green base. They have a golden throat and a vivid scarlet style. Hardy.

General care: Plant in autumn with the top of the corm about 8cm (3in) deep.

Height: 8cm (3in) **Spread:** 5cm (2in)

Site: Sun. Gritty, well-drained soil

Compost: Soil-based (John Innes No. 1) with added grit

Use: Container, raised bed, rock garden, sunny bed

Good companions: *Crocus chrysanthus* 'Zwanenburg Bronze', *Iris danfordiae, Iris histrioides* 'Major'

9 Galanthus 'Atkinsii'

Snowdrop

Strong-growing early flowering snowdrop hybrid that does not set seed, but quickly forms colonies from offsets. Often one segment of the white drooping flowers is malformed. Each of the smaller inner segments carries a green heart-shaped mark. Hardy.

General care: Plant in early spring immediately after flowering and before leaves die down with the top of the bulbs about 8cm (3in) deep.

Height: 20cm (8in)

Spread: 8cm (3in)

Site: Partial shade. Humus-rich and moist but well-drained soil

Compost: Soil-based (John Innes No. 2) with added leaf-mould

Use: Container, planting in grass, rock garden, underplanting for shrubs and trees

Good companions: *Bergenia* 'Ballawley', *Narcissus* 'Dove Wings', *Pulmonaria saccharata* 'Frühlingshimmel'

11

10 Galanthus elwesii

Snowdrop

Late-flowering honey-scented snowdrop with grey-green broad leaves. Each inner segment has two green marks that are often merged. Hardy.

General care: As for 9, above.

Height: 20cm (8in) **Spread:** 8cm (3in)

Site: Partial shade. Humus-rich and moist but well-drained soil

Compost: Soil-based (John Innes No. 2) with added leaf-mould

Use: As for 9, above

Good companions: *Colchicum speciosus* 'Album', *Crocus speciosus, Crocus tommasinianus* 'Whitewell Purple'

11 Galanthus nivalis

Common snowdrop

The scented pendulous flowers are globular and the inner segments bear a green inverted V-shaped mark. Colonies expand from offsets and seeding, especially in light woodland. Hardy.

General care: As for 9, above.

Height: 10cm (4in) **Spread:** 8cm (3in)

Site: Partial shade. Humus-rich and moist but well-drained soil

Compost: Soil-based (John Innes No. 2) with added leaf-mould

Use: As for 9, above

Good companions: *Asplenium scolopendrium, Hamamelis* x *intermedia* 'Pallida', *Scilla bifolia*

12 Galanthus 'S. Arnott'

Snowdrop

This vigorous, sweetly scented snowdrop flowers in late winter or early spring. The relatively large blooms just reveal a green inverted V on the inner segments. The leaves are grey-green. Hardy.

General care: As for 9, above.

Height: 20cm (8in) **Spread:** 8cm (3in)

Site: Partial shade. Humus-rich and moist but well-drained soil

Compost: Soil-based (John Innes No. 2) with added leaf-mould

Use: As for 9, above

Good companions: *Colchicum* 'The Giant', *Leucojum vernum, Scilla mischtschenkoana*

12

dwarf irises

Hardy reticulata irises form the largest group of dwarf irises. Their fragile-looking flowers, composed of inner petals (standards) and outer petals (falls), usually appear in late winter, but stand up to inclement weather. Plant in autumn in well-drained sunny borders, raised beds or rock gardens, with the top of the bulb 8cm (3in) deep. In containers use soil-based compost (John Innes No. 2) with added grit.

1 Iris 'Natascha'

There is a hint of blue in the white of this slender flower and blue lines surround the orange crests on the falls.

Height: 5cm (2in) **Spread:** 8cm (3in)

Good companions: *Origanum amanum, Tulipa humilis* Violacea Group, *Tulipa saxatilis* Bakeri Group 'Lilac Wonder'

2 Iris danfordiae

Sturdy greenish yellow flowers appear in mid to late winter before the leaves. Very small standards give the flowers a squat appearance. Happiest in small groups.

Height: 10cm (4in) **Spread:** 5cm (2in)

Good companions: *Crocus imperati* subsp. *imperati* 'De Jager', *Lavandula angustifolia* 'Hidcote', *Tulipa clusiana*

3 Iris reticulata

This species, a parent of numerous dwarf hybrids, has slender, deep violet-blue flowers with a yellow ridge on each fall. They are scented and appear while the leaves are still short.

Height: 15cm (6in) **Spread:** 5cm (2in)

Good companions: *Armeria juniperifolia, Iris* 'Joyce', *Pulsatilla vulgaris*

4 Iris histrioides 'Major'

In mid to late winter this sturdy iris produces one or two large flowers before the leaves appear. They are royal blue with deeper markings and have a yellow ridge on the falls.

Height: 13cm (5in) **Spread:** 8cm (3in)

Good companions: *Crocus laevigatus* 'Fontenayi', *Gypsophila repens* 'Rosa Schönheit', *Tulipa* 'Heart's Delight'

5 Iris 'Joyce'

Deep sky-blue flowers, with bright yellow crests over white markings on the falls, appear when the leaves are just emerging.

Height: 13cm (5in) **Spread:** 8cm (3in)

Good companions: *Artemisia schmidtiana* 'Nana', *Ipheion uniflorum* 'Wisley Blue', *Tulipa* 'Shakespeare'

6 Iris 'J.S. Dijt'

Slender but vigorous iris that produces scented red-purple flowers with an orange-yellow ridge on the falls. Leaves are short at flowering time.

Height: 13cm (5in) **Spread:** 8cm (3in)

Good companions: *Crocus chrysanthus* 'Zwanenburg Bronze', *Geranium cinerium* subsp. *subcaulescens, Helianthemum* 'Wisley Primrose'

7 Iris 'Katharine Hodgkin'

This vigorous hybrid has flowers of unusual colouring. The pale creamy blue petals are overlaid by yellow and sea-green and the standards are marked with blue. It usually flowers in midwinter.

Height: 13cm (5in) **Spread:** 8cm (3in)

Good companions: *Dianthus alpinus* 'Joan's Blood', *Iris* 'Natascha', *Tulipa* 'Red Riding Hood'

8 Iris 'George'

Vigorous plant with relatively large flowers. The standards are red-purple and the darker falls are marked with yellow on white.

Height: 13cm (5in) **Spread:** 8cm (3in)

Good companions: *Armeria maritima* 'Düsseldorfer Stolz', *Crocus chrysanthus* 'Ladykiller', *Iris* 'J.S. Dijt'

climbers

Climbers twine, cling with aerial roots or clasp with tendrils. Trained on architectural supports or other plants, they assert the vertical dimension of the garden. Plant in the dormant season.

blue, violet and purple

1 Ampelopsis glandulosa var. brevipedunculata

This deciduous tendril climber is worth growing for its handsome lobed foliage alone, but where summers are warm enough, bead-like fruits form and persist after the leaves have fallen They ripen from green to purple-pink then blue. Hardy.

General care: If necessary to restrict growth prune in early spring.

Height: 5m (15ft) **Spread:** 4m (12ft)

Site: Sun, partial shade. Moist, well-drained soil

Use: Pergola, tree climber, wall

Good companions: *Clematis armandii* 'Snowdrift', *Rosa* 'Parade', *Solanum laxum* 'Album'

red and russet

2 Clematis cirrhosa 'Freckles'

Evergreen twining climber with leaves composed of three to six leaflets. Nodding, creamy pink flowers heavily speckled with red are borne in late winter or early spring. Silky seedheads follow. Not fully hardy.

General care: Plant with the base in shade. Prune immediately after flowering.

Height: 3m (10ft) **Spread:** 1.5m (5ft)

Site: Sun, partial shade. Fertile, humus-rich and well-drained soil. Good on lime

Use: Screen, shrub climber, tripod, wall

Good companions: *Clematis* 'Etoile Rose', *Forsythia suspensa*, *Narcissus* 'Jack Snipe'

3 Euonymus fortunei 'Coloratus'

Like most other cultivars of the evergreen shrub *E. fortunei*, 'Coloratus' is capable of performing as a climber. The usually green leaves turn red-purple in winter, especially on poor soils. Hardy.

General care: If necessary to restrict growth prune in early spring.

Height: 5m (15ft) **Spread:** 4m (12ft)

Site: Sun, partial shade. Well-drained soil

Use: Ground cover, tree climber, wall

Good companions: *Cotoneaster conspicuus* 'Decorus', *Ilex* x *altaclerensis* 'Golden King', *Prunus lusitanica*

silver

4 Clematis vitalba

Traveller's joy

Rampant, twining deciduous climber. Small, lightly scented greenish white flowers in late summer or early autumn are followed by fluffy seedheads that last through winter. Hardy.

General care: If necessary cut back stems to near ground level in early spring.

Height: 9m (30ft) **Spread:** 5m (15ft)

Site: Sun, partial shade. Well-drained soil. Good on lime

Use: Wild garden

Good companions: *Cotoneaster salicifolia* 'Rothschildianus', *Euonymus europaeus* 'Red Cascade', *Philadelphus* 'Belle Etoile'

green

5 Hedera colchica 'Dentata'

Bullock's heart ivy, Persian ivy

In its long-lasting juvenile stage, evergreen Persian ivy is self clinging. This cultivar has large dark green leaves and purplish stems. When it reaches the non-clinging mature stage, it bears clusters of yellow-green autumn flowers, which are followed by poisonous black fruits. Hardy.

General care: Prune at any time to restrict growth.

Height: 9m (30ft) **Spread:** 6m (20ft)

Site: Partial shade, sun, shade. Well-drained soil

Use: Ground cover, wall

Good companions: *Camellia* 'Freedom Bell', *Camellia* x *williamsii* 'Francis Hanger', *Rhododendron* 'Cilpinense'

6 Hedera colchica 'Sulphur Heart'

Bullock's heart ivy, Persian ivy

This cultivar of Persian ivy (see 5, above) has large plain leaves that are light green with patches of lighter green and yellow. Poisonous black fruits follow yellow-green autumn flowers. Hardy.

General care: Prune at any time to restrict growth.

Height: 9m (30ft) **Spread:** 6m (20ft)

Site: Sun, partial shade. Well-drained soil

Use: Ground cover, wall

Good companions: *Aucuba japonica* 'Rozannie', *Choisya ternata*, *Fatsia japonica*

2

4

1

3

5

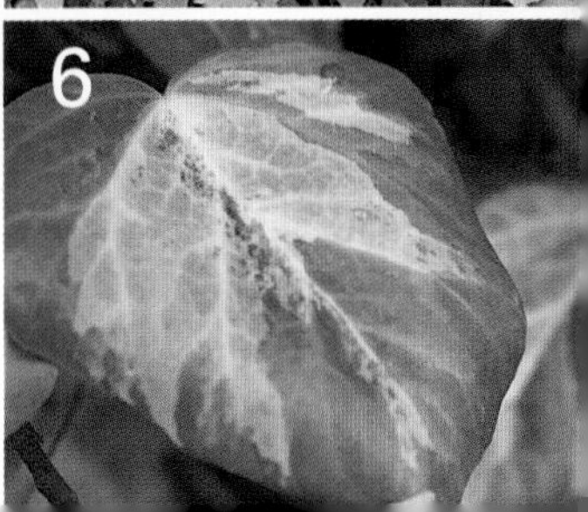
6

common or english ivy

The common ivy is an evergreen climber and its many cultivars offer a wide variety of leaf size, shape and colour. Leaves in the juvenile stage are usually lobed and stems cling by aerial roots. Plants may develop the adult bushy form, without aerial roots; they produce unlobed leaves and in autumn heads of yellow-green flowers, followed by poisonous black fruits. Ivy generally prefers partial shade and well-drained soil, but will tolerate sun and shade; variegated forms need a well-lit position. In containers, use soil-based (John Innes No. 2) or soil-less compost.

1 Hedera helix 'Adam'

Small shallow-lobed leaves with grey-green mottling and creamy white margins. Hardy.
Height: 5m (15ft) **Spread:** 2.5m (8ft)
Use: Container, houseplant, wall
Good companions: *Fuchsia* 'Leonora', *Hydrangea macrophylla* 'Madame Emile Mouillère', *Skimmia japonica* 'Rubella'

1

2 Hedera helix 'Manda's Crested'

The large five-lobed leaves have downward-pointing tips and waved edges. In summer they are mid-green, but take on bronze tints in winter. Not fully hardy.
Height: 2m (6ft) **Spread:** 1.2m (4ft)
Use: Ground cover, wall
Good companions: *Epimedium* x *versicolor* 'Sulphureum', *Euphorbia amygdaloides* 'Purpurea', *Pachysandra terminalis*

3 Hedera helix 'Parsley Crested'

The medium-sized, glossy deep green leaves are almost rounded and if there are lobes these are obscured by the strongly waved and crimped margins. Not fully hardy.
Height: 2m (6ft) **Spread:** 1m (3ft)
Use: Wall
Good companions: *Celastrus orbiculatus, Chaenomeles speciosa* 'Nivalis', *Osmanthus delavayi*

4 Hedera helix 'Goldheart' (syn. 'Oro di Bogliasco')

The neat, finely tapered, three-lobed leaves of medium size are rich green with an irregular bright yellow central splash. Young shoots are tinted pink. Hardy.
Height: 8m (25ft) **Spread:** 5m (15ft)
Use: Wall
Good companions: *Chimonanthus praecox, Clematis* 'Bill MacKenzie', *Clematis* 'Perle d'Azur'

5 Hedera helix 'Ivalace'

Versatile ivy with medium-sized, glossy dark green leaves that have five shallow lobes and are stiffly waved. Hardy.
Height: 1.2m (4ft) **Spread:** 75cm (2ft 6in)
Use: Container, ground cover, houseplant, wall
Good companions: *Fargesia nitida, Fatsia japonica, Viburnum davidii*

6 Hedera helix 'Buttercup'

Slow-growing ivy with large five-lobed leaves. In full sun, young leaves are bright yellow, older leaves yellow-green; in shade, leaves are pale or deeper green. Hardy.
Height: 2m (6ft) **Spread:** 1m (3ft)
Use: Wall
Good companions: *Clematis alpina* 'Frances Rivis', *Coronilla valentina* subsp. *glauca, Ipheion uniflorum* 'Wisley Blue'

7 Hedera helix 'Goldchild'

The small three to five-lobed leaves have an irregular centre with various overlays of green surrounded by a creamy yellow margin. Not fully hardy.
Height: 1.2m (4ft) **Spread:** 75cm (2ft 6in)
Use: Container, houseplant, wall
Good companions: *Clematis alpina* 'Frances Rivis', *Clematis* 'Gipsy Queen', *Clematis* 'Helsingborg'

11

12

9 Hedera helix 'Pittsburgh'

The glossy dark green leaves are of medium size and elegantly cut into five lobes. Not fully hardy.

Height: 1.2m (4ft) **Spread:** 75cm (2ft 6in)

Use: Container, ground cover, houseplant, wall

Good companions: *Epimedium* x *rubrum*, *Euphorbia griffithii* 'Fireglow', *Fargesia murielae*

10 Hedera helix 'Atropurpurea'

Purple-leaved ivy

The pattern of green veins stands out against the purple-green of the large five-lobed leaves. Hardy.

Height: 6m (20ft) **Spread:** 4m (12ft)

Use: Wall

Good companions: *Forsythia suspensa*, *Jasminum nudiflorum*, *Rosa* 'Madame Alfred Carrière'

10

8 Hedera helix 'Pedata'

Bird's foot ivy

The medium-sized glossy leaves are divided into five narrow lobes. Hardy.

Height: 4m (12ft) **Spread:** 2m (6ft)

Use: Wall

Good companions: *Jasminum nudiflorum*, *Lonicera periclymenum* 'Belgica', *Lonicera periclymenum* 'Serotina'

11 Hedera helix 'Glacier'

The small three to five-lobed leaves are grey-green with silvery grey markings and cream variegation. Hardy.

Height: 2.5m (8ft) **Spread:** 2m (6ft)

Use: Container, ground cover, houseplant, wall

Good companions: *Chaenomeles* x *superba* 'Pink Lady', *Clematis* 'Jackmanii', *Clematis macropetala* 'Maidwell Hall'

12 Hedera helix 'Glymii'

The medium-sized three-lobed or unlobed leaves, are often curled, especially in cold weather. They are glossy dark green, but in winter become red-purple with conspicuous green veins. Hardy.

Height: 2m (6ft) **Spread:** 1.5m (5ft)

Use: Wall

Good companions: *Clematis* 'Alba Luxurians', *Garrya elliptica* 'James Roof', *Lunaria annua*

9

6

7

8

shrubs & trees

Shrubs and trees are the mainstay of the winter garden. Whether with leaves or without, they bring substance and shape, and evergreen foliage also gives colour. Late fruits and colourful stems add their rich tones, and early blossom heralds new life. Plant in the dormant season, preferably in autumn or early spring.

purple and blue-grey

1 Chamaecyparis lawsoniana 'Ellwoodii'

Lawson cypress

The species is a large columnar evergreen conifer, but this form makes a compact cone densely packed with sprays of grey-green foliage, which in winter turns blue-grey. Hardy.

Height: 9m (30ft) **Spread:** 8m (25ft)

Site: Sun, partial shade. Humus-rich and moist but well-drained soil, preferably lime-free

Use: Avenue, heather garden, large rock garden

Good companions: *Camellia japonica* 'Lavinia Maggi', *Pieris japonica* 'Debutante', *Rhododendron* 'Praecox'

2 Cornus alba 'Kesselringii'

The young stems of this deciduous shrub are striking purplish black in winter. In autumn the green leaves turn red-purple. Hardy.

General care: To maintain a supply of young wood, cut all or a proportion of stems to near ground level in early spring.

Height and spread: 3m (10ft)

Site: Sun. Well-drained, preferably moist soil

Use: Sunny border, waterside

Good companions: *Astilbe* x *arendsii* 'Irrlicht', *Miscanthus sacchariflorus, Salix gracilistyla*

3 Picea pungens 'Hoopsii'

Colorado spruce

Several forms of the colorado spruce, a broadly conical evergreen conifer, have silvery blue foliage. The stiff needles of dense-growing 'Hoopsii' are silvery white when young but become more blue as they age. The cones, 10cm (4in) long, are green at first, later pale brown. Hardy.

Height: 15m (50ft) **Spread:** 5m (15ft)

Site: Sun. Moist but well-drained soil, preferably lime-free

Use: Canopy in mixed planting, specimen tree

Good companions: *Bergenia* 'Ballawley', *Chamaecyparis lawsoniana* 'Tamariscifolia', *Cotoneaster conspicuus* 'Decorus'

4 Salix daphnoides

Violet willow

In winter the stems of this fast-growing, deciduous small tree are a conspicuous violet-purple overlaid with a white bloom. Grey catkins are borne in late winter or early spring before the leaves emerge. Hardy.

Height: 9m (30ft) **Spread:** 8m (25ft)

Site: Sun, partial shade. Humus-rich and moist but well-drained soil, preferably lime-free

Use: Canopy in mixed planting, specimen tree

Good companions: *Eupatorium purpureum, Salix gracilistyla* 'Melanostachys', *Salix irrorata*

5 Viburnum davidii

Spreading evergreen shrub that makes a mound of dark green foliage. The leaves have three prominent veins that run to a pointed tip. Metallic blue egg-shaped berries follow the dull white flowers of early summer. For a good show of these long-lasting inedible fruits grow several plants together. Hardy.

Height: 1.2m (4ft) **Spread:** 1.5m (5ft)

Site: Sun, partial shade. Humus-rich and moist but well-drained soil

Use: Front of border, ground cover, underplanting for shrubs and trees

Good companions: *Bergenia* 'Sunningdale', *Betula utilis* var. *jacquemontii* 'Silver Shadow', *Helleborus argutifolius*

pink and mauve

6 Acer pensylvanicum 'Erythrocladum'

Moosewood, Striped maple

This small deciduous tree is outstanding for the brilliant pink of its young shoots, which become striped white with age. The white-striped green bark of *A. pensylvanicum* itself is also arresting. The leaves of both trees have forward-pointing lobes and turn bright yellow in autumn. Hardy.

Height: 9m (30ft) **Spread:** 8m (25ft)

Site: Sun, partial shade. Humus-rich and moist but well-drained soil, preferably lime-free

Use: Canopy in mixed planting, specimen tree

Good companions: *Acer griseum, Enkianthus campanulatus, Fothergilla major* Monticola Group

7 Camellia x williamsii 'J.C. Williams'

Between late winter and mid-spring this camellia bears soft pink single flowers with a conspicuous cluster of stamens. Flowers fall when they are over. Glossy green evergreen foliage. Hardy.

Height: 4m (12ft) **Spread:** 3m (10ft)

Site: Partial shade. Lime-free, humus-rich and moist but well-drained soil

Compost: Soil-based (ericaceous)

Use: Container, shady border, underplanting for trees

Good companions: *Camellia* x *williamsii* 'Donation', *Eucryphia* x *nymansensis* 'Nymansay', *Rhododendron* 'Cilpinense'

8 Chaenomeles speciosa 'Moerloosei'

This deciduous shrub makes a spreading bush of tangled spiny branches, but is also suitable for training against a wall. The first of its pink-and-white flowers open in late winter, before the leaves appear, but the display continues, with thick clusters, into spring. Hardy.

General care: Prune immediately after flowering, on wall-trained specimens cutting back flowered shoots to within three or four buds of a permanent framework of branches.

Height: 2.5m (8ft) **Spread:** 4m (12ft)

Site: Sun, partial shade. Well-drained soil

Use: Sunny or lightly shaded border, wall

Good companions: *Garrya elliptica* 'James Roof', *Muscari armeniacum, Narcissus* 'Dove Wings'

9 Daphne bholua 'Jacqueline Postill'

Upright evergreen or semi-evergreen shrub with narrow leathery leaves. Dense clusters of sweetly scented, small pink flowers open in mid and late winter from purplish red buds. Not fully hardy.

Height: 2.5m (8ft) **Spread:** 1.5m (5ft)

Site: Sun, partial shade. Humus-rich and moist but well-drained soil

Use: Border, woodland garden

Good companions: *Magnolia stellata, Prunus subhirtella* 'Autumnalis', *Sorbus cashmiriana*

10 Daphne odora 'Aureomarginata'

This variegated evergreen shrub, with a fine cream line edging its leaves, is said to be hardier than the plain-leaved species. Fragrant, small, pink-purple flowers are in tight clusters. Half hardy.

Height and spread: 1.5m (5ft)

Site: Sun, partial shade. Humus-rich and moist but well-drained soil

Use: Border

Good companions: *Anemone blanda, Galanthus nivalis, Primula* 'Miss Indigo'

11 Prunus incisa 'February Pink'
Fuji cherry

This form of the deciduous shrubby Fuji cherry often starts flowering in midwinter and continues into early spring. The pale pink blossom is rarely followed by fruit. The leaves are bronzed when young and orange-red in autumn. Hardy.

Height: 8m (25ft) **Spread:** 6m (20ft)

Site: Sun. Moist but well-drained soil

Use: Canopy in border, specimen tree

Good companions: *Galanthus* 'Atkinsii', *Narcissus* 'Dove Wings', *Scilla siberica* 'Spring Beauty'

12 Prunus x subhirtella 'Autumnalis'
Higan cherry, Rosebud cherry

From late autumn to early spring this deciduous small tree provides a trickle and in late winter a flush of pink-tinged white blossom. When the leaves first appear they are lightly bronzed; after their summer green they turn yellow. Hardy.

Height and spread: 8m (25ft)

Site: Sun. Moist but well-drained soil

Use: Canopy in border, specimen tree

Good companions: *Crocus speciosus, Crocus tommasinianus* 'Whitewell Purple', *Cyclamen hederifolium*

pink and mauve (continued)

1 Rhododendron mucronulatum

The bare branches of this deciduous dwarf shrub carry clusters of pink-purple funnel-shaped flowers throughout winter. Hardy.

Height and spread: 1m (3ft)

Site: Sun or partial shade. Lime-free and moist but well-drained soil

Use: Sunny or lightly shaded border, woodland garden

Good companions: *Camellia* 'Cornish Snow', *Halesia carolina, Magnolia* x *loebneri* 'Leonard Messel'

2 Rhododendron 'Praecox'

Small-leaved evergreen shrub bearing clusters of red-purple funnel-shaped flowers at the end of stems in late winter or early spring. Hardy.

Height and spread: 1.2m (4ft)

Site: Sun or partial shade. Lime-free, moist but well-drained soil

Use: Sunny or lightly shaded garden, rock garden, woodland garden

Good companions: *Acer palmatum* var. *dissectum* Dissectum Viride Group, *Kalmia latifolia* 'Ostbo Red', *Rhododendron* 'Bow Bells'

3 Viburnum x bodnantense 'Dawn'

The naked stems of this upright deciduous shrub carry tight clusters of powerfully scented pink flowers from late autumn to early spring. Hardy.

Height: 3m (10ft) **Spread:** 2m (6ft)

Site: Sun, partial shade. Moist but well-drained soil

Use: Border, woodland garden

Good companions: *Ceratostigma willmottianum, Geranium* 'Johnson's Blue', *Viburnum davidii*

4 Viburnum tinus 'Gwenllian'

Compact form of an evergreen bushy shrub. From late autumn to early spring small pale pink flowers open from tight heads of carmine buds. Inedible blue-black fruits follow. Hardy.

General care: Trim or hard prune in spring only if required.

Height and spread: 3m (10ft)

Site: Sun, partial shade. Moist, well-drained soil

Compost: Soil-based (John Innes No. 3)

Use: Container, border, informal hedge, topiary

Good companions: *Hydrangea macrophylla* 'Blue Wave', *Prunus serrula, Rhamnus alaternus* 'Argenteovariegata'

bronze and maroon

5 Cryptomeria japonica 'Elegans Compacta'

Japanese cedar

This form of the Japanese cedar, a fast-growing, columnar evergreen conifer, is compact and retains its soft juvenile foliage when it matures. In winter the foliage changes from blue-green to purplish or reddish bronze. Hardy.

Height: 8m (25ft) **Spread:** 5.5m (18ft)

Site: Sun, partial shade. Moist but well-drained soil

Use: Heather garden, specimen tree or shrub, woodland garden

Good companions: *Acer palmatum* 'Corallinum', *Corylus avellana* 'Contorta', *Nandina domestica* 'Fire Power'

6 Leucothoe Scarletta

Graceful evergreen shrub grown for its glossy foliage. In summer the lance-shaped leaves are dark green, but are red-purple when young and in winter turn dark bronze. Hardy.

Height: 1.2m (4ft) **Spread:** 1.5m (5ft)

Site: Partial shade, shade. Lime-free, moist but well-drained soil

Use: Woodland garden

Good companions: *Eucryphia* x *nymansensis* 'Nymansay', *Gaultheria mucronata* 'Wintertime', *Uvularia grandiflora*

red and russet

7 Acer griseum

Paper-bark maple

The three-lobed leaves of this slow-growing deciduous tree turn brilliant shades of red in autumn, but of lasting beauty is the peeling bark.

Brown-coloured old bark curls back to reveal orangey new bark beneath. Hardy.
Height and spread: 9m (30ft)
Site: Sun, partial shade. Moist but well-drained soil
Use: Specimen tree, woodland garden
Good companions: *Erythronium californicum* 'White Beauty', *Galanthus* 'S. Arnott', *Primula vulgaris*

8 Arbutus x andrachnoides
Strawberry tree
This evergreen tree has a tapering canopy of dark green, finely toothed leaves above trunks and branches with peeling red-brown bark. Hardy.
Height: 8m (25ft)
Spread: 6m (20ft)
Site: Sun. Well-drained soil
Use: Canopy in border, specimen tree, woodland garden
Good companions: *Bergenia* 'Sunningdale', *Colchicum* 'The Giant', *Ribes laurifolium*

9 Berberis x carminea 'Buccaneer'
Spiny deciduous or semi-evergreen shrub with small yellow flowers in late spring or early summer followed by dense clusters of glowing scarlet berries. Hardy.
Height: 1.5m (5ft)
Spread: 2.5m (8ft)
Site: Sun, partial shade. Well-drained soil
Use: Border, informal hedge
Good companions: *Berberis* x *stenophylla*, *Cytisus* x *praecox* 'Allgold', *Genista aetnensis*

10 Calluna vulgaris 'Robert Chapman'
Heather, Ling
The heathers are low evergreens valued for their long-lasting flowers in late summer and autumn and in some cases for their richly coloured foliage. That of 'Robert Chapman' turns from gold in summer to red in winter; the flowers, from midsummer to autumn, are soft purple. Hardy.
General care: Clip over in early spring.
Height: 25cm (10in) **Spread:** 60cm (2ft)
Site: Sun. Lime-free, humus-rich, well-drained soil
Compost: Soil-based (ericaceous)
Use: Container, ground cover, heather garden, raised bed, rock garden
Good companions: *Calluna vulgaris* 'Darkness', *Erica carnea* 'Vivellii', *Gaultheria mucronata* 'Bell's Seedling'

11 Chaenomeles x superba 'Knap Hill Scarlet'
Flowering quince, Japanese quince, Japonica
Spreading deciduous shrub that often starts flowering in late winter. Hardy.
General care: Prune immediately after flowering; on wall-trained specimens cut back flowered shoots to within three or four buds of the permanent framework of branches.
Height: 1.5m (5ft) **Spread:** 2m (6ft)
Site: Sun or partial shade. Well-drained soil
Use: Sunny or lightly shaded border, wall
Good companions: *Clematis* 'Helsingborg', *Rosa* 'Parade', *Solanum laxum* 'Album'

12 Cornus alba 'Sibirica'
Red-barked dogwood
Thickets of glossy red stems are the main feature of this deciduous suckering shrub in winter. The leaves turn red and orange in autumn. Hardy.
General care: To maintain a supply of young wood, cut all or a proportion of stems to near ground level in early spring.
Height and spread: 3m (10ft)
Site: Sun. Well-drained, preferably moist soil
Use: Sunny border, waterside
Good companions: *Cornus stolonifera* 'Flaviramea', *Salix alba* subsp. *vitellina* 'Britzensis', *Salix irrorata*

10

11

12

red and russet (continued)

1 Cotoneaster frigidus 'Cornubia'

Vigorous semi-evergreen shrub or small tree with arching branches and dark green leaves that turn purplish bronze in winter. Clusters of small white flowers in summer are followed by prodigious crops of inedible bright red fruits in autumn, which weigh down the branches. The brilliant display continues well into winter. Hardy.

Height and spread: 6m (20ft)
Site: Sun, partial shade. Well-drained soil
Use: Canopy in border, specimen tree or shrub
Good companions: *Berberis* x *carminea* 'Buccaneer', *Bergenia* 'Ballawley', *Cotoneaster conspicuus* 'Decorus'

2 Cotoneaster 'Hybridus Pendulus'

Low-growing, spreading evergreen or semi-evergreen shrub with glossy leaves. Inedible, long-lasting brilliant red fruits follow the clusters of small white flowers of early summer. It is sometimes grown as a standard on a stem to make a small weeping tree about 2.5m (8ft) high. Hardy.

Height: 1.2m (4ft) **Spread:** 2m (6ft)
Site: Sun, partial shade. Well-drained soil
Use: Canopy in border, ground cover, large rock garden, raised bed, specimen tree
Good companions: *Bergenia* Ballawley', *Galanthus elwesii, Helleborus foetidus*

3 Cotoneaster lactaeus

Large evergreen shrub with leathery oval leaves that are dark green with grey undersides. Clusters of small creamy flowers in summer are followed by berries that ripen red in late autumn and remain colourfully conspicuous until midwinter. Hardy.

Height and spread: 4m (12ft)
Site: Sun, partial shade. Well-drained soil
Use: Canopy in border, specimen shrub
Good companions: *Berberis darwinii, Choisya ternata, Syringa vulgaris* 'Katherine Havemeyer'

4 Fagus sylvatica

Common beech

This large deciduous tree is magnificent in broad landscapes, as are purple-leaved forms such as 'Riversii'. In gardens, however, it is excellent for hedges 2–5m (6–15ft) high. When trimmed in the summer it retains its dead leaves until the following spring, when their warm copper gives way to the acid-green of young foliage. Hardy.

General care: Trim hedges in late summer.
Height: 25m (80ft) **Spread:** 15m (50ft)
Site: Sun, partial shade. Well-drained soil. Good on chalk and lime but also on acid soils
Use: Hedge, specimen tree
Good companions: *Ilex aquifolium* 'Pyramidalis', *Pachysandra terminalis, Taxus baccata*

5 Gaultheria mucronata 'Bell's Seedling'

Compact evergreen shrub that makes thickets of wiry stems covered with glossy deep green leaves and flowers in late spring and early summer. The edible berries are produced by female plants if a male plant is growing nearby, but 'Bell's Seedling' is hermaphrodite and produces long-lasting dark red berries if grown on its own. Hardy.

Height and spread: 1.2m (4ft)
Site: Partial shade, sun. Lime-free, moist but well-drained soil

Use: Ground cover, raised bed, woodland garden
Good companions: *Camellia* 'Freedom Bell', *Camellia* x *williamsii* 'Francis Hanger', *Rhododendron* 'Palestrina'

6 Hamamelis x intermedia 'Diane'
Witch hazel

Deciduous large shrub or tree that bears small, fragrant spidery flowers of rich copper-red in winter or early spring. In autumn the leaves usually colour well. Hardy.
Height and spread: 4m (12ft)
Site: Sun, partial shade. Moist but well-drained soil, preferably lime-free
Use: Canopy in border, specimen tree, woodland garden
Good companions: *Cornus mas, Disanthus cercidifolius, Magnolia* 'Elizabeth'

7 Malus x robusta 'Red Sentinel'
Crab apple

Deciduous small tree with arching branches that make a spreading canopy. White blossom in late spring is followed by edible, shiny scarlet crab apples, which persist through winter. Hardy.
Height and spread: 6m (20ft)
Site: Sun. Moist but well-drained soil
Use: Canopy in border, specimen tree
Good companions: *Digitalis purpurea, Hyacinthoides non-scripta, Lunaria annua*

8 Nandina domestica 'Fire Power'
Heavenly bamboo

This compact form of an evergreen bamboo-like shrub is grown mainly for its attractive foliage. The large leaves, composed of elegantly pointed leaflets, turn red in autumn and remain colourful throughout winter. Not fully hardy.

Height: 45cm (18in) **Spread:** 60cm (2ft)
Site: Sun, partial shade. Moist, well-drained soil
Use: Border, ground cover
Good companions: *Epimedium* x *rubrum, Osmanthus delavayi, Viburnum* x *bodnantense*

9 Parrotia persica
Persian ironwood

Spreading deciduous tree that usually branches close to the ground. On old wood the bark flakes off in patches, creating a grey-and-beige pattern. In late winter or early spring tiny petal-less flowers with red stamens are borne on the naked branches. In autumn leaves turn yellow and orange, shaded with purple and crimson. Hardy.
Height: 9m (30ft) **Spread:** 10m (33ft)
Site: Sun, partial shade. Moist but well-drained soil, preferably lime-free
Use: Specimen tree, woodland garden
Good companions: *Acer japonicum* 'Vitifolium', *Amelanchier canadensis, Prunus sargentii*

10 Prunus serrula
Ornamental cherry

The bark of this deciduous tree is its main ornamental feature. A pattern of rough bands breaks up the polished red-brown surface of new bark. White flowers appear in mid to late spring at the same time as the tapered leaves. Hardy.
Height and spread: 9m (30ft)
Site: Sun. Moist but well-drained soil
Use: Specimen tree
Good companions: *Cryptomeria japonica* 'Elegans Compacta', *Hydrangea macrophylla* 'Blue Wave', *Ilex* x *altaclerensis* 'Camelliifolia'

11 Pyracantha 'Mohave'

Bushy and spiny evergreen shrub. Heavy crops of red berries follow the dense clusters of small white flowers of early summer. Although eventually eaten by birds, the display usually persists well into winter. Hardy.
General care: Trim hedges and prune wall-trained specimens in the first half of summer.
Height: 4m (12ft) **Spread:** 5m (15ft)
Site: Sun, partial shade. Well-drained soil
Use: Border, hedge, wall
Good companions: *Hedera colchica* 'Sulphur Heart', *Kerria japonica* 'Pleniflora', *Pyracantha* 'Soleil d'Or'

1 Salix alba subsp. vitellina 'Britzensis'
White willow

White willows are fast-growing deciduous trees. They bear slender catkins in spring and their leaves are silky-hairy when young, giving them a general silvery appearance. The main ornamental feature of this male clone is the brilliant orange-red of its young shoots, a supply of which can be maintained by severe pruning; this will also keep it below the dimensions given. Hardy.

General care: For a supply of strongly coloured young growths cut back stems to a permanent framework every two or three years.

Height: 18m (60ft) **Spread:** 12m (40ft)

Site: Sun. Moist but well-drained soil

Use: Specimen tree, waterside

Good companions: *Cornus alba* 'Kesselringii', *Osmunda regalis, Rodgersia pinnata* 'Superba'

2 Skimmia japonica 'Rubella'

Female and hermaphrodite clones of *Skimmia japonica*, usually domed evergreen shrubs, are grown for their fragrant white flowers in spring, which are followed by inedible, long-lasting red fruits. This male form has dark green leaves edged in red and red-tinted stems. From autumn through winter it carries eye-catching heads of red flower buds. Hardy.

Height: 1m (3ft) **Spread:** 1.2m (4ft)

Site: Partial shade, shade. Humus-rich and moist but well-drained soil

Compost: Soil-based (John Innes No. 3)

Use: Container, shady border, woodland garden

Good companions: *Hydrangea* 'Preziosa', *Sarcococca hookeriana* var. *digyna, Sorbus hupehensis*

3 Sorbus aucuparia 'Beissneri'
Mountain ash, Rowan

The amber or russet bark and red shoots of this form of the mountain ash make it an arresting deciduous tree in winter, but it is attractive at other seasons, too. In spring and summer the rather upright branches are clothed in ferny yellow-green leaves, which colour well in autumn. Heavy crops of inedible bright red fruits ripen in late summer. Hardy.

Height: 9m (30ft) **Spread:** 5m (15ft)

Site: Sun, partial shade. Moist but well-drained soil, preferably lime-free

Use: Canopy in border, specimen tree

Good companions: *Cornus mas, Mahonia japonica, Malus* 'Winter Gold'

yellow and orange

4 Aucuba japonica 'Crotonifolia'
Spotted laurel

Although very tolerant of a wide range of conditions, this variegated evergreen shrub does best in a well-lit position, where it will make a dense rounded bush well covered with large leaves heavily spotted and blotched with rich yellow. If there is a male plant nearby this female clone produces inedible berries that ripen red in spring. Hardy.

Height and spread: 2.5m (8ft)

Site: Sun, partial shade. Well-drained soil

Compost: Soil-based (John Innes No. 2)

Use: Border, container, specimen shrub, underplanting for trees

Good companions: *Lonicera fragrantissima, Mahonia aquifolium* 'Apollo', *Taxus* x *media* 'Hicksii'

5 Calluna vulgaris 'Beoley Gold'
Heather, Ling

The ever-gold foliage earns this vigorous low-growing shrub a place in the winter garden. There are white flowers in autumn. Hardy.

General care: Trim in early to mid-spring.

Height: 40cm (16in) **Spread:** 60cm (2ft)

Site: Sun. Lime-free, humus-rich soil

Compost: Soil-based (ericaceous)

Use: Container, front of sunny border, ground cover, heather garden, wild garden

Good companions: *Calluna vulgaris* 'Firefly', *Pinus mugo* 'Mops', *Thuja occidentalis* 'Rheingold'

6 Calluna vulgaris 'Firefly'
Heather, Ling

In autumn there are short sprays of deep mauve flowers, but the foliage makes this low evergreen attractive throughout the year. In summer it is red-brown, but in winter it turns a more intense rust-orange. Hardy.

General care: Trim in early to mid-spring.

Height: 45cm (18in) **Spread:** 60cm (2ft)

Site: Sun. Lime-free, humus-rich soil

Compost: Soil-based (ericaceous)

Use: Container, front of sunny border, ground cover, heather garden, wild garden

Good companions: *Calluna vulgaris* 'Robert Chapman', *Juniperus communis* 'Hibernica', *Juniperus* x *pfitzeriana* 'Wilhelm Pfitzer'

7 Chimonanthus praecox
Wintersweet

Deciduous large but twiggy shrub grown for the spicy scent of its winter flowers. These are waxy and pale yellow with purplish centres, somewhat larger and more deeply coloured in 'Grandiflorus'. Hardy.

General care: Shorten growths of wall-trained plants immediately after flowering.

Height: 4m (12ft) **Spread:** 3m (10ft)

Site: Sun. Well-drained soil

Use: Border, specimen shrub, wall

Good companions: *Alchemilla mollis, Clematis* 'Abundance', *Galanthus nivalis*

8 Cornus mas
Cornelian cherry

Deciduous twiggy shrub or small tree that bears numerous small yellow flowers on naked stems in late winter and early spring. Edible red fruits sometimes follow the blooms and the foliage

frequently colours well in autumn. Hardy.
Height: 5m (15ft) **Spread:** 4m (12ft)
Site: Sun, partial shade. Well-drained soil
Use: Canopy in border, specimen shrub or tree, woodland garden
Good companions: *Cornus alba* 'Elegantissima', *Hyacinthoides non-scripta, Mahonia aquifolium* 'Apollo'

9 Coronilla valentina subsp. glauca

Lightweight evergreen shrub with blue-green foliage. It bears scented yellow pea-flowers in late winter and early spring, and again in summer. Benefits from the favourable conditions at the base of a warm wall. Hardy.
General care: No regular pruning required but to rejuvenate leggy plants cut hard back in mid-spring.
Height and spread: 1.5m (5ft)
Site: Sun. Well-drained soil
Use: Border
Good companions: *Clematis* 'Bill MacKenzie', *Narcissus obvallaris, Solanum crispum* 'Glasnevin'

10 Corylus avellana 'Contorta'

Corkscrew hazel

In late winter and early spring yellow catkins dangle from the twisted stems of this deciduous tree-like shrub. Cut stems provide interesting material for arrangements. Hardy.
Height: 3m (10ft) **Spread:** 2.5m (8ft)
Site: Sun, partial shade. Well-drained soil. Good on lime
Use: Border, specimen shrub
Good companions: *Buddleja* 'Lochinch', *Caryopteris* x *clandonensis* 'Heavenly Blue', *Cercis siliquastrum*

11 Elaeagnus pungens 'Maculata'

Evergreen shrub with lustrous leaves with a bold yellow mark in the centre. In autumn small silvery flowers, hidden among the leaves, are betrayed by their intense scent. Hardy.
General care: Remove promptly any green-leaved shoots. Trim hedges in early summer and again in early autumn.
Height: 3m (10ft) **Spread:** 4m (12ft)
Site: Sun, partial shade. Well-drained soil
Use: Border, hedge
Good companions: *Genista aetnensis, Potentilla fruticosa* 'Tangerine', *Prunus lusitanica*

1 Euonymus fortunei 'Emerald 'n' Gold'

The various cultivars of evergreen *E. fortunei* make bushy shrubs or, when given support, vigorous climbers. They are mainly valued for their foliage. This cultivar is usually seen as a low bush with deep green leaves that are edged yellow, often with a pink flush in cold winters. Hardy.

Height and spread: 1m (3ft)
Site: Sun. Well-drained soil
Compost: Soil-based (John Innes No. 3)
Use: Border, container, ground cover
Good companions: *Allium* 'Globemaster', *Cytisus* x *praecox* 'Allgold', *Helianthemum* 'Wisley Primrose'

2 Forsythia giraldiana

This is a more lanky deciduous shrub than the later-flowering forsythias, but its early display of pale yellow flowers hanging from arching naked stems in late winter or early spring gives it special value. Grey to mid-green oval leaves follow the flowers. Hardy.

General care: Immediately after flowering cut back to base up to a quarter of old stems and cut back all remaining shoots that have borne flowers.
Height and spread: 4m (12ft)
Site: Sun, partial shade. Moist, well-drained soil
Use: Border, wall
Good companions: *Lonicera* x *purpusii* 'Winter Beauty', *Rosa* 'Golden Wings', *Rosa xanthina* 'Canary Bird'

3 Hamamelis x intermedia 'Arnold Promise'

Witch hazel

Like other hybrid witch hazels, this deciduous shrub or small tree is principally grown for its scented flowers. In mid and late winter the naked stems are encrusted with small ribbon-like petals that are bright yellow. The rounded leaves usually turn yellow in autumn. Hardy.

Height and spread: 4m (12ft)
Site: Sun, partial shade. Moist but well-drained soil, preferably lime-free
Use: Canopy in border, specimen tree, woodland garden
Good companions: *Fothergilla major* Monticola Group, *Sarcoccoca hookeriana* var. *digyna, Sorbus cashmiriana*

4 Hamamelis x intermedia 'Pallida'

Witch hazel

The spreading canopy of naked branches thickly covered with lemon-yellow spidery flowers is a luminous sight in a dark winter garden. The scent of the flowers is delicate but sweet. Hardy.

Height and spread: 4m (12ft)
Site: Sun, partial shade. Moist but well-drained soil, preferably lime-free
Use: Canopy, specimen tree, woodland garden

Good companions: *Hosta sieboldiana* var. *elegans*, *Narcissus* 'Jack Snipe', *Pulmonaria angustifolia* 'Munstead Blue'

5 Hamamelis mollis
Chinese witch hazel

Deciduous large shrub or small tree with a somewhat irregular canopy of ascending and spreading branches. In mid to late winter the bare stems are covered with small, bright yellow many-petalled flowers. Their sweet scent carries well. The rounded soft leaves turn yellow in autumn. Hardy.
Height and spread: 4m (12ft)
Site: Sun, partial shade. Moist but well-drained soil, preferably lime-free
Use: Canopy in border, specimen tree, woodland garden
Good companions: *Cryptomeria japonica* 'Elegans Compacta', *Hamamelis* x *intermedia* 'Diane', *Prunus serrula*

6 Hippophae rhamnoides
Sea buckthorn

Bushy, spiny deciduous shrub, sometimes tree-like, with narrow silvery leaves. If a male plant is present, female plants bear thickly clustered crops of inedible bright orange berries that remain on the branches through winter. Hardy.
Height and spread: 6m (20ft)
Site: Sun. Moist but well-drained soil
Use: Border, hedge, windbreak
Good companions: *Escallonia* 'Apple Blossom', *Fuchsia* 'Riccartonii', *Griselinia littoralis* 'Variegata'

7

7 Jasminum nudiflorum
Winter jasmine

Deciduous shrub with lax green stems and bright yellow scentless flowers, red tinted in bud, between late autumn and early spring. Hardy.
General care: Immediately after flowering remove up to a quarter of old stems and trim back all shoots that have flowered to strong buds.
Height and spread: 3m (10ft)
Site: Sun, partial shade. Well-drained soil
Use: Bank, wall
Good companions: *Cotoneaster conspicuus* 'Decorus', *Hedera helix* 'Goldheart', *Pyracantha* 'Soleil d'Or'

8 Lonicera nitida 'Baggesen's Gold'

Bushy evergreen shrub that in sunny positions is an alternative to shade-tolerant plain green forms. The small leaves are yellow in summer and yellow-green in autumn and winter. Hardy.
General care: Trim hedges at least twice between early summer and early autumn.
Height and spread: 1.5m (5ft)
Site: Sun, partial shade. Well-drained soil
Use: Hedge, ground cover
Good companions: *Epimedium* x *versicolor* 'Sulphureum', *Forsythia* x *intermedia* 'Lynwood', *Lonicera* x *purpusii* 'Winter Beauty'

9 Mahonia japonica

Evergreen shrub with rosettes of bold leaves composed of dark green, leathery spiny leaflets. It flowers between late autumn and early spring, the lax sprays of small yellow blooms falling over the leaves. The sweet scent carries well on the air. Strings of inedible dark blue fruits follow. Hardy.
Height: 3m (10ft) **Spread:** 4m (12ft)
Site: Partial shade, shade, sun. Moist but well-drained soil
Use: Border, specimen shrub, woodland garden
Good companions: *Aconitum* 'Ivorine', *Aucuba japonica* 'Crotonifolia', *Hydrangea quercifolia*

10 Mahonia x media 'Winter Sun'

This hybrid bears many similarities to one of its parents (see 9, above), but its flowers are not so strongly fragrant and are borne in sprays that are more upright. Hardy.
Height: 5m (15ft) **Spread:** 4m (12ft)
Site: Partial shade, shade, sun. Moist but well-drained soil
Use: Border, specimen shrub, woodland garden
Good companions: *Elaeagnus pungens* 'Maculata', *Forsythia giraldiana*, *Geranium* x *magnificum*

11 Malus 'Winter Gold'
Crab apple

Small deciduous tree with a rounded canopy. The white blossom opens from pink buds in the second half of spring. The edible lemon-yellow crab apples that follow remain on the tree well into winter. Hardy.
Height and spread: 6m (20ft)
Site: Sun. Moist but well-drained soil
Use: Canopy in border, specimen tree
Good companions: *Narcissus* 'Actaea', *Narcissus* 'Cedric Morris', *Tulipa sprengeri*

8

9

10

11

4

1 **Prunus maackii**

Manchurian cherry

The lasting feature of this deciduous tree or large shrub is the bark; the old layer peels away to reveal yellow-brown new bark beneath. Inedible, glossy black spherical fruits follow scented white spring flowers. Hardy.

Height: 9m (30ft) **Spread:** 8m (25ft)

Site: Sun. Moist but well-drained soil

Use: Canopy in border, specimen tree

Good companions: *Anemone blanda*, *Crocus vernus* 'Pickwick', *Narcissus* 'Dove Wings'

2 **Pyracantha 'Orange Glow'**

Evergreen spiny shrub of upright but irregular shape. Numerous clusters of inedible orange fruits follow dense heads of small, white late spring flowers and last well into winter. Hardy.

General care: Trim hedges and prune wall-trained specimens in the first half of summer.

Height and spread: 3m (10ft)

Site: Sun, partial shade. Well-drained soil

Use: Border, hedge, wall

Good companions: *Forsythia suspensa*, *Hedera colchica* 'Dentata Variegata', *Pyracantha* 'Mohave'

3 Pyracantha 'Soleil d'Or'

Moderately vigorous evergreen shrub with red-tinted spiny stems and glossy green leaves. Large clusters of inedible amber-yellow fruits follow heads of small white early summer flowers and persist for many weeks. Hardy.
General care: Trim hedges and prune wall-trained specimens in the first half of summer.
Height: 3m (10ft) **Spread:** 2.5m (8ft)
Site: Sun, partial shade. Well-drained soil
Use: Border, hedge, wall
Good companions: *Jasminum nudiflorum*, *Narcissus* 'Tête-à-Tête', *Tulipa* 'Orange Emperor'

4 Stachyurus praecox

Deciduous shrub with red-brown stems, from which hang stiff sprays studded with pale yellow buds from late autumn until they open as bell-shaped flowers in late winter or early spring. Tapered leaves emerge after the flowers. Hardy.
Height and spread: 3m (10ft)
Site: Sun, partial shade. Moist but well-drained soil, preferably lime-free
Use: Border, woodland garden
Good companions: *Hamamelis* x *intermedia* 'Diane', *Smilacina racemosa*, *Sorbus sargentiana*

cream and white

5 Abeliophyllum distichum

Deciduous shrub best grown against a sunny wall to encourage flowering. The sprays of fragrant, white four-petalled flowers open from pink-tinted buds in late winter or early spring. The rounded leaves usually turn purple before falling. Hardy.
General care: After flowering cut back all shoots to a low framework or, if wall trained, to within three or four buds of a permanent framework.
Height and spread: 1.5m (5ft)
Site: Sun. Well-drained soil
Use: Border, wall
Good companions: *Clematis armandii* 'Snowdrift', *Clematis* 'Etoile Rose', *Ribes speciosum*

6 Acer grosseri var. hersii

Snakebark maple

Small deciduous tree with variable lobed leaves that turn orange and yellow in autumn. Dangling clusters of fruits are often conspicuous in late summer and autumn, but the main feature is the bold white striation of the bark, which is particularly eye-catching in winter. Hardy.
Height: 9m (30ft) **Spread:** 8m (25ft)
Site: Sun, partial shade. Humus-rich and moist but well-drained soil, preferably lime-free
Use: Canopy in mixed planting, specimen tree, woodland garden
Good companions: *Acer palmatum* 'Corallinum', *Chionodoxa luciliae* Gigantea Group, *Colchicum* 'Rosy Dawn'

7 Camellia 'Cornish Snow'

Evergreen shrub with tapered leaves that emerge bronze before turning dark green. Small white single flowers, tinted very pale pink, are borne profusely in late winter and early spring. Hardy.
Height: 3m (10ft) **Spread:** 1.5m (5ft)
Site: Partial shade. Lime-free, humus-rich and moist but well-drained soil
Compost: Soil-based (ericaceous)
Use: Container, shady border, underplanting for trees
Good companions: *Camellia japonica* 'Bob's Tinsie', *Gaultheria mucronata* 'Wintertime', *Rhododendron* 'Razorbill'

8 Daphne mezereum f. alba

Mezereon

In late winter and early spring the naked shoots of this upright deciduous shrub are densely clad with small white stemless flowers. It is a well scented alternative to the usual mezereon, which has purplish pink flowers. Poisonous fleshy yellow fruits follow the flowers. Hardy.
Height: 1.2m (4ft) **Spread:** 1m (3ft)
Site: Sun, partial shade. Humus-rich, well-drained soil
Use: Border, woodland garden
Good companions: *Anemone blanda*, *Exochorda* x *macrantha* 'The Bride', *Geranium sanguineum*

9 Eucalyptus pauciflora subsp. niphophila

Alpine snow gum, Snow gum

In late summer and autumn the grey-and-brown bark of this evergreen tree flakes to reveal colourful patches of new bark. Rounded grey-green juvenile leaves give way to scimitar-shaped pendent leaves with a blue-green bloom. Hardy.
Height: 9m (30ft) **Spread:** 6m (20ft)
Site: Sun. Well-drained soil, preferably lime-free
Use: Specimen tree
Good companions: *Artemesia arborescens*, *Ceanothus thyrsiflorus* var. *repens*, *Cistus ladanifer*

10 Euonymus fortunei 'Emerald Gaiety'

Evergreen bushy foliage shrub. The leaves have bright green and grey-green centres and irregular white margins, often tinged pink in winter. Hardy.
Height and spread: 1.5m (5ft)
Site: Sun. Well-drained soil
Compost: Soil-based (John Innes No. 3)
Use: Border, container, ground cover
Good companions: *Choisya ternata*, *Fatsia japonica*, *Hypericum* 'Hidcote'

11 Gaultheria mucronata 'Wintertime'

This evergreen shrub makes dense thickets of wiry stems covered with small, glossy deep green leaves and bears white flowers in late spring. This female clone bears heavy crops of long-lasting, white fruits if grown near a male plant. Hardy.
Height and spread: 1.2m (4ft)
Site: Partial shade, sun. Lime-free, moist but well-drained soil
Use: Ground cover, raised bed, woodland garden
Good companions: *Gaultheria mucronata* 'Bell's Seedling', *Ledum groenlandicum*, *Rhododendron* 'Praecox'

12 Lonicera x purpusii 'Winter Beauty'

Shrubby honeysuckle

Deciduous or semi-evergreen rounded shrub. From midwinter sweetly scented cream flowers are borne over several weeks on naked stems. Hardy.
General care: Immediately after flowering cut out up to a quarter of old stems and cut back remaining stems that have flowered to a strong bud.
Height: 2m (6ft) **Spread:** 2.5m (8ft)
Site: Sun, partial shade. Well-drained soil
Use: Border
Good companions: *Campanula lactiflora* 'Prichard's Variety', *Geranium pratense* 'Mrs Kendall Clark', *Rosa* 'Golden Wings'

1 Prunus davidiana

Small deciduous tree of upright growth worth planting in a sheltered position for its early blossom. The white or pink saucer-shaped flowers appear on leafless stems from midwinter. The glossy dark green leaves are finely tapered. Hardy.
Height and spread: 8m (25ft)
Site: Sun. Moist but well-drained soil
Use: Canopy in border, specimen tree
Good companions: *Anemone blanda, Crocus vernus* 'Jeanne d'Arc' and 'Remembrance'

2 Rhamnus alaternus 'Argenteovariegata'
Italian buckthorn

Evergreen shrub grown mainly for its foliage. The green and grey-green leaves have an irregular bright white margin. It requires hot sunny summers to produce fruits, which are red then black. All parts are harmful if ingested. Hardy.
Height: 5m (15ft) **Spread:** 4m (12ft)
Site: Sun, partial shade. Well-drained soil
Use: Border
Good companions: *Ceanothus* 'Italian Skies', *Euonymus alatus* 'Compactus', *Ruta graveolens* 'Jackman's Blue'

3 Rhododendron 'Christmas Cheer'

Compact evergreen hybrid that bears trusses of pink buds, which open to white trumpet-shaped flowers in late winter and early spring. If grown under glass it can be brought into flower by early winter, hence its name. Hardy.
Height and spread: 2m (6ft)
Site: Sun or partial shade. Lime-free, moist but well-drained soil
Compost: Soil-based (ericaceous)
Use: Container, sunny or lightly shaded border, rock garden, woodland garden
Good companions: *Acer palmatum* 'Sango-kaku', *Omphalodes cappadocica, Viburnum carlesii* 'Aurora'

4 Rhododendron moupinense

A parent of many compact hybrids, this evergreen dwarf species has shiny, mid-green rounded leaves that are light coloured and scaly on the underside. The white or pink funnel-shaped flowers, sometimes speckled red, are borne in twos or threes in late winter or early spring. Hardy.
Height and spread: 1.2m (4ft)
Site: Sun, partial shade. Lime-free, moist but well-drained soil
Compost: Soil-based (ericaceous)
Use: Container, sunny or lightly shaded border, rock garden, woodland garden
Good companions: *Kalmia latifolia* 'Ostbo Red', *Rhododendron* 'Palestrina', *Rhododendron* 'Vanessa Pastel'

5 Sarcococca hookeriana var. digyna
Christmas box, Sweet box

This evergreen shrub makes a dense thicket of upright green stems that are well covered with narrow tapered leaves. Small, pink-tinged white flowers add a delicious fragrance to the winter garden. Inedible black fruits follow. Hardy.
Height: 1.5m (5ft) **Spread:** 2m (6ft)
Site: Shade, partial shade. Humus-rich and moist but well-drained soil
Use: Informal hedge, underplanting for shrubs and trees, woodland garden
Good companions: *Cercidiphyllum japonicum, Saxifraga fortunei, Viburnum davidii*

6 Sorbus cashmiriana

Deciduous small tree with an open canopy and leaves up to 20cm (8in) long composed of numerous narrow leaflets. White or pale pink flowerheads in late spring are followed by drooping clusters of inedible, white, or pink-tinged, berries that last well into winter. Hardy.
Height: 8m (25ft) **Spread:** 6m (20ft)
Site: Sun, partial shade. Moist but well-drained soil, preferably lime-free
Use: Canopy in border, specimen tree
Good companions: *Hydrangea macrophylla* 'Madame Emile Mouillère', *Magnolia soulangeana, Viburnum opulus* 'Roseum'

7 Symphoricarpos x doorenbosii 'White Hedge'
Snowberry

Hybrid deciduous shrub that makes a steadily increasing thicket. Inconspicuous summer flowers are followed by long-lasting, eye-catching white fruits. These are suitable for indoor arrangements, but harmful if ingested. Hardy.
Height: 1.5m (5ft) **Spread:** Indefinite
Site: Sun, partial shade. Well-drained soil
Use: Border, informal hedge
Good companions: *Cotinus* 'Flame', *Euonymus europaeus* 'Red Cascade', *Euonymus fortunei* 'Emerald Gaiety'

8 Viburnum farreri

Deciduous shrub with very upright main stems, although mature plants develop a rounded outline. The oval leaves are bronze-tinted when they open. Sweetly scented, white tubular flowers, sometimes tinted pink, are borne in small clusters over a remarkably long period from late autumn until early or even mid-spring. Hardy.
Height: 3m (10ft) **Spread:** 2.5m (8ft)
Site: Sun, partial shade. Moist but well-drained soil
Use: Border
Good companions: *Epimedium* x *youngianum* 'Niveum', *Galanthus nivalis, Geranium* 'Johnson's Blue'

silver and grey

9 Betula utilis var. jacquemontii 'Silver Shadow'
Himalayan birch

The trunk and ascending branches of this deciduous tree are silvery white but terminate in a haze of dark twigs. The large drooping leaves are dark green. Hardy.
Height: 18m (60ft) **Spread:** 9m (30ft)
Site: Sun. Moist but well-drained soil
Use: Specimen tree, woodland garden
Good companions: *Clerodendrum trichotomum* var. *fargesii, Taxus baccata, Tsuga heterophylla*

10 Juniperus communis 'Hibernica'

Common juniper

Evergreen conifer that forms a dense slender column of grey-green foliage in which there is a hint of blue. The vertical accent remains shapely without any training or clipping. Hardy.

Height: 4m (12ft) **Spread:** 30cm (12in)

Site: Sun. Well-drained soil

Use: Avenue, heather garden, rock garden, specimen shrub

Good companions: *Erica carnea* 'Vivellii', *Erica arborea* var. *alpina*, *Euonymus alatus* 'Compactus'

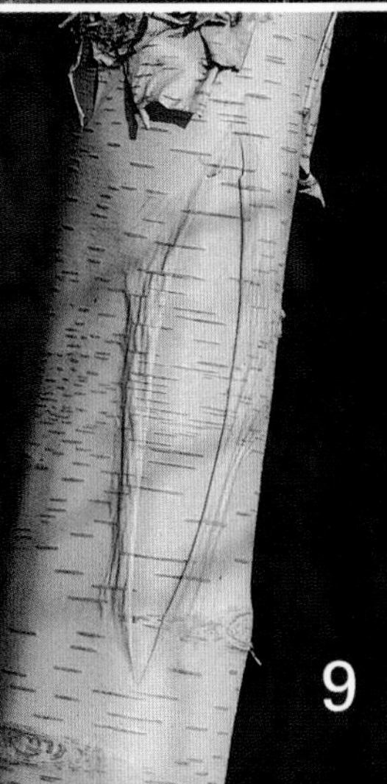

11 Rubus cockburnianus

White-stemmed bramble

Deciduous shrub that forms thickets of arching purple stems. These are conspicuous in winter because of the overlay of white bloom. The ferny leaves are dark green, grey-white on the underside. Purple flowers in summer are followed by unpalatable black fruits. The larger, more spreading white-washed bramble (*R. biflorus*) produces edible yellow fruits. Hardy.

General care: For the best stem colour cut all growths back to near ground level in early spring.

Height and spread: 2.5m (8ft)

Site: Sun, partial shade. Moist, well-drained soil

Use: Border, woodland garden

Good companions: *Anemone nemorosa*, *Omphalodes verna*, *Taxus baccata*

12 Salix irrorata

Willow

Deciduous shrub of upright growth. Purple stems covered with a white bloom, which are particularly conspicuous in winter, are its main ornamental feature. Grey catkins appear in spring before the leaves; the male catkins have red anthers that turn yellow. Hardy.

General care: For a supply of young growths, cut back stems to a permanent framework every two or three years.

Height: 3m (10ft) **Spread:** 4m (12ft)

Site: Sun. Moist but well-drained soil

Use: Border, waterside

Good companions: *Alnus glutinosa* 'Imperialis', *Cornus alba* 'Sibirica', *Salix daphnoides*

1 **Buxus sempervirens**

Common box

Slow-growing evergreen shrub or small tree with dense, glossy dark green foliage, traditionally used for hedging and topiary. The numerous cultivars include 'Suffruticosa', which because of its compact slow growth is used as a clipped edging as little as 15cm (6in) high. The dimensions may, after many years, exceed those given below. Hardy.

Height: 3m (10ft) **Spread:** 2m (6ft)
Site: Partial shade, sun. Well-drained soil
Compost: Soil-based (John Innes No. 3)
Use: Border, container, hedging, topiary
Good companions: *Rosa* 'Céleste', *Rosa* 'Louise Odier', *Viola cornuta* Alba Group

2 **Cedrus deodara**

Deodar cedar

Magnificent evergreen conifer for large gardens and landscapes. It is broadly conical, with spreading branches and drooping sprays of needle-like leaves that vary in colour from grey-green to dark green. Hardy.

Height: 25m (80ft) **Spread:** 8m (25ft)
Site: Sun. Well-drained soil
Use: Specimen tree
Good companions: *Crataegus persimilis* 'Prunifolia', *Liquidambar styraciflua* 'Worplesdon', *Prunus sargentii*

3 **Chamaecyparis lawsoniana 'Tamariscifolia'**

Lawson cypress

The species is a columnar evergreen conifer of considerable vigour, but this slow-growing form is of irregular spreading growth with no main stem and branches that splay out from a high centre. The foliage is deep green with a hint of blue. Hardy.

Height: 3m (10ft) **Spread:** 4m (12ft)
Site: Sun. Moist but well-drained soil, preferably lime-free
Use: Sunny bank, border, ground cover, large rock garden
Good companions: *Berberis* x *stenophylla*, *Cotinus* 'Flame', *Cotoneaster salicifolius* 'Rothschildianus'

4 **Cornus stolonifera 'Flaviramea'**

Red osier dogwood

Deciduous shrub that makes a thicket from a base of spreading underground stems. After the elegantly tapered leaves have coloured red and fallen, the bare greenish yellow stems remain conspicuous throughout winter. Hardy.

General care: To maintain a supply of young wood, cut all or a proportion of stems to near ground level in early spring.
Height: 3m (10ft) **Spread:** 4m (12ft)
Site: Sun. Moist but well-drained soil
Use: Border, waterside
Good companions: *Cornus alba* 'Sibirica', *Metasequoia glyptostroboides*, *Salix* x *sepulcralis* var. *chrysocoma*

5 **Garrya elliptica 'James Roof'**

Silk-tassel bush

Evergreen shrub or small tree with leathery leaves. In late winter and early spring, male specimens bear pale green to grey-green dangling catkins up to 20cm (8in) long. The silver-grey female catkins are smaller and less showy, but are followed by inedible purplish fruits. Hardy.

Height: 4m (12ft) **Spread:** 3m (10ft)
Site: Sun, partial shade. Well-drained soil
Use: Border, wall
Good companions: *Clematis* 'Gipsy Queen', *Myrtus communis* subsp. *tarentina*, *Vitis* 'Brant'

6 **Juniperus x pfitzeriana 'Wilhelm Pfitzer'**

This evergreen conifer has tiers of branches that rise at an angle of 45 degrees to make a somewhat flat-topped shrub. The scale-like leaves are green or grey-green. The fruits are purplish. Hardy.

Height: 1.2m (4ft) **Spread:** 2.5m (8ft)
Site: Sun, partial shade. Well-drained soil
Use: Border, ground cover, heather garden, large rock garden, specimen shrub
Good companions: *Artemisia* 'Powis Castle', *Buddleja davidii* 'Black Knight', *Cistus ladanifer*

7 **Picea breweriana**

Brewer spruce

Evergreen conifer of broad conical shape with horizontal main branches and hanging shoots that make a curtain of deep green or blue-green foliage. The backs of the flattened leaves are marked by two white lines. Mature specimens bear female cones that are green at first and later purple-brown. Hardy.

Height: 12m (40ft) **Spread:** 6m (20ft)
Site: Sun. Moist but well-drained soil
Use: Specimen tree
Good companions: *Betula utilis* var. *jacquemontii* 'Silver Shadow', *Parrotia persica*, *Quercus coccinea* 'Splendens'

8 Prunus lusitanica
Portugal laurel

Evergreen large shrub or small tree grown mainly for its dense foliage. The glossy dark green leaves have red stalks. Upright sprays of small white flowers with a cloying scent are borne in early summer, followed by inedible red fruits that turn black. Specimens can be clipped to make simple topiary shapes. Hardy.

General care: Clip topiary in early to mid-spring.
Height: 9m (30ft) **Spread:** 6m (20ft)
Site: Sun, partial shade. Moist but well-drained soil
Use: Canopy in border, specimen tree, topiary
Good companions: *Bergenia* 'Sunningdale', *Helleborus argutifolius, Pachysandra terminalis*

9 Quercus ilex
Evergreen oak, Holm oak

Majestic evergreen broad-leaved tree with a trunk or sometimes several stems supporting a large canopy of dark green leaves that are lighter on the underside. The bark is dark grey. Bears acorns, singly or in twos or threes. Suitable for trimming into simple geometric shapes. Hardy.

General care: Trim shaped specimens in late summer.
Height: 25m (80ft) **Spread:** 20m (65ft)
Site: Sun. Fertile, well-drained soil
Use: Hedge, shelter belt, specimen tree, topiary
Good companions: *Arbutus unedo, Cytisus* x *praecox* 'Allgold', *Genista aetnensis*

10 Ribes laurifolium
Flowering currant

Evergreen shrub with smooth, dark green leathery leaves. It flowers in late winter or early spring, the yellow-green male or female blooms being borne on separate bushes. The larger male flowers are carried in drooping sprays. The smaller female flowers are more upright and may be followed by inedible red fruits that ripen to black. Hardy.

Height: 1m (3ft) **Spread:** 1.5m (5ft)
Site: Partial shade, sun. Well-drained soil
Use: Border, underplanting for shubs and trees
Good companions: *Cyclamen hederifolium, Iris foetidissima, Osmanthus delavayi*

11 Taxus baccata 'Fastigiata'
Florence court yew, Irish yew

The yews are impressive and long-lived evergreen conifers that make large shrubs or trees, many being excellent for hedging and topiary. This female form is best grown to show it off as a dark green column composed of densely packed branches. As a young plant it is narrow but steadily acquires girth. In autumn it carries seeds with a bright red fleshy covering (aril), which is the only part of the plant that is not poisonous. Hardy.

Height: 9m (30ft) **Spread:** 6m (20ft)
Site: Sun, partial shade. Fertile, well-drained soil
Use: Avenue, specimen tree
Good companions: *Prunus* 'Taihaku', *Pyrus calleryana* 'Chanticleer', *Sorbus cashmiriana*

12 Tsuga heterophylla
Western hemlock

Tall-growing evergreen conifer of narrowly conical growth, with purplish brown bark and dense dark green foliage that hangs from slightly upturned branches. Small, pale brown female cones develop on mature trees. Excellent for hedging, but too large as a specimen tree for most gardens and will eventually exceed the dimensions given. Hardy.

General care: Trim hedges in summer.
Height: 25m (80ft) **Spread:** 8m (25ft)
Site: Sun, partial shade. Humus-rich and moist but well-drained soil
Use: Hedge, specimen tree
Good companions: *Aconitum* 'Ivorine', *Fuchsia magellanica* 'Versicolor', *Hydrangea macrophylla* 'Madame Emile Mouillère'

holly

The best-known hollies are hardy evergreen shrubs and trees grown for their glossy, often spined leaves and colourful inedible berries. For a crop of berries, most female plants require a male plant nearby. Grow in sun or partial shade on moist, well-drained soil. Clip hedges and topiary specimens in spring or late summer.

1 Ilex aquifolium 'Handsworth New Silver'

Common holly, English holly

Female large shrub or small tree with purplish stems. The long spiny leaves are green and grey-green with cream margins. Heavy crops of red berries.

Height: 8m (25ft) **Spread:** 5m (15ft)

Good companions: *Anemone hupehensis* 'Hadspen Abundance', *Aster* x *frikartii* 'Mönch', *Kolkwitzia amabilis* 'Pink Cloud'

2 Ilex crenata 'Convexa'

Box-leaved holly, Japanese holly

Slow-growing female shrub with small, dark green convex leaves and shiny black berries. Suitable as a low hedge or for a border or rock garden.

Height: 2m (6ft) **Spread:** 1.5m (5ft)

Good companions: *Dicentra* 'Langtrees', *Nandina domestica* 'Fire Power', *Tiarella wherryi*

3 Ilex aquifolium 'Ferox Argentea'

Hedgehog holly

This relatively slow-growing male cultivar has small puckered leaves that bristle with numerous spines. These, like the leaf margins, are white.

Height: 8m (25ft) **Spread:** 5m (15ft)

Good companions: *Anemone* x *hybrida* 'Whirlwind', *Aster pringlei* 'Monte Cassino', *Deutzia* x *rosea*

4 Ilex x meserveae 'Blue Princess'

Blue holly

Female shrub with blue-tinted spiny leaves and glossy red berries if there is a male plant, such as 'Blue Prince', nearby. Useful as specimen, canopy in border or for a woodland garden.

Height: 3m (10ft) **Spread:** 2.5m (8ft)

Good companions: *Betula utilis* var. *jacquemontii* 'Silver Shadow', *Lonicera* x *purpusii* 'Winter Beauty', *Nandina domestica* 'Fire Power'

5 Ilex aquifolium 'Bacciflava'

Common holly, English holly

Female tree or large shrub with dark green spiny leaves. Heavy crops of long-lasting bright yellow berries.

Height: 6m (20ft) **Spread:** 5m (15ft)

Good companions: *Epimedium* x *versicolor* 'Sulphureum', *Epimedium* x *warleyensis* 'Orangekönigin', *Hosta fortunei* var. *albopicta*

6 Ilex aquifolium 'J.C. van Tol'

Dark green leaves, which have few spines, and large crops of bright red berries. Self-fertile. Best used as a specimen shrub or tree.

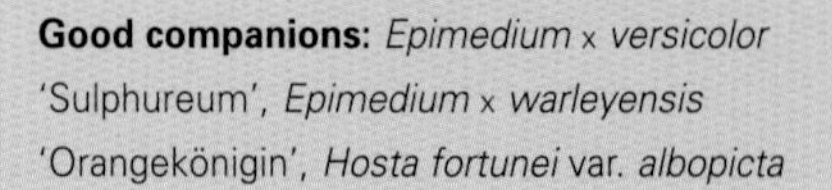

Height: 8m (25ft) **Spread:** 4m (12ft)

Good companions: *Amelanchier canadensis*, *Crataegus persimilis* 'Prunifolia', *Prunus sargentii*

7 Ilex aquifolium 'Pyramidalis'

Common holly, English holly

This self-fertile shrub or small tree is narrowly conical when young, more open when mature. It has green stems, spiny or spineless leaves and heavy crops of long-lasting bright red berries. Useful as a specimen or for topiary. For a formal shape, clip in summer.

Height: 6m (20ft) **Spread:** 5m (15ft)

Good companions: *Bergenia* 'Sunningdale', *Hedera helix* 'Ivalace', *Skimmia japonica* 'Rubella'

8 Ilex x altaclerensis 'Golden King'

Female tree or large shrub with almost spineless leaves that are rich green with an irregular bright yellow margin or sometimes entirely yellow. Heavy crops of red berries.

Height: 6m (20ft) **Spread:** 5m (15ft)

Good companions: *Doronicum orientale* 'Magnificum', *Eranthis hyemalis*, *Narcissus obvallaris*

heaths

These low-growing evergreen shrubs resemble heathers (*Calluna vulgaris*), but most flower from winter to spring. Although many are natives of acid moorland or heathland, those described here are tolerant of lime. Most are hardy and require a sunny well-drained site; in a container use soil-based, preferably lime-free (ericaceous) compost. Trim in spring after flowering.

1 **Erica carnea 'Springwood White'**
Alpine heath, Winter heath
From midwinter white flowers almost hide the small bright green leaves.
Height: 25cm (10in) **Spread:** 50cm (20in)
Good companions: *Calluna vulgaris* 'Peter Sparkes', *Erica* x *darleyensis* 'White Perfection', *Gaultheria mucronata* 'Mulberry Wine'

2 **Erica x darleyensis 'Arthur Johnson'**
Darley dale heath
Long-flowering heath with long slender sprays of pink flowers that are good for cutting.
Height: 30cm (12in) **Spread:** 60cm (2ft)
Good companions: *Cotoneaster conspicuus* 'Decorus', *Erica carnea* 'Vivellii', *Juniperus communis* 'Green Carpet'

3 **Erica x darleyensis 'White Perfection'**
Darley dale heath
Bright green foliage and spikes of pure white, urn-shaped flowers that open between early and late winter and last for many weeks.
Height: 40cm (16in) **Spread:** 75cm (2ft 6in)
Good companions: *Chamaecyparis lawsoniana* 'Ellwoodii', *Erica arborea* var. *alpina*, *Picea glauca* var. *albertina* 'Conica'

4 **Erica x darleyensis 'Furzey'**
Darley dale heath
Deep green leaves and deep pink flowers. Can flower over a long period, sometimes starting in late autumn and continuing until mid-spring.
Height: 30cm (12in) **Spread:** 60cm (2ft)
Good companions: *Calluna vulgaris* 'Robert Chapman', *Erica* x *darleyensis* 'White Perfection', *Juniperus communis* 'Compressa'

5 **Erica carnea 'King George'**
Alpine heath, Winter heath
This is one of the first heaths to flower, with dark pink blooms in early winter. Hardy.
Height and spread: 25cm (10in)
Good companions: *Calluna vulgaris* 'Peter Sparkes', *Erica carnea* 'Springwood White', *Picea pungens* 'Montgomery'

6 **Erica erigena 'Brightness'**
Irish heath, Mediterranean heath
The dense foliage of this heath takes on a purple tint in winter. Honey-scented, deep pink flower spikes from late winter until mid or late spring. Not fully hardy.
Height: 1.2m (4ft) **Spread:** 1m (3ft)
Good companions: *Erica carnea* 'Springwood White', *Juniperus communis* 'Compressa', *Picea glauca* var. *albertiana* 'Conica'

7 **Erica carnea 'Vivellii'**
Alpine heath, Winter heath
Compact plant with bronze-red foliage and deep carmine flowers in winter.
Height: 15cm (6in) **Spread:** 35cm (14in)
Good companions: *Erica arborea* var. *alpina*, *Erica carnea* 'King George', *Erica* x *darleyensis* 'Furzey'

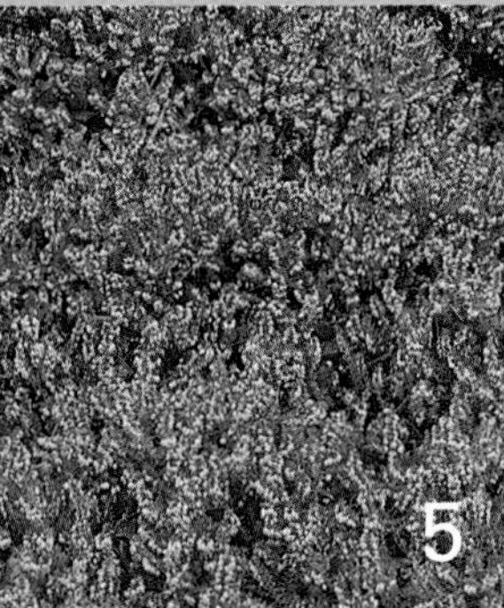

7

1

2

3

6

5

4

alpines

Small perennials and shrubs that thrive in well-drained conditions look good in a raised bed or rock garden and many are suitable for containers or paving. Most can be planted during any mild spell in the dormant season, but dwarf conifers are best planted in late autumn or mid-spring.

pink and mauve

1 Primula nana (syn. P. edgeworthii)

In winter the leaves of this perennial form a congested rosette covered with a mealy powder. They extend in summer and become mid-green. Clusters of yellow-eyed, usually mauve flowers are borne in late winter or early spring. Hardy.

General care: Protect from excessive wet in winter.

Height: 10cm (4in) **Spread:** 15cm (6in)

Site: Partial shade or shade. Lime-free, moist but gritty and sharply drained soil

Compost: Soil-based (John Innes No. 2) with added leaf-mould and grit

Use: Container, raised bed, rock garden

Good companions: *Acer palmatum* var. *dissectum* Dissectum Viride Group, *Leucojum vernum, Salix* 'Boydii'

2 Saxifraga 'Johann Kellerer'

Kabschia saxifrage

Evergreen perennial with grey-green wedge-shaped leaves packed in small silvery rosettes. In late winter and early spring there are sprays of tubular pink flowers. Valued as an early flowering saxifrage for the alpine house, but can be grown successfully outdoors. Hardy.

General care: Plant in early autumn or early spring.

Height and spread: 15cm (6in)

Site: Partial shade. Moist but gritty and sharply drained soil. Good on lime

Compost: Soil-based (John Innes No. 1) with added limestone chippings

Use: Container, raised bed, rock garden

Good companions: *Primula marginata, Saxifraga* 'Gloria', *Scilla mischtschenkoana*

yellow and orange

3 Adonis amurensis

The yellow bowl-shaped flowers of this perennial are borne in late winter and early spring. They can have as many as 30 petals, sometimes bronzed on the backs. The fern-like leaves develop fully after the flowers are over. Hardy.

General care: Plant in autumn with the crown about 2–3cm (1in) deep.

Height: 35cm (14in) **Spread:** 30cm (12in)

Site: Partial shade. Humus-rich and moist but well-drained soil

Use: Raised bed, rock garden, shaded border

Good companions: *Alchemilla conjuncta, Cyclamen hederifolium, Erythronium californicum* 'White Beauty'

4 Chamaecyparis lawsoniana 'Minima Aurea'

Lawson cypress

One of many dwarf cultivars of the Lawson cypress, a large, evergreen conical conifer much used as a specimen tree and for hedging and shelter belts. It is globular to conical with erect sprays of soft golden foliage. Hardy.

Height and spread: 1m (3ft)

Site: Sun. Moist but well-drained soil

Compost: Soil-based (John Innes No. 3)

Use: Container, heather garden, raised bed, rock garden, sunny border

Good companions: *Campanula cochleariifolia, Hebe cupressoides* 'Boughton Dome', *Narcissus* 'Tête-à-tête'

5 Thuja occidentalis 'Rheingold'

White cedar

This slow-growing dwarf form of the white cedar, a medium-sized evergreen conifer, is of roughly conical shape. Young leaves are tinged pink, but the deep old-gold colouring of mature foliage

makes it a good contrast to deep greens, particularly in winter. Hardy.
Height: 1.5m (5ft) **Spread:** 1m (3ft)
Site: Sun. Moist but well-drained soil
Compost: Soil-based (John Innes No. 3)
Use: Container, heather garden, raised bed, rock garden, sunny border
Good companions: *Salix reticulata*, *Thuja occidentalis* 'Hetz Midget', *Viola biflora*

cream and white

6 Saxifraga 'Gloria'
Kabschia saxifrage
Perennial with tight rosettes of grey-green spiky leaves that make firm lime-encrusted cushions. In late winter or early spring yellow-centred white flowers stand on reddish stems. Hardy.
General care: Plant in early autumn or in early spring.
Height: 5cm (2in) **Spread:** 15cm (6in)
Site: Partial shade. Moist but gritty and sharply drained soil. Good on lime
Compost: Soil-based (John Innes No. 1) with added limestone chippings
Use: Container, raised bed, rock garden
Good companions: *Campanula carpatica*, *Gentiana verna*, *Saxifraga* 'Johann Kellerer'

silver, grey and blue

7 Juniperus squamata 'Blue Star'
Flaky juniper
Dwarf evergreen conifer that makes a hummock of silver-blue narrow leaves. It is most silvery when growing in relatively dry conditions. Hardy.
Height: 40cm (16in) **Spread:** 1m (3ft)
Site: Sun, partial shade. Well-drained soil
Compost: Soil-based (John Innes No. 3)
Use: Container, ground cover, heather garden, raised bed, rock garden
Good companions: *Geranium cinereum* 'Ballerina', *Tulipa saxatilis* Bakeri Group 'Lilac Wonder', *Tulipa turkestanica*

8 Picea mariana 'Nana'
Black spruce
This dwarf form of the black spruce, a slow-growing evergreen conifer, makes a dense mound composed of radiating stems closely covered with small blue-grey leaves. If bruised leaves smell of menthol. Hardy.
Height: 45cm (18in) **Spread:** 60cm (2ft)
Site: Sun, partial shade. Moist but well-drained soil
Compost: Soil-based (John Innes No. 3)
Use: Container, heather garden, raised bed, rock garden
Good companions: *Erica carnea* 'King George', *Erica carnea* 'Vivellii', *Picea glauca* var. *albertiana* 'Conica'

green

9 Juniperus communis 'Compressa'
Common juniper
The common juniper is a very variable evergeen shrubby conifer that has several compact upright forms. The miniature column of the slow-growing 'Compressa' is composed of erect, closely held sprays of dull green to blue-green leaves. Hardy.
Height: 75cm (2ft 6in) **Spread:** 35cm (14in)
Site: Sun, partial shade. Well-drained soil
Compost: Soil-based (John Innes No. 3)
Use: Container, front of border, heather garden, raised bed, rock garden
Good companions: *Aubrieta* 'Greencourt Purple', *Helianthemum* 'Wisley Primrose', *Tulipa* 'Cape Cod'

10 Picea abies 'Little Gem'
Christmas tree, Norway spruce
One of several dwarf forms of the Norway spruce, a tall-growing evergreen conifer, this makes an almost globular bush of tiny, tightly packed dark green leaves. Hardy.
Height and spread: 40cm (16in)
Site: Sun. Moist but well-drained soil
Compost: Soil-based (John Innes No. 3)
Use: Container, heather garden, raised bed, rock garden
Good companions: *Chamaecyparis lawsoniana* 'Gimbornii', *Picea glauca* var. *albertiana* 'Conica', *Thuja occidentalis* 'Danica'

11 Picea glauca var. albertiana 'Conica'
White spruce
This slow-growing form of the white spruce, a large blue-green evergreen conifer, usually makes a remarkably symmetrical cone of dense bright green foliage. It may take more than 30 years to achieve the dimensions given. Hardy.
Height: 2m (6ft) **Spread:** 1.2m (4ft)
Site: Sun. Moist but well-drained soil
Compost: Soil-based (John Innes No. 3)
Use: Container, front of border, heather garden, raised bed, rock garden
Good companions: *Calluna vulgaris* 'Firefly', *Calluna vulgaris* 'Robert Chapman', *Erica* x *darleyensis* 'Furzey'

12 Pinus mugo 'Mops'
Dwarf mountain pine
This is a slow-growing globular form of the dwarf mountain pine, an evergreen conifer that usually develops as a gnarled shrub. Hardy.
Height: 35cm (14in) **Spread:** 50cm (20in)
Site: Sun. Well-drained soil
Compost: Soil-based (John Innes No. 3)
Use: Container, heather garden, raised bed, rock garden
Good companions: *Crocus chrysanthus* 'Ladykiller', *Cytisus* x *beanii*, *Pulsatilla vulgaris*

herbs, vegetables & fruit

In winter the kitchen garden provides a store of hearty vegetables and flavourings that are the basis of sustaining recipes. It is also the season to make sowings, as weather permits, of early succulent crops.

herbs

1 Horseradish
Armoracia rusticana

The hot, pungent flavour of this robust perennial's roots is used to flavour sauces and dips. Mild in spring but fiery in autumn. Hardy.

General care: Sow or plant in spring. Control spread of older plants by chopping out wayward roots before they establish. To grow as an annual, plant root cuttings in spring for lifting in late autumn or winter.

Height: 1m (3ft) **Spread:** Indefinite

Site: Sun or dappled shade. Light moist soil

Use: Herb or vegetable garden

2 Sage
Salvia officinalis

Aromatic shrubby evergreen with grey-green leaves used as a flavouring, especially for stuffing and meat dishes. Milder-flavoured variegated and coloured kinds are good for shrub borders. Hardy.

General care: Prune hard to shape in spring and trim after flowering. Replace after four to five years. Sow under glass in March and plant out after the last severe frosts 45cm (18in) apart or take softwood cuttings in early summer. Protect in the first winter.

Height and spread: 1m (3ft)

Site: Sun. Well-drained soil, not acid

Compost: Soil-based (John Innes No. 3) or soil-less, both with added grit

Use: Border, container, herb garden

3 Salad burnet
Sanguisorba minor

Drought-tolerant evergreen perennial best treated as an annual for culinary use. The soft divided leaves have a fresh nutty flavour and are useful in salads. Naturalises well in grass. Hardy.

General care: Sow indoors in spring or autumn and plant out 30cm (12in) apart. Cut young leaves from early summer onwards; frequent cutting encourages plenty of young growth.

Height: 60cm (2ft) **Spread:** 30cm (12in)

Site: Sun or light shade. Well-drained soil

Compost: Soil-based (John Innes No. 3)

Use: Container, edging, herb garden, wild garden

4 Scented-leaved pelargonium
Pelargonium species and cultivars

A huge range of very different pelargoniums has soft, sometimes variegated leaves packed with aromatic oils that smell variously of mint, lemon, eucalyptus, eau-de-cologne or spicy nutmeg; these can be used as culinary flavouring. Pink or white flowers in summer. Grow in pots and harvest young leaves as required. Half hardy.

General care: Take cuttings in summer, pot up individually when rooted and overwinter in a cool room or greenhouse. Feed and trim to shape regularly. Keep fairly dry over winter, but well watered at other times.

Height and spread: 30cm–1m (1–3ft)

Site: Sunny, sheltered and frost-free

Compost: Soil-based (John Innes No. 3) or soil-less, both with added grit

Use: Container, houseplant, sunny patio

vegetables

5 Brussels sprout, late
Brassica oleracea Gemmifera Group

As mid-season varieties finish cropping in early winter, late varieties, such as 'Wellington' and 'Fortress', extend supplies until spring. Hardy.

Site: Sun or light shade, sheltered. Deep, rich very firm soil, limed to pH7 or higher

How to grow: Sow in late April in a nursery bed outdoors and thin seedlings to 8cm (3in) apart. Transplant 60cm (2ft) apart each way when five to six weeks old. Water freely in dry weather; use a high-potash feed in midsummer only. Stake leafy plants in windy sites. Remove yellow leaves and net against birds. Harvest from the bottom up, or pull up whole stems for stripping indoors. Harvest leafy tops to eat as greens.

6 Cabbage, winter
Brassica oleracea Capitata Group

These often large plants have solid heads and a distinctive flavour. Many varieties have dark crinkled leaves, often tinted blue or red. Hardy.

Site: Sun. Rich firm soil, limed to pH7

How to grow: Sow in late April in a nursery bed outdoors and thin seedlings to 8cm (3in) apart. Transplant 50cm (20in) apart each way when six to eight weeks old. Water in dry weather and protect from birds. In exposed gardens earth up the stems for stability in early winter. Cut heads as required or pull up with the roots and suspend in a frost-free shed if bad weather is forecast. Use by early spring.

7 **Celeriac**
Apium graveolens var. rapaceum
Rugged vegetable with celery-flavoured bulbous stem. The firm flesh is delicious in winter stews or grated raw in salads. Hardy.
Site: Sun or light shade. Rich moist soil
How to grow: Sow indoors in mid-spring and prick out seedlings individually into cell trays or small pots. Plant out 30cm (12in) apart when about 8cm (3in) tall. Water freely in dry weather and mulch. Gently pull off lower leaves and any secondary growing tips every few weeks. Harvest from autumn onwards, when large enough, and leave in the ground over winter.

8 **Chicory, heading**
Cichorium intybus
Crunchy salad crop with a slightly bitter flavour. The large green 'sugar loaf' type and various red chicories, often called radicchio, are both outdoor crops for autumn and early winter, or throughout winter if grown under cover. Not fully hardy.
Site: Sun. Fertile and well-drained soil
How to grow: Sow in succession from April to July for harvesting from August to December. Plants can be sown *in situ* and thinned to 25–30cm (10–12in) apart each way; transplant midsummer thinnings to a coldframe or cool greenhouse for winter use. Water well in dry weather. Harvest complete heads as required.

9 **Chicory, witloof**
Cichorium intybus
This produces loose heads of leaves and thick roots that can be dug up and forced in an airing cupboard or cellar to produce fat buds called chicons. Surplus plants can be left to produce exquisite blue flowers the following year and may be transplanted to a wild garden. Hardy.
Site: Sun. Fertile and well-drained soil
How to grow: Sow outdoors in mid to late spring and thin seedlings to 23–25cm (9–10in) apart each way. Water well in dry weather. In early winter, dig up a few roots at a time, trim the thickest to 15cm (6in) long and cut off the leaves about 2–3cm (1in) from their base. Pack the roots upright in a box or pot of moist soil and put in a dark place; chicons will appear after three to six weeks in a warm place, twice that in a cool place. Cut when 10–15cm (4–6in) long; discard exhausted roots.

10 **Claytonia**
Montia perfoliata
An undemanding salad plant with succulent, mildly flavoured leaves, stems and flowers. This annual can self-sow and naturalise in the garden. Needs some shelter in cold gardens. Hardy.
Site: Sun or shade. Most soils
How to grow: For winter use, sow in August, indoors in cell trays or outdoors in rows 15cm (6in) apart. Plant out or thin to clusters 10–15cm (4–6in) apart, and transplant some seedlings to a coldframe or unheated greenhouse. Cut the whole plant when large enough, leaving a 2–3cm (1in) basal tuft of stems to regrow and provide several more pickings throughout winter. Can be sown in May for summer use.

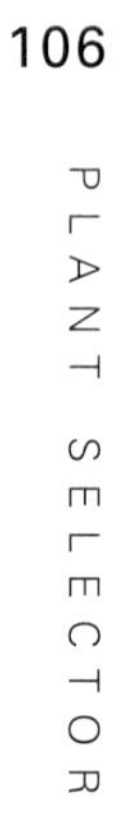

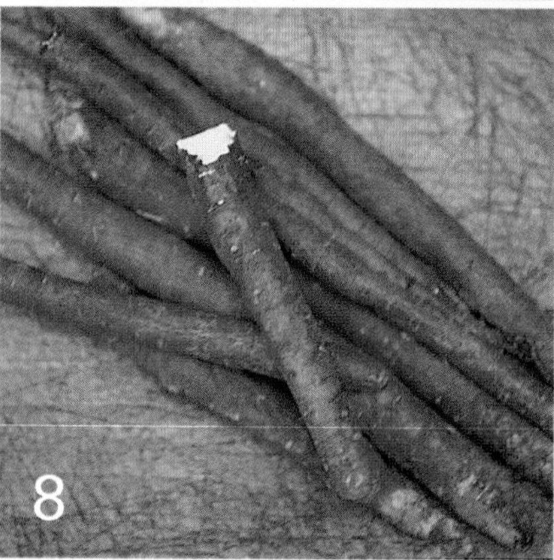

vegetables (continued)

1 Kale
Brassica oleracea Acephala Group

This annual or biennial leaf crop often supplies juicy 'greens' when other vegetables have succumbed in a hard winter. Different varieties have plain, sometimes red-tinted leaves or curly green or rich red foliage that is tightly crimped like parsley. Hardy.

Site: Sun. Most, even light soils with added compost or rotted manure

How to grow: Sow outdoors in May in a nursery bed and thin seedlings to 8cm (3in) apart. Transplant when about eight weeks old, 60cm (2ft) apart and keep well watered. Surplus kale can be transplanted to flower borders for winter bedding. Pick young leaves and whole shoots regularly from November until April.

2 Land cress, upland cress
Barbarea verna

Biennial usually grown as an annual that resembles watercress but is a brighter green. Ready about eight weeks after sowing, it remains green all winter and can be used like spinach. Young shoots can be added to salads. Hardy.

Site: Most soils, with plenty of added compost

How to grow: Sow in July or August, indoors in cell trays or outdoors in rows 15cm (6in) apart, and thin or transplant 10–15cm (4–6in) apart. Transplant some seedlings to a coldframe or greenhouse or cover outdoor sowings with cloches where winters are very cold. Cut or pick young leaves. May also be sown in early spring for early summer crops.

3 Leek, late
Allium porrum

Versatile and richly flavoured undemanding crop that can withstand the harshest weather. Winter leek varieties are bulkier than early ones, with thicker squat stems and dark, sometimes steely blue or purple-tinted foliage; 'Cortina', 'Apollo', 'Giant Winter' and 'Bleu de Solaise' are all good. Hardy.

Site: Sun or light shade. Deep, rich soil with plenty of added compost

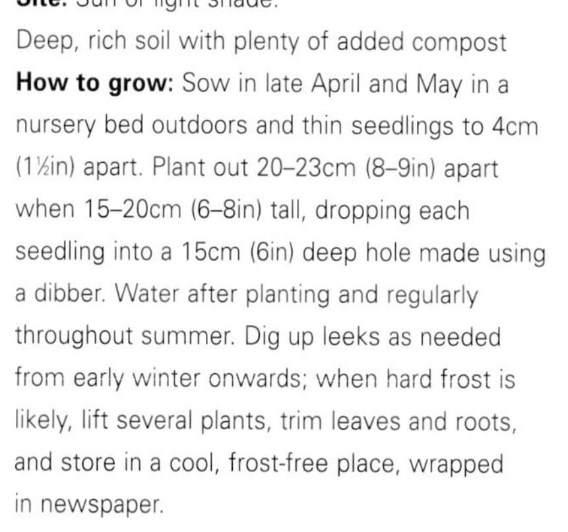

How to grow: Sow in late April and May in a nursery bed outdoors and thin seedlings to 4cm (1½in) apart. Plant out 20–23cm (8–9in) apart when 15–20cm (6–8in) tall, dropping each seedling into a 15cm (6in) deep hole made using a dibber. Water after planting and regularly throughout summer. Dig up leeks as needed from early winter onwards; when hard frost is likely, lift several plants, trim leaves and roots, and store in a cool, frost-free place, wrapped in newspaper.

4 **Lettuce, winter**
Lactuca sativa
Fresh lettuce can be available even in the depths of winter by using greenhouse varieties that are tolerant of short days and low light levels, such as 'Kellys', 'Novita' and 'Valdor'. In mild gardens these may be grown outdoors, preferably under cloches. Hardy.
Site: Sun. Moist and well-drained soil
How to grow: Sow in September in modular trays indoors and transplant 20–25cm (8–10in) apart each way when 5–8cm (2–3in) high. Keep moist, but avoid overwatering. Ventilate freely if under glass except in frosty weather. Cut either complete heads or a few leaves from each young plant as loose-leaf lettuce.

5 **Parsnip**
Pastinaca sativa
Sweetly flavoured and popular as a roast vegetable, parsnips are a reliable winter root that improves as the season progresses. Long varieties such as 'Tender and True' suit deep, light soils, but for shallow soils a shorter kind like 'Avonresister' is preferable. Always use fresh seeds, as they do not keep well. Hardy.
Site: Sun. Deeply dug soil that is not acid or recently manured
How to grow: Sow outdoors in March to May in rows 30cm (12in) apart and thin seedlings to 8–15cm (3–6in) apart, depending on the size of root required. Water regularly in dry weather to prevent splitting, and pull weeds by hand – hoeing can damage the tops of roots and admit canker disease. Start digging up roots in mid-autumn. To make lifting easier in a severe winter, cover rows with straw or leaves.

6 **Radish, winter**
Raphanus sativus
Although small summer radishes may still be available in a cold frame or greenhouse, the most reliable kinds for winter use are the large Spanish or Chinese varieties, such as 'China Rose' or red-fleshed 'Manhangtong', and the long white Japanese mooli or daikon. Flavour and use are as for summer radishes. Not fully hardy.
Site: Sun. Light soil
How to grow: Sow outdoors in August, in rows 25cm (10in) apart, and thin seedlings to about 15cm (6in) apart according to variety. Keep moist, but avoid over-watering. Crops are mature after about three months' growth and can be lifted as required.

7 **Salsify**
Tragopogon porrifolius
A biennial crop with delicious white-skinned roots for winter use and edible flower buds in summer followed by pretty purple daisy-like flowers. The roots are best skinned after cooking. High in insulin, a sugar acceptable to diabetics. Hardy.
Site: Sun. Deeply dug light soil, not recently manured
How to grow: Sow outdoors in April, in rows 15cm (6in) apart, and thin seedlings to 10cm (4in) apart. Keep well watered during dry weather, and feed with high-potash fertiliser in midsummer to encourage large roots. Start lifting as required from late autumn onwards; remaining roots can be left in the ground.

8 **Scorzonera**
Scorzonera hispanica
Winter crop with slim black-skinned roots that have a delicate, slightly nutty flavour and are high in insulin, a sugar acceptable to diabetics. Bright yellow summer flowers. Hardy.
Site: Sun. Deeply dug light soil, not recently manured
How to grow: As for salsify (see 7, Salsify). Plants can be left for a further year for larger roots, but older plants become woody.

9 **Spinach, winter**
Spinacia oleracea
Fast-growing annual leaf vegetable. Varieties such as 'Bergola' and 'Sigmaleaf' are available from December, but with cloche protection can be cropped throughout winter. In very cold gardens, perpetual spinach or spinach beet (see Early Spring, Leaf beet) may be a more productive alternative. Hardy.
Site: Sun. Fertile, well-drained soil
How to grow: Sow outdoors in August and September, in rows 30cm (12in) apart, and thin seedlings to clusters 15cm (6in) apart. Keep well watered at all times. Cover with cloches from late October. Harvest a few leaves from each plant.

10 **Swede**
Brassica napus var. napobrassica
This sweet yellow-fleshed root needs a long growing season. Swedes can be overwintered in the ground, but keep their quality better if stored in boxes of sand. Ridging up surplus roots with soil in midwinter will produce young, semi-blanched 'spring greens'. Hardy.
Site: Sun or light shade. Rich, moist soil, limed to pH7
How to grow: Sow outdoors in June for winter use and in April for autumn use. Space rows 40cm (16in) apart and thin seedlings to 25cm (10in) apart. Water regularly in dry weather. Dig roots as required; lift for storing in early winter.

fruit

11 **Rhubarb, forced**
Rheum x hybridum
Established crowns are covered with cloches where they grow for early spring use, but can be forced in warmth and darkness for an even earlier harvest. Plants are useless after forcing, but divisions can be taken for replanting before forcing takes place. Hardy.
Site: Dark frost-free place
How to grow: Dig up two to three year old crowns in November. Leave on the soil surface exposed to frost for two to three weeks then pack side by side in soil, old potting compost, straw or leaves and put in a dark place. Water well and do not allow to dry out. Ready to harvest after five to six weeks at 10ºC (50ºF), or a little longer at lower temperatures.

the greenhouse

In the protected environment of a greenhouse or conservatory you can defy the season and grow plants that would never survive outdoors or force others that in the open garden would not flower until later.

purple, blue and violet

1 Hyacinthus orientalis 'Delft Blue'

Hyacinth

Specially prepared hyacinth bulbs can be made to produce their spikes of fragrant waxy flowers in winter. 'Delft Blue' bears soft blue, tubular to bell-shaped flowers with mauve tints. Other cultivars are white, yellow, pink, red and blue. Hardy.

General care: Plant prepared bulbs in early autumn with the tip just above the surface of the compost. Keep cool and dark until growths are 2–3cm (1in) long, then bring into light and slowly increase the temperature.

Height: 25cm (10in) **Spread:** 10cm (4in)

Under glass: Full light. Soil-based compost (John Innes No. 2)

Use: Conservatory or greenhouse minimum 2°C (36°F), container, houseplant

pink and mauve

2 Begonia rex hybrids

Begonia rex, an evergreen rhizomatous perennial, is a parent of numerous begonias that are grown for their varied foliage. The mainly dark green background colour can be partly or wholly obscured by patterning in silver and shades of pink, red, brown and other greens. Metallic sheen, puckering and veining add to the rich effect of the foliage. Tender.

General care: Water sparingly in winter. Plants can be moved outdoors in summer.

Height: 25cm (10in) **Spread:** 30cm (12in)

Under glass: Full light, partial shade. Soil-based compost (John Innes No. 2)

Use: Conservatory or greenhouse minimum 10°C (50°F), houseplant, patio

3 Cyclamen persicum

The florists' cyclamens are derived from this tuberous species. It has variable, often marbled leaves and flowers from early winter to early spring when in leaf. The large 'shuttlecock' blooms are pink, carmine or white with twisted petals and are scented. The flowers of most cultivars are large, sometimes double or ruffled and often scentless, but are valued for their long showy display. Dimensions refer to these. Tender.

General care: Plant during the dormant season, with the top of the tuber just above the surface of the compost. Reduce watering and dry off as leaves wither after flowering.

Height and spread: 20cm (8in)

Under glass: Bright light. Soil-based compost (John Innes No. 2)

Use: Conservatory or greenhouse minimum 10°C (50°F), houseplant

4 Freesia hybrids

The hybrid freesias produce fans of narrow blade-like leaves, above which rise sprays of usually scented, upright funnel-shaped flowers in a wide range of colours. Under glass they flower in late winter or early spring. Half hardy.

General care: Plant in autumn with the top of the corm about 5cm (2in) deep.

Height: 40cm (16in) **Spread:** 8cm (3in)

Under glass: Full light. Soil-based compost (John Innes No. 2) with added grit

Use: Conservatory or greenhouse minimum 2°C (36°F), sunny bed or border

5 Hippeastrum 'Apple Blossom'

This hybrid grows from a large bulb that produces strap-shaped leaves and a stout stem bearing four to six outward-facing trumpet-shaped flowers, which are white shaded with pink and up to 15cm (6in) across. Other hybrids with white pink or red flowers are also available. Tender.

General care: Plant in autumn, leaving half the bulb exposed.

Height: 45cm (18in) **Spread:** 30cm (12in)

Under glass: Full light. Soil-based compost (John Innes No. 2)

Use: Conservatory or greenhouse minimum 13°C (55°F), houseplant

6 Laelia anceps

Epiphytic orchid with a large pseudobulb bearing one or, rarely, two large leaves. In winter an arching stem carries two to five mauve-pink flowers with a purple lip and dark-streaked yellow throat. Tender.

General care: Sit pseudobulb in surface of compost. Water sparingly in winter but maintain a humid atmosphere in summer.

Height: 50cm (20in) **Spread:** 30cm (12in)

Under glass: Full light. Soil-less (epiphytic orchid) compost

Use: Conservatory or greenhouse minimum 10°C (50°F)

7 Pericallis hybrids

Florists' cineraria

These short-lived dome-shaped perennials are usually grown as biennials for their long-lasting colourful displays in winter and early spring. Dark green leaves make a sober base for packed bunches of daisy-like flowerheads in shades of pink, red, blue and purple. Some are bicoloured with bold white bands. The compact Spring Glory Series is early flowering. Tender.

General care: Discard plants when flowering is over.

Height: 20cm (8in) **Spread:** 25cm (10in)

Under glass: Full light. Soil-based compost (John Innes No. 2)

Use: Conservatory or greenhouse minimum 5°C (40°F), container, houseplant

8 Pleione Eiger

Hybrid terrestrial or rock-perching orchid with a squat pseudobulb that produces large flowers close to the ground. These are pink with a boldly

4

9

6

10

12

11

7

8

marked, fringed trumpet-shaped lip. Half hardy.
General care: Plant in late spring with two-thirds of the pseudobulb exposed.
Height: 13cm (5in) **Spread:** 10cm (4in)
Under glass: Indirect light. Soil-based compost (John Innes No. 1) with added leaf-mould, or soil-less (epiphytic orchid) compost
Outdoor site: Partial shade. Well-drained soil with added leaf-mould
Use: Conservatory or greenhouse minimum 2°C (36°F), sheltered rock garden

9 Primula malacoides
Fairy primrose

Evergreen perennial usually grown as an annual. The pale green downy leaves have a scalloped margin. In winter and spring stems carry tiers of scented, single or double starry flowers in mauve, pink, purple or white. Half hardy.
General care: Keep plants moist at all times.
Height: 40cm (16in) **Spread:** 20cm (8in)
Under glass: Full light. Soil-based compost (John Innes No. 2) or soil-less
Use: Conservatory or greenhouse minimum 5°C (40°F), houseplant

10 Primula obconica

Perennial species with large-flowered strains that are usually grown as annuals. The light green, slightly hairy leaves are roughly heart-shaped with a scalloped margin. The flowers, in a wide range of colours and often with lightly frilled petals, are borne in clusters during winter and early spring. Contact with the foliage may cause allergic skin reactions. Not fully hardy.
General care: Keep plants moist at all times.
Height: 35cm (14in) **Spread:** 25cm (10in)
Under glass: Full light. Soil-based compost (John Innes No. 2) or soil-less
Use: Conservatory or greenhouse minimum 2°C (36°F), houseplant

11 Rhododendron indicum hybrids
Indian azalea

These small-leaved, bushy evergreen shrubs can be forced under glass to flower in winter; outdoors their season is late spring. The many single or double flowers are mainly white, red or pink and up to 8cm (3in) across, many with ruffled petals. Not fully hardy.
General care: Plunge in a lightly shaded frame or sheltered corner in summer, but for winter flowers bring under glass in autumn and mist buds.
Height: 1.2m (4ft) **Spread:** 1m (3ft)
Under glass: Bright light. Soil-based (ericaceous) compost
Outdoor site: Partial shade. Lime-free, moist but well-drained soil
Use: Conservatory or greenhouse minimum 13°C (55°F), houseplant, lightly shaded border

red and russet

12 Ardisia crenata
Coralberry, Marlberry, Spiceberry

Upright evergreen shrub grown mainly for its clusters of inedible, red waxy fruits, which are shown off by the glossy dark green scalloped leaves. They follow fragrant, white or pink starry flowers borne in summer and persist for many weeks. Half hardy.
General care: Prune to restrict growth in late spring.
Height: 1.5m (5ft) **Spread:** 60cm (2ft)
Under glass: Bright light. Soil-based compost (John Innes No. 3)
Use: Conservatory or greenhouse minimum 2°C (36°F)

red and russet
(continued)

1 Camellia japonica 'Adolphe Audusson'
Common camellia

Evergreen shrub with glossy tapering leaves. The large, red semi-double flowers are often damaged in the open garden whereas in a cold greenhouse they can be enjoyed for several weeks. Hardy.
Height: 3m (10ft) **Spread:** 2.5m (8ft)
Under glass: Bright light. Soil-based (ericaceous) compost
Outdoor site: Partial shade. Lime-free, humus-rich and moist but well-drained soil
Use: Container, conservatory or greenhouse, shady border, underplanting for trees

2 Euphorbia pulcherrima
Mexican flame leaf, Poinsettia

The slender branches of this deciduous shrub bear terminal clusters of insignificant flowers surrounded by petal-like bracts up to 15cm (6in) long. These are usually deep crimson, but the colour range includes red and pink as well as white. The dimensions given are for normal pot-grown specimens, but in the wild the plant can grow more than 4m (12ft) high. Tender.
General care: Plants are best discarded after flowering.
Height: 1.2m (4ft) **Spread:** 75cm (2ft 6in)
Under glass: Full light. Soil-based compost (John Innes No. 3) or soil-less
Use: Conservatory or greenhouse minimum 13°C (55°F)

3 Kalanchoe 'Tessa'
Trailing perennial succulent with slender red stems and red-margined oval leaves. In late winter and early spring it bears numerous drooping clusters of coral-red tubular flowers. For best effect grow in a hanging basket. Tender.
Height: 30cm (12in) **Spread:** 60cm (2ft)
Under glass: Bright light. Soil-based compost (John Innes No. 2) with added grit
Use: Conservatory or greenhouse minimum 12°C (54°F)

4 Primula Joker Series
Polyanthus

The numerous strains of Primrose-Polyanthus primulas include several that are mainly grown as biennials for early colourful displays under glass. In the Joker Series the flowers come in a wide range of colours, including some bicoloured, and make a low bunch just above the rosette of deeply veined spoon-shaped leaves. Half hardy.
General care: Keep moist when in growth. Discard after flowering.
Height: 10cm (4in) **Spread:** 20cm (8in)
Under glass: Full light. Soil-based compost (John Innes No. 2) with added leaf-mould and grit or soil-less
Use: Conservatory or greenhouse minimum 2°C (36°F), houseplant

5 Schlumbergera hybrids
Christmas cactus

The numerous hybrids in this genus of epiphytic cacti have flat jointed stems with toothed leaf-like segments. In winter they bear at their tips lop-sided tubular flowers with reflexed petals and protruding stamens, usually in pink, magenta or red. Suitable for hanging baskets. Tender.
General care: Too much light can retard flowering.
Height: 30cm (12in) **Spread:** 40cm (16in)
Under glass: Bright but indirect light. Soil-based compost (John Innes No. 2) or soil-less, both with added grit
Use: Conservatory or greenhouse minimum 5°C (40°F)

6 Solanum pseudocapsicum
Christmas cherry, Jerusalem cherry, Winter cherry

Evergreen shrub grown as an annual for its inedible spherical fruits, which follow insignificant white summer flowers. They are dark green at first, then yellow and eventually scarlet. Tender.
General care: Cut back by a third in early spring to retain for another year or discard in late winter.
Height: 35cm (14in) **Spread:** 30cm (12in)
Under glass: Full light or bright indirect light. Soil-based compost (John Innes No. 2)
Use: Conservatory or greenhouse minimum 5°C (40°F), houseplant

yellow and orange

7 Acacia dealbata
Mimosa, Silver wattle

Where there is space this evergreen tree makes a splendid specimen. When young the grey-green fern-like leaves are covered with silvery down. The tiny, fragrant yellow flowers are packed into fluffy balls that are carried in dense sprays. In the wild this tree can grow to 30m (100ft). Half hardy.
General care: Prune lightly after flowering.
Height: 8m (25ft) **Spread:** 3m (10ft)
Under glass: Full light. Soil-based compost (John Innes No. 2)
Outdoor site: Sun. Well-drained soil
Use: Conservatory or greenhouse minimum 4°C (39°F), sunny sheltered wall

8 x Citrofortunella microcarpa
Calamondin, Panama orange

Large evergreen shrub or small tree with bright green leathery leaves. It can bear its fragrant, waxy white flowers at almost any time, but the

main season is late spring and summer. The inedible, decorative spherical fruits that follow ripen from yellow to orange and are usually about 2–3cm (1in) across. Half hardy.
General care: Stand outdoors in summer.
Height: 1.5m (5ft) **Spread:** 1m (3ft)
Under glass: Full light. Soil-based compost (John Innes No. 2)
Use: Conservatory or greenhouse minimum 5°C (40°F), houseplant, sunny patio

7

8

9

9 Echinocactus grusonii
Golden barrel cactus, Mother-in-law's cushion

The main value of this spherical cactus lies in the pattern of 30 or more ridges and their creamy yellow spines. Yellow flowers are produced by plants 30 or more years old. Tender.
General care: Do not water from mid-autumn to mid-spring.
Height: 1m (3ft) **Spread:** 1.2m (4ft)
Under glass: Full light. Soil-based compost (John Innes No. 2) or soil-less, both with added grit
Use: Conservatory or greenhouse minimum 10°C (50°F)

10 Lachenalia aloides var. aurea
Cape cowslip

This South African bulb flowers between winter and early spring. The soft orange-yellow tubular bells dangle from purplish stems above strap-shaped leaves. The flowers of the species itself are scarlet-tipped yellow and the stems and leaves are spotted with purple. Half hardy.
General care: Plant in late summer or early autumn with the top of the bulb about 2–3cm (1in) deep. Keep dry after the leaves have died down.
Height: 25cm (10in) **Spread:** 8cm (3in)
Under glass: Full light. Soil-based compost (John Innes No. 2)
Use: Conservatory or greenhouse minimum 2°C (36°F), houseplant

10

11

11 Camellia japonica 'Nobilissima'
Common camellia

Evergreen shrub with glossy leaves that taper to an elegant point. The white peony-like flowers have crowded centres and are shaded with yellow. In the open garden camellia blooms may start to open in early winter and are often damaged by frost, snow or wind, but in a cold greenhouse the flowers escape such inclement weather and can be enjoyed for several weeks in perfect condition. Hardy.
Height: 3m (10ft) **Spread:** 2.5m (8ft)
Under glass: Bright light. Soil-based and lime-free (ericaceous) compost
Outdoor site: Partial shade. Lime-free, humus-rich and moist but well-drained soil
Use: Container, conservatory or greenhouse, shady border, underplanting for trees

12 Coelogyne cristata

Evergreen epiphytic orchid with leathery strap-shaped leaves. Between early winter and spring trailing stems carry up to seven scented flowers that are pure white but for an orange-yellow mark on the lip. Tender.
General care: Do not water in winter. In summer place in bright light and maintain a humid atmosphere.
Height: 30cm (12in) **Spread:** 60cm (2ft)
Under glass: Full light. Soil-less (epiphytic orchid) compost
Use: Conservatory or greenhouse minimum 10°C (50°F)

12

cream and white (continued)

1 Hyacinthus orientalis 'L'Innocence'
Hyacinth

Specially prepared bulbs (see 1, *Hyacinthus orientalis* 'Delft Blue', page 108) will produce spikes of fragrant white flowers in winter. Hardy.

General care: As for 1, *Hyacinthus orientalis* 'Delft Blue', page 108.

Height: 25cm (10in) **Spread:** 10cm (4in)

Under glass: Full light. Soil-based compost (John Innes No. 2)

Outdoor site: Sun, partial shade. Fertile, well-drained soil

Use: Conservatory or greenhouse minimum 2°C (36°F), container, formal bedding, houseplant

2 Jasminum polyanthum

Twining evergreen climber with dark green leaves composed of five to seven leaflets. Under glass the airy sprays of sweetly scented white flowers are borne generously in airy sprigs between late autumn and early spring. Half hardy.

General care: To promote early flowering maintain a minimum temperature of 10°C (50°F).

Height: 3m (10ft) **Spread:** 1.5m (5ft)

Under glass: Full light. Soil-based compost (John Innes No. 2)

Use: Conservatory or greenhouse minimum 5°C (40°F), houseplant

3 Narcissus papyraceus
Paper-white narcissus

Sturdy stems carry up to 10 sweetly scented, clean white flowers in winter. Not fully hardy.

General care: Plant in early autumn with the top of the bulb just showing or set among pebbles in a bowl of water. Keep cool, moist and dark. When shoots are 5cm (2in) long move into full light and gradually increase temperature to 10°C (50°F).

Height: 35cm (14in) **Spread:** 8cm (3in)

Under glass: Full light. Soil-based compost (John Innes No. 2) or soil-less

Use: Conservatory or greenhouse minimum 5°C (40°F), houseplant

4 Odontoglossum crispum

Evergreen epiphytic orchid with a pseudobulb about 10cm (4in) long that produces two narrow leaves. Usually flowers in late winter and early spring, when an arching stem, up to 60cm (2ft) long, carries large glistening white flowers, about 8cm (3in) across and with a coloured lip. Tender.

General care: Water sparingly in winter. In summer place in bright light and maintain a humid atmosphere.

Height: 50cm (20in) **Spread:** 25cm (10in)

Under glass: Full light. Soil-less (epiphytic orchid) compost

Use: Conservatory or greenhouse minimum 10°C (50°F)

5 Phalaenopsis amabilis
Moth orchid

Epiphytic orchid with large leaves on a short stem. Arching stems up to 75cm (2ft 6in) long each carry up to 15 very long-lasting blooms. These are brilliant white with yellow edging to the lip and red markings in the throat. Tender.

General care: Water sparingly in winter but maintain a humid atmosphere all year round.

Height: 30cm (12in) **Spread:** 75cm (2ft 6in)

Under glass: Bright light. Soil-less (epiphytic orchid) compost

Use: Conservatory or greenhouse minimum 18°C (64°F)

silver and grey

6 Cephalocereus senilis
Old man cactus

Slow-growing columnar cactus covered in white hairs. Plants more than 20 years old may bear short-lived pink nocturnal flowers. In the wild can grow to 1.5m (5ft). Tender.

Height: 1.2m (4ft) **Spread:** 20cm (8in)

Under glass: Full light. Gritty soil-less compost with added limestone chippings

Use: Conservatory or greenhouse minimum 10°C (50°F), houseplant

green

7 Agave victoriae-reginae
Queen Victoria century plant, Royal agave

Evergreen perennial succulent with numerous spine-tipped and facetted leaves that are dark green with bold white markings. In summer mature plants, usually 20–30 years old, produce cream flowers in a spike up to 4m (12ft) high. Tender.

General care: Do not water in winter. Move outdoors in summer.

Height and spread: 50cm (20in)

Under glass: Full light. Soil-based compost (John Innes No. 2) or soil-less, both with added grit

Use: Conservatory or greenhouse minimum 10°C (50°F), container, sunny patio

8 Asparagus densiflorus Sprengeri Group

Feathery foliage plant best displayed in a hanging basket. The wiry stalks are armed with prickles and arch over with glossy leaf-like growth. Bright red berries follow inconspicuous pink summer flowers. Tender.

General care: Water sparingly in winter.

Height: 1m (3ft) **Spread:** 1.2m (4ft)

3

4

2

1

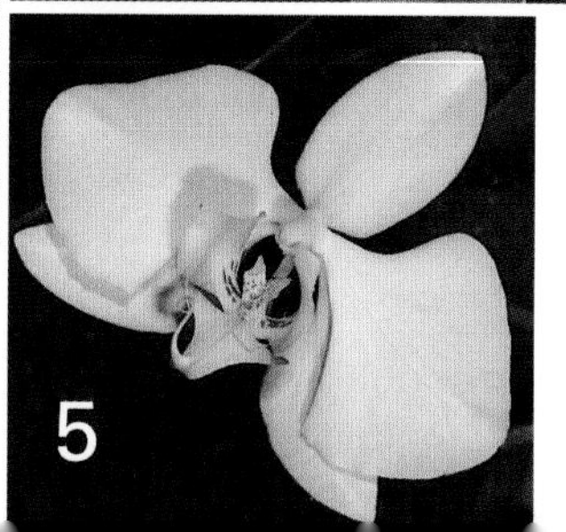
5

6

7

8

9

Under glass: Bright light. Soil-based compost (John Innes No. 2)
Use: Conservatory or greenhouse minimum 7°C (45°F), houseplant

9 Cymbidium hybrids

The hundreds of winter and spring-flowering cymbidium hybrids are easy to grow. The wide range of colours includes shades of green and maroon. Typical of the large hybrids, for which dimensions are given, is 'Thurso', which has green flowers with a red-flecked lip. Tender.
General care: Water sparingly in winter. In summer place in bright light.
Height: 60cm (2ft) **Spread:** 1m (3ft)
Under glass: Full light. Soil-less (epiphytic or terrestrial orchid) compost
Use: Conservatory or greenhouse minimum 10°C (50°F), houseplant

10 Ficus pumila

Climbing fig, Creeping fig

Evergreen perennial climber that clings by aerial roots. In cultivation it is usually seen in its juvenile state, either climbing or trailing, when leaves are small, pointed and dark green and can be kept well below the dimensions given. Mature plants are large leaved and produce hairy figs. Tender.
General care: Trim to restrict growth in mid to late spring.
Height: 5m (15ft) **Spread:** 4m (12ft)
Under glass: Full light, partial shade. Soil-based compost (John Innes No. 3)
Use: Conservatory or greenhouse minimum 5°C (40°F)

10

11 Paphiopedilum insigne

Slipper orchid

Evergreen terrestrial orchid with strap-shaped yellow-green leaves. It flowers in autumn and winter, usually with a single waxy bloom to each dark stem. The most conspicuous feature is the shiny yellow-green slipper or pouch, which is usually flushed brown, as are the wings. Tender.
General care: Water sparingly in winter. In summer place in bright light and maintain a humid atmosphere.
Height and spread: 25cm (10in)
Under glass: Full light. Soil-less (terrestrial orchid) compost
Use: Conservatory or greenhouse minimum 10°C (50°F)

11

12 Philodendron scandens

Heart leaf, Sweetheart plant

Evergreen climber that clings by aerial roots. It rarely flowers in cultivation, but is valued for its dark green foliage with a silky sheen. The leaves are about 15cm (6in) long on young plants, nearly twice this on mature plants. Harmful if ingested and contact with the sap can cause allergic skin reactions. Tender.
General care: In winter water sparingly. Prune to restrict growth in mid to late spring.
Height: 4m (12ft) **Spread:** 1m (3ft)
Under glass: Indirect light, partial shade. Soil-less compost
Use: Conservatory or greenhouse minimum 15°C (60°F), houseplant

12

choosing the best plants

The following plant lists draw on all the plants described in the preceding pages of the Plant Selector, but they are grouped together here to help you choose plants for particular conditions, situations and uses.

plants for acid soils

Plants in the following list that are marked with an asterisk* will only grow satisfactorily on soils that are free of lime. Other plants in the list thrive on acid soils, although they may also grow satisfactorily on soils that are neutral or to some degree alkaline.

- *Acer* (most)
- *Calluna vulgaris**
- *Camellia* (all)*
- *Chamaecyparis lawsoniana* (all)
- *Erica carnea* (all)
- *Erica* x *darleyensis* (all)
- *Erica erigena* 'Brightness'
- *Eucalyptus pauciflora* subsp. *niphophila*
- *Gaultheria mucronata* (all)*
- *Hamamelis* (all)
- *Leucothoe* Scarletta*
- *Parrotia persica*
- *Picea pungens* 'Hoopsii'
- *Rhododendron* (all)*
- *Salix daphnoides*
- *Sorbus* (most)
- *Stachyurus praecox**

plants for sandy or gravelly soil

The following plants require free drainage and are generally drought tolerant, although bulbs generally require a good supply of moisture in the growing season. The range of plants that can be grown in dry sunny gardens can be enlarged if the soil is improved by the addition of organic matter.

- *Anemone blanda*
- *Calluna vulgaris* (all)
- *Cotoneaster* (all)
- *Crocus* (most)
- *Iris* (most)
- *Juniperus* (all)
- *Pinus mugo* 'Mops'
- *Tulipa humilis* Violacea Group

plants for dry chalky soil

A large number of plants are automatically excluded from this list because they will not tolerate alkaline (limy) soil. The improvement of shallow chalky soil by the addition of moisture-retaining organic matter allows lime-tolerant but moisture-loving plants, notably hellebores and clematis, to be grown successfully. Some lime-loving plants, including many saxifrages, require plentiful moisture as well as gritty free-draining conditions.

- *Anemone blanda*
- *Aucuba japonica* 'Crotonifolia'
- *Bergenia*
- *Cornus mas*
- *Cotoneaster*
- *Crocus* (many)
- *Cyclamen coum*
- *Euonymus fortunei*
- *Iris* (all)
- *Juniperus communis*
- *Juniperus* x *pfitzeriana* 'WilhelmPfitzer'
- *Lonicera nitida* 'Baggesen's Gold'
- *Lonicera* x *purpusii* 'Winter Beauty'
- *Pinus mugo* 'Mops'
- *Pyracantha* (all)
- *Symphoricarpos* x *doorenbosii* 'White Hedge'
- *Taxus baccata*

Crocus imperati subsp. *imperati* 'De Jager'

plants for clay soil

Although the following plants generally succeed on close-textured clay soils, they do better when the ground has been improved by the addition of grit and organic matter such as garden compost.

- *Acer* (all)
- *Aucuba japonica* 'Crotonifolia'
- *Berberis* x *carminea* 'Buccaneer'
- *Bergenia* (all)
- *Chaenomeles* (all)
- *Chamaecyparis lawsoniana* (all)
- *Cornus* (all)
- *Cotoneaster* (all)
- *Euonymus* (all)
- *Forsythia giraldiana*
- *Galanthus* (most)
- *Garrya elliptica* 'James Roof'
- *Hamamelis* (all)
- *Hedera* (all)
- *Helleborus* (all)
- *Ilex* (all)
- *Juniperus* (all)
- *Lonicera* (all)
- *Mahonia* (all)
- *Malus* (all)
- *Prunus* (all)
- *Pyracantha* (all)
- *Salix* (all)
- *Sorbus* (all)
- *Taxus baccata* 'Fastigiata'
- *Viburnum* (all)

Viburnum x *bodnantense* 'Dawn'

plants for moist shade

The following plants thrive in moist soils and tolerate partial shade and, in a few cases, full shade. Many will also grow in full sun provided the soil is reliably moist.

- *Acer* (all)
- *Adonis amurensis*
- *Arum italicum* subsp. *italicum* 'Marmoratum'
- *Camellia* (all)
- *Cryptomeria japonica* 'Elegans Compacta'
- *Gaultheria mucronata* (all)
- *Hamamelis* (all)
- *Helleborus* (all)
- *Leucothoe* Scarletta
- *Mahonia japonica*
- *Mahonia* x *media* 'Winter Sun'
- *Nandina domestica* 'Fire Power'
- *Polystichum munitum*
- *Primula* Polyanthus Group
- *Pulmonaria angustifolia* 'Munstead Blue'
- *Pulmonaria rubra* 'Redstart'
- *Rhododendron* (all)
- *Rubus cockburnianus*
- *Sarcococca hookeriana* var. *digyna*
- *Skimmia japonica* 'Rubella'
- *Stachyurus praecox*
- *Viburnum davidii*
- *Viola* (all)

plants for ground cover

Close planting of shrubs and perennials can create a weed-excluding cover. However, effective cover can be achieved only by planting into soil from which every trace of perennial weed has been eliminated.

- *Bergenia* 'Ballawley'
- *Bergenia* x *schmidtii*
- *Calluna vulgaris* (all)
- *Chamaecyparis lawsoniana* 'Tamariscifolia'
- *Cotoneaster* 'Hybridus Pendulus'
- *Erica* (all)
- *Gaultheria mucronata* (all)
- *Hedera* (most)
- *Juniperus* x *pfitzeriana* 'Wilhelm Pfitzer'
- *Juniperus squamata* 'Blue Star'
- *Lonicera nitida* 'Baggesen's Gold'
- *Nandina domestica* 'Fire Power'

plants for coastal sites

Where windbreaks and hedges give protection from salt-laden winds, a wide range of plants can be grown in coastal gardens, including many that benefit from the sea's moderating influence on temperatures.

- *Anemone blanda*
- *Calluna vulgaris* (all)
- *Chaenomeles* (all)
- *Chamaecyparis lawsoniana* (all)
- *Cornus stolonifera* 'Flaviramea'
- *Crocus* (most)
- *Elaeagnus pungens* 'Maculata'
- *Erica* (all)
- *Euonymus fortunei* (all)
- *Garrya elliptica* 'James Roof'
- *Hippophae rhamnoides*
- *Ilex* x *altaclerensis* (all)
- *Ilex aquifolium* (all)
- *Iris* (most)
- *Juniperus* (all)
- *Lonicera nitida* 'Baggesen's Gold'
- *Pinus mugo* 'Mops'
- *Pyracantha* (all)
- *Quercus ilex*
- *Rhamnus alaternus* 'Argenteovariegata'
- *Salix alba* subsp. *vitellina* 'Britzensis'
- *Sorbus aucuparia* 'Beissneri'
- *Viburnum tinus*

flowers for cutting

Several spring-flowering shrubs and trees provide excellent material if cut judiciously in winter, while winter-flowering pansies and early bulbs suit small displays.

- *Abeliophyllum distichum*
- *Chaenomeles* (all)
- *Chimonanthus praecox*
- *Forsythia giraldiana*
- *Galanthus* (all)
- *Hamamelis* (all)
- *Helleborus niger*
- *Jasminum nudiflorum*
- *Mahonia japonica*
- *Narcissus* 'Cedric Morris'
- *Narcissus* 'Rijnveld's Early Sensation'
- *Primula* Polyanthus Group
- *Prunus incisa* 'February Pink'
- *Prunus* x *subhirtella* 'Autumnalis'
- *Viburnum* x *bodnantense* 'Dawn'
- *Viburnum davidii*

plants with aromatic foliage

In the case of many aromatic plants the scent of the leaves is only detectable when they are bruised.

- *Chamaecyparis lawsoniana*
- *Eucalyptus pauciflora* subsp. *niphophila*
- *Hedera colchica*
- *Pelargonium* (scented-leaved forms)
- *Picea mariana* 'Nana'
- *Picea pungens* 'Hoopsii'
- *Rhododendron* 'Praecox'
- Sage *(Salvia officinalis)*
- *Skimmia japonica* 'Rubella'
- *Thuja occidentalis* 'Rheingold'

trees for small gardens

None of the following plants is really suitable for very small gardens, but some can be grown as large shrubs rather than as trees.

- *Acer griseum*
- *Acer grosseri* var. *hersii*
- *Acer pensylvanicum* 'Erythrocladum'
- *Arbutus* x *andrachnoides*
- *Chamaecyparis lawsoniana* 'Ellwoodii'
- *Cornus mas*
- *Cotoneaster* 'Hybridus Pendulus'
- *Cryptomeria japonica* 'Elegans Compacta'
- *Eucalyptus pauciflora* subsp. *niphophila*
- *Garrya elliptica* 'James Roof'
- *Hamamelis* x *intermedia* (all)
- *Hamamelis mollis*
- *Ilex* (most)
- *Malus* 'Winter Gold'
- *Prunus* (most)
- *Salix daphnoides*

Prunus incisa 'February Pink'

choosing the best plants/2

plants with variegated foliage

The leaves of the following plants are edged, spotted or otherwise marked white, cream or yellow.

- *Arum italicum* subsp. *italicum* 'Marmoratum'
- *Aucuba japonica* 'Crotonifolia'
- *Daphne odora* 'Aureomarginata'
- *Elaeagnus pungens* 'Maculata'
- *Euonymus fortunei* 'Emerald Gaiety'
- *Hedera colchica* 'Suphur Heart'
- *Hedera helix* 'Adam'
- *Hedera helix* 'Glacier'
- *Hedera helix* 'Goldheart'
- *Ilex* x *altaclerensis* 'Golden King'
- *Ilex aquifolium* 'Ferox Argentea'
- *Ilex aquifolium* 'Handsworth New Silver'
- *Rhamnus alternus* 'Argenteovariegata'

plants with large and bold leaves

The following plants have impressively large leaves and bold shapes that make a strong impact in the garden. The foliage of other plants with cut and lobed leaves, particularly the maples (*Acer*) and ivies (*Hedera*), adds interesting textures.

- *Ampelopsis glandulosa* var. *brevipedunculata*
- *Arum italicum* subsp. *italicum* 'Marmoratum'
- *Bergenia* 'Ballawley'
- *Hedera colchica* 'Dentata'
- *Hedera colchica* 'Sulphur Heart'
- *Helleborus argutifolius*
- *Helleborus foetidus* Wester Flisk Group
- *Mahonia japonica*
- *Mahonia* x *media* 'Winter Sun'
- *Nandina domestica*
- *Polystichum munitum*

Helleborus argutifolius

plants with colourful foliage

The colour of leaves often changes significantly from one season to the next. Some of the plants listed below are notable for the bronze tints they develop in cold weather. For other colourful foliage see Shrubs and Trees for Autumn and Winter Colour and Plants with Variegated Foliage.

- *Bergenia* 'Ballawley'
- *Calluna vulgaris* 'Beoley Gold'
- *Calluna vulgaris* 'Firefly'
- *Calluna vulgaris* 'Robert Chapman'
- *Chamaecyparis lawsoniana* 'Ellwoodii'
- *Chamaecyparis lawsoniana* 'Minima Aurea'
- *Cryptomeria japonica* 'Elegans Compacta'
- *Cyclamen coum*
- *Eucalyptus pauciflora* subsp. *niphopila*
- *Euonymus fortunei* 'Coloratus'
- *Hedera helix* 'Atropurpurea'
- *Hedera helix* 'Buttercup'
- *Hedera helix* 'Glymii'
- *Hedera helix* 'Manda's Crested'
- *Ilex* x *meserveae* 'Blue Princess'
- *Juniperus squamata* 'Blue Star'
- *Leucothoe* Scarletta
- *Lonicera nitida* 'Baggesen's Gold'
- *Picea pungens* 'Hoopsii'
- *Picea mariana* 'Nana'
- *Thuja occidentalis* 'Rheingold'

shrubs and trees for autumn and winter colour

In addition to the interest they provide in winter, in most years the following deciduous plants have colourful autumn foliage. The display is always more reliable in a frost-free climate.

- *Abeliophyllum distichum*
- *Acer griseum*
- *Acer grosseri* var. *hersii*
- *Acer pensylvanicum* 'Erythrocladum'
- *Cornus* alba 'Kesselringii'
- *Cornus* alba 'Sibirica'
- *Hamamelis* (all)
- *Parrotia persica*
- *Prunus incisa* 'February Pink'
- *Sorbus* (all)

shrubs, trees and climbers with ornamental fruits, berries or seed heads

The ornamental value of the fruits or seed heads of the following plants is often in addition to other features.

- *Ampelopsis glandulosa* var. *brevipedunculata*
- *Arum italicum* subsp. *italicum* 'Marmoratum'
- *Aucuba japonica* 'Crotonifolia'
- *Berberis* x *carminea* 'Buccaneer'
- *Clematis cirrhosa* 'Freckles'
- *Clematis vitalba*
- *Cotoneaster frigidus* 'Cornubia'
- *Cotoneaster* 'Hybridus Pendulus'
- *Cotoneaster lacteaus*
- *Daphne mezereum* f. *alba*
- *Gaultheria mucronata* 'Bell's Seedling'
- *Gaultheria mucronata* 'Wintertime'
- *Hippophae rhamnoides*
- *Ilex* x *altaclerensis* 'Golden King'
- *Ilex aquifolium* 'Bacciflava'
- *Ilex aquifolium* 'Handsworth New Silver'
- *Ilex aquifolium* 'J.C. van Tol'
- *Ilex aquifolium* 'Pyramidalis'
- *Ilex crenata* 'Convexa'
- *Ilex* x *meserveae* 'Blue Princess'
- *Mahonia japonica*
- *Malus* 'Winter Gold'
- *Nandina domestica* 'Fire Power'
- *Pyracantha* (all)
- *Sorbus* (all)
- *Symphoricarpos* x *doorenbosii* 'White Hedge'
- *Viburnum davidii*

Gaultheria mucronata 'Wintertime'

evergreen shrubs and trees

The following are useful for creating a year-round structure.

- *Arbutus* x *andrachnoides*
- *Aucuba japonica* 'Crotonifolia'
- *Buxus* (all)
- *Calluna vulgaris* (all)
- *Camellia* (all)
- *Cedrus deodara*
- *Chamaecyparis* (all)
- *Coronilla valentina* subsp. *glauca*
- *Cotoneaster* 'Hybridus Pendulus'
- *Cotoneaster lactaeus*
- *Cryptomeria japonica* 'Elegans Compacta'
- *Daphne bholua* 'Jacqueline Postill'
- *Daphne odora* 'Aureomarginata'
- *Elaeagnus pungens* 'Maculata'
- *Erica* (all)
- *Eucalyptus pauciflora* subsp. *niphophila*
- *Euonymus fortunei* (all)
- *Garrya elliptica* 'James Roof'
- *Gaultheria mucronata* (all)
- *Ilex* (all)
- *Juniperus* (all)
- *Leucothoe Scarletta*
- *Lonicera nitida* 'Baggesen's Gold'
- *Mahonia* (all)
- *Nandina domestica* 'Fire Power'
- *Picea glauca* (all)
- *Pinus mugo* 'Mops'
- *Prunus lusitanica*
- *Pyracantha* (all)
- *Quercus ilex*
- *Rhamnus alaternus* 'Argenteovariegata'
- *Rhododendron* (all)
- *Sarcococca hookeriana* var. *digyna*
- *Skimmia japonica* 'Rubella'
- *Solanum pseudocapsicum*
- *Taxus baccata* 'Variegata'
- *Thuja occidentalis* 'Rheingold'
- *Tsuga heterophylla*
- *Viburnum davidii*
- *Viburnum tinus* 'Gwenllian'

Pyracantha 'Mohave'

shrubs and trees with ornamental twigs or bark

Twigs or bark that are strongly coloured or attractively patterned or shaped stand out in the winter garden.

- *Acer griseum*
- *Acer grosseri* var. *hersii*
- *Acer pensylvanicum* 'Erythrocladum'
- *Betula utilis* var. *jacquemontii* 'Silver Shadow'
- *Cornus alba* 'Kesselringii'
- *Cornus alba* 'Sibirica'
- *Cornus stolonifera* 'Flaviramea'
- *Corylus avellana* 'Contorta'
- *Eucalyptus pauciflora* subsp. *niphophila*
- *Parrotia persica*
- *Prunus maackii*
- *Prunus serrula*
- *Rubus cockburnianus*
- *Salix alba* subsp. *vitellina* 'Britzensis'
- *Salix daphnoides*
- *Salix irrorata*
- *Sorbus aucuparia* 'Beissneri'

flowering plants for containers

As well as the plants listed here, a number of alpine or rock garden plants are suitable for troughs, and all the greenhouse plants described on pages 108–113 can be grown in containers.

- *Calluna vulgaris* (all)
- *Camellia* (all)
- *Crocus* (all)
- *Cyclamen coum*
- *Erica* (most)
- *Galanthus* (all)
- *Iris* (all)
- *Narcissus* (all)
- *Primula* Polyanthus Group
- *Scilla mischtschenskoana*
- *Tulipa humilis* Violacea Group
- *Viola* x *wittrockiana* (all)

Iris 'Natascha'

plants with fragrant flowers

Age of flower, time of day, temperature and other factors affect the strength of floral scents and their appreciation is highly personal. Some of the following are worth siting to give the best chance of their perfume being enjoyed, but the fragrance of others can only be fully appreciated close to.

- *Abeliophyllum distichum*
- *Acacia dealbata*
- *Chimonanthes praecox*
- *Coelogyne cristata*
- *Coronilla valentina* subsp. *glauca*
- *Crocus chrysanthus* (all)
- *Cyclamen persicum*
- *Daphne* (all)
- *Elaeagnus pungens* 'Maculata'
- *Erica erigena* 'Brightness'
- *Freesia* hybrids
- *Galanthus elwesii*
- *Galanthus* 'S. Arnott'
- *Hamamelis* (all)
- *Hyacinthus orientalis* (all)
- *Iris reticulata*
- *Jasminum polyanthum*
- *Lonicera* x *purpusii* 'Winter Beauty'
- *Mahonia japonica*
- *Narcissus* (all)
- *Primula malacoides*
- *Primula* Polyanthus Group
- *Prunus maackii*
- *Sarcococca hookeriana* var. *digyna*
- *Skimmia japonica* 'Rubella'
- *Viburnum* x *bodnentense* 'Dawn'
- *Viola odorata*

Galanthus elwesii

garden projects

Of all the seasons, winter is the most telling when it comes to structure and design. Now is the time, without the distraction of summer growth, to analyse, plan and put pencil to paper for new garden projects. Siting a shed for storage, or a greenhouse in which to raise next season's plants, both require careful consideration. You might want to embark on a woodworking project, such as making your own plant supports. And as the nights draw in, out come the seed catalogues, inspiring dreams of colourful summer flowers and tasty fresh vegetables. Winter is also the time to get the kitchen garden ready for sowing and planting, or to create deep beds and start off the no-dig system of cultivation.

planning a new garden

For most of us, the chance to design a garden from scratch happens only once or twice in a lifetime. Whether you have a virgin plot or want to make radical changes to an established garden, it's worth making a proper plan.

Wish list
- seating area in sun
- barbecue with storage under
- water feature
- wide patio near house
- lawn - poss. circular?
- pergola with climbers
- shed for storage; dustbin store
- compost bins
- herb garden; vegetable area?
- electric lighting and water supply
- play areas for the children

Take your time, and write down your thoughts about what you want from a new garden before you begin the planning stage. This will prove an invaluable exercise.

deciding what you want

Faced with the prospect of a complete garden makeover, some people hire a garden designer. But it could be more fun – as well as more challenging and satisfying – to do it yourself. First, focus your thoughts by writing down what you want from your garden. Think carefully about how you and your family will use it, day to day. Do you like eating outdoors? Do you want a children's play area? Must you have a shed? For inspiration, look at other people's gardens, and garden design books and magazines that show a range of solutions for different shapes and sizes of garden. Visit plant nurseries for ideas about plants, features and materials.

assessing what you have

Next, carry out a critical assessment of what you actually have in your plot or existing garden. Take your time over this important stage as you may find you have many plants and materials worth saving. Try to allow a full year before you finalise your plans, so you can see what plants are growing in different parts of the garden, and how they perform season by season.

The soil has a great influence on which plants can be grown. Both the soil pH (its level of acidity or alkalinity) and its type can vary enormously from place to place, so it is a good idea to test the soil in different parts of your garden at this stage (see Autumn).

Look at your garden from an upstairs window, if possible, to get an overview of its layout. A covering of snow will enable you to see the basic structure clearly, with all extraneous detail obliterated.

re-using plants and materials

If you inherit well-established plants, they can give the garden a sense of maturity. Neglected plants will need rejuvenating by renovation pruning – or they may have to be taken out altogether. Try to identify those you are considering keeping.

Materials can be recycled too. For example, good-quality paving slabs from an unwanted patio can be used for a path or stepping stones across a lawn, while cheap concrete slabs will make a good base for a new shed or greenhouse.

orientation, sun and shade

Use a compass to find north and ascertain the aspect of different parts of the garden. Take into account the shade cast by large trees and by neighbouring buildings, and do not grow sun-loving plants there. Remember that in summer the sun is high in the sky, reducing the amount of shade cast in winter.

what to include?

All gardens include structural features – some practical, such as a shed or a patio, and others of aesthetic value, like a pond, planting beds or a pergola. They need to be juggled successfully into a new layout, so list the features you want in order of priority and plan in your essentials first, so that the layout is not compromised by having to accommodate too many features.

- **patios and paved areas** make a great focus for relaxing, entertaining and eating outside, as well as being a level space for children to play. Paving slabs create a hard-wearing surface for a flat area, while timber decking is excellent for sloping sites or a garden on different levels. A patio is usually adjacent to the house for convenience, but another area might be better to take advantage of sun, shelter or a view. If there is space, you could have more than one patio to enjoy the sun at different times of day.
- **paths** are a key part of a garden's structure. They link different areas but not necessarily by the most direct route – it is preferable that a path leads you around the garden. They are usually surfaced with a hard material such as paving, gravel or stepping stones.
- **a lawn** is not compulsory, though it remains a traditional choice, especially if you have children. For those who wish to give up the regular chore of mowing, and especially in small gardens or where the grass is overshadowed or quickly gets worn, alternatives do exist. Consider materials such as paving slabs, bricks, paviors, timber decking, granite setts, gravel or slate chippings. Chipped bark can provide a soft surface for a children's play area. Bear in mind that the ground surfaces of a garden set an overall style, in much the same way as choice of flooring affects the look of a room.
- **beds and borders** provide the growing space for your selection of plants. The choice is very personal, but with the variety now available it is possible to have some plants of interest throughout the year (see page 126).
- **boundaries** create shelter and privacy. Plan new boundaries (see Autumn) as an integral part of the garden's design. Check out materials to see what might look good and work best in your area.
- **dividing a garden** into separate areas or 'rooms', each with a distinct character, can work well in all but very small plots. If you do not see the whole garden at a glance, you are encouraged to step out and explore.
- **vertical structures** create visual interest as well as extra growing space, which is especially useful in a small garden. They might include a pergola to cast dappled shade over a sunny patio; an arbour for a secluded seat; arches over gates and paths; trellis or screens to divide up the garden; or obelisks for climbing plants.
- **a pond or water feature** can be made to any size and design to suit the garden. Moving water generally requires access to electricity.
- **lighting** aids security and allows greater use of the garden at night in summer. Unless solar-powered lights are used, access to electricity is needed.
- **conservatory or summer house:** if you think you may want to add one at a later date, make a note to allow sufficient space in the design.
- **storage** is essential for a lawn mower, tools, garden furniture, bicycles and toys. Site a shed out of sight if at all possible.
- **screening off** dark or awkward corners allows you to hide a shed, compost heap or dustbins behind planting, trellis or willow hurdles.
- **a greenhouse** is an essential item for plant enthusiasts, but needs careful siting (see page 136).

A gravel surface requires little upkeep. Here, it is edged with bricks, with stepping stones across, to provide a hard-wearing seating area between the house and a lawn.

planning a new garden/2

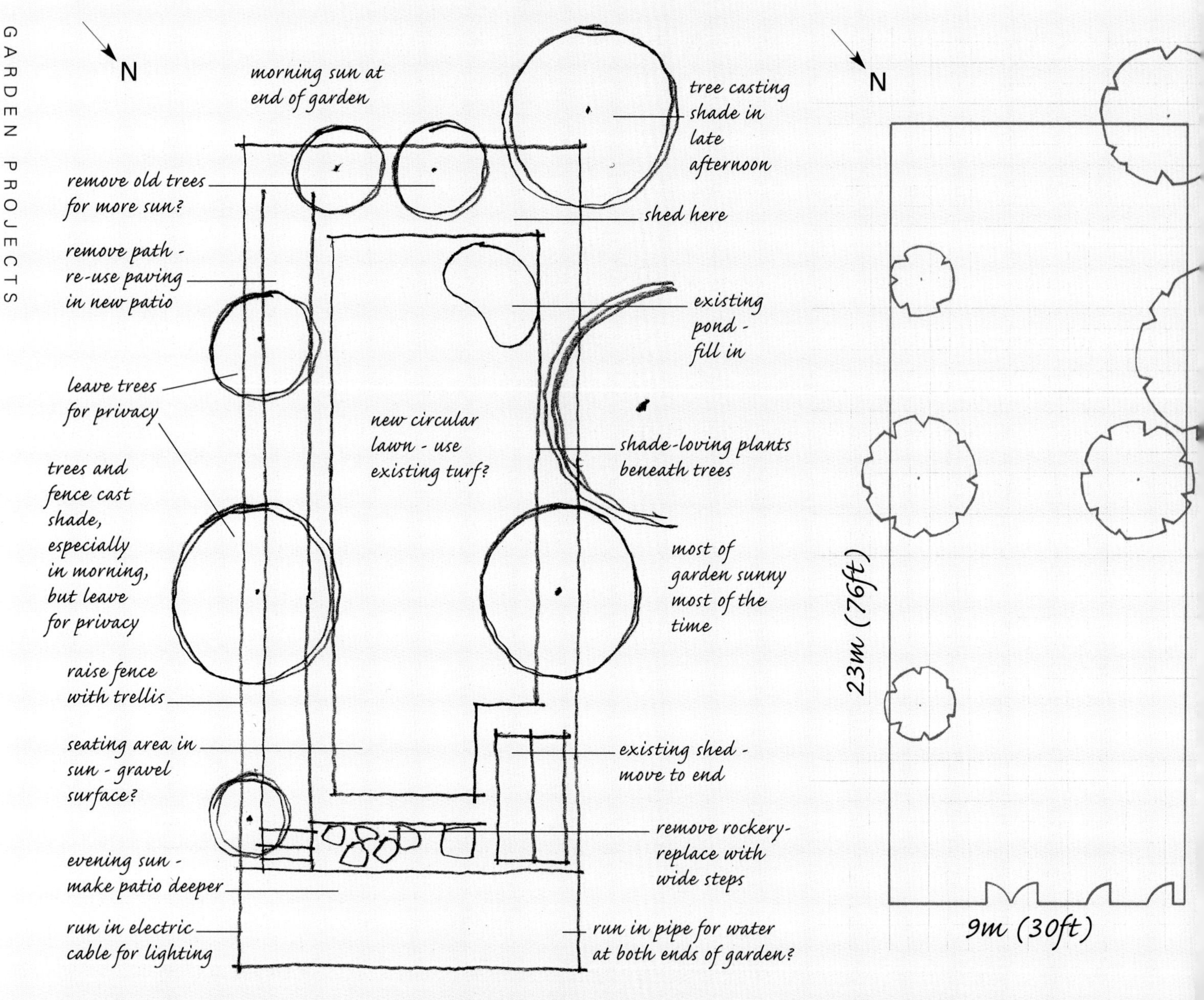

making an initial sketch

Start by drawing a rough sketch of your existing garden, using a sheet of paper large enough to jot down plenty of comments. Note which areas are sunny or shady at different times of day and year. Where would you like to sit throughout the day, according to sun, privacy and proximity to the house? For planting, note which spots are sheltered and warm, or cold and exposed: plants vary in their preferences for growing conditions, and you want to ensure that they will perform at their best.

drawing up an accurate plan

Planning your garden on paper enables you to correct potential mistakes before they become a reality. The drawing must be to scale in order to get an accurate picture of the layout. A scale of 2cm = 1 metre is good for most gardens, or 1cm = 2ft if working in imperial measures. You will need a long tape measure (or preferably two), a piece of paper for the outline sketch, graph paper and tracing paper, pencil, ruler, rubber and a pair of compasses for drawing circles.

working outdoors:

- **make an outline sketch** of your plot.
- **measure the site down the centre,** starting from the house and working outwards. Note down all measurements and distances between key features.
- **indicate all existing features** that you want to keep, such as paving, paths and garden buildings, as well as plants.
- **make a note** of anything outside the garden that influences your plot, such as a tree overhanging from next door, creating shade and taking up moisture.
- **indicate north** on the sketch.

indoors, at your leisure:

- **on graph paper**, use your measurements to make a scale drawing (see left) of the outline of your garden and retained features.
- **secure a sheet of tracing paper** over the outline, and sketch on your new layout (see right). This allows you to do several different versions of the layout, without spoiling your scale outline.
- **you could cut out and label** 'footprints' of larger features, like garden buildings, on card so you can move them around on your plan before finally siting them.

the family garden

This garden (sketched right, illustrated page 124) is designed for a family with growing children and takes into account their need for safe play areas and soft surfaces. The rectangular plot has been broadly divided into three areas, giving a large paved patio near the house on which toddlers can play, in view of the kitchen window, and an area behind the main lawn for a climbing frame and swing for older children.

In between, a gravelled patio takes advantage of a sunny spot on which to sit and eat outdoors, while the circular lawn gives a soft surface for activities from sunbathing to ball games. The shed is sited behind the lawn, screened off by climbers and shrubs, while the dustbin store is conveniently near the back door.

Advantage has been taken of a sloping site to introduce a change of level and a visual break part way up the garden, with steps up to the gravelled patio. Some trees have been retained, to give the garden a sense of maturity, and shrubs on the boundary have also been kept, to help block out the view of buildings beyond.

Mixed borders soften boundaries and allow the adults to indulge an interest in plants, with a herb bed and children's own 'garden' area close to the kitchen.

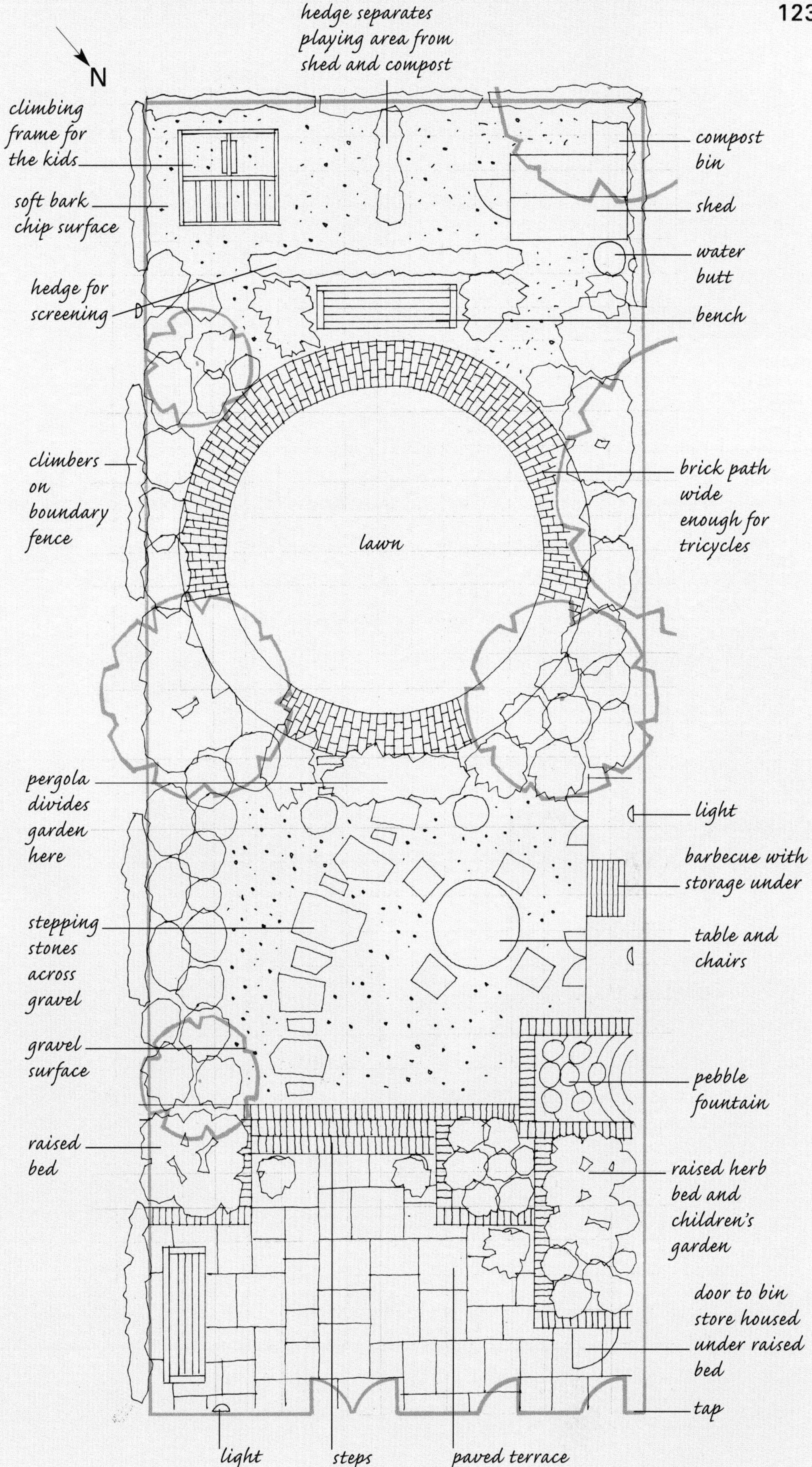

planning a new garden/3

the finished scheme

All successful gardens cater for the interests of the owners, but the best designs have the flexibility to allow for changing priorities. Here, the same plot is shown meeting three very different sets of requirements.

family garden

This design provides safe play areas for growing children and room for adults to enjoy the garden too.

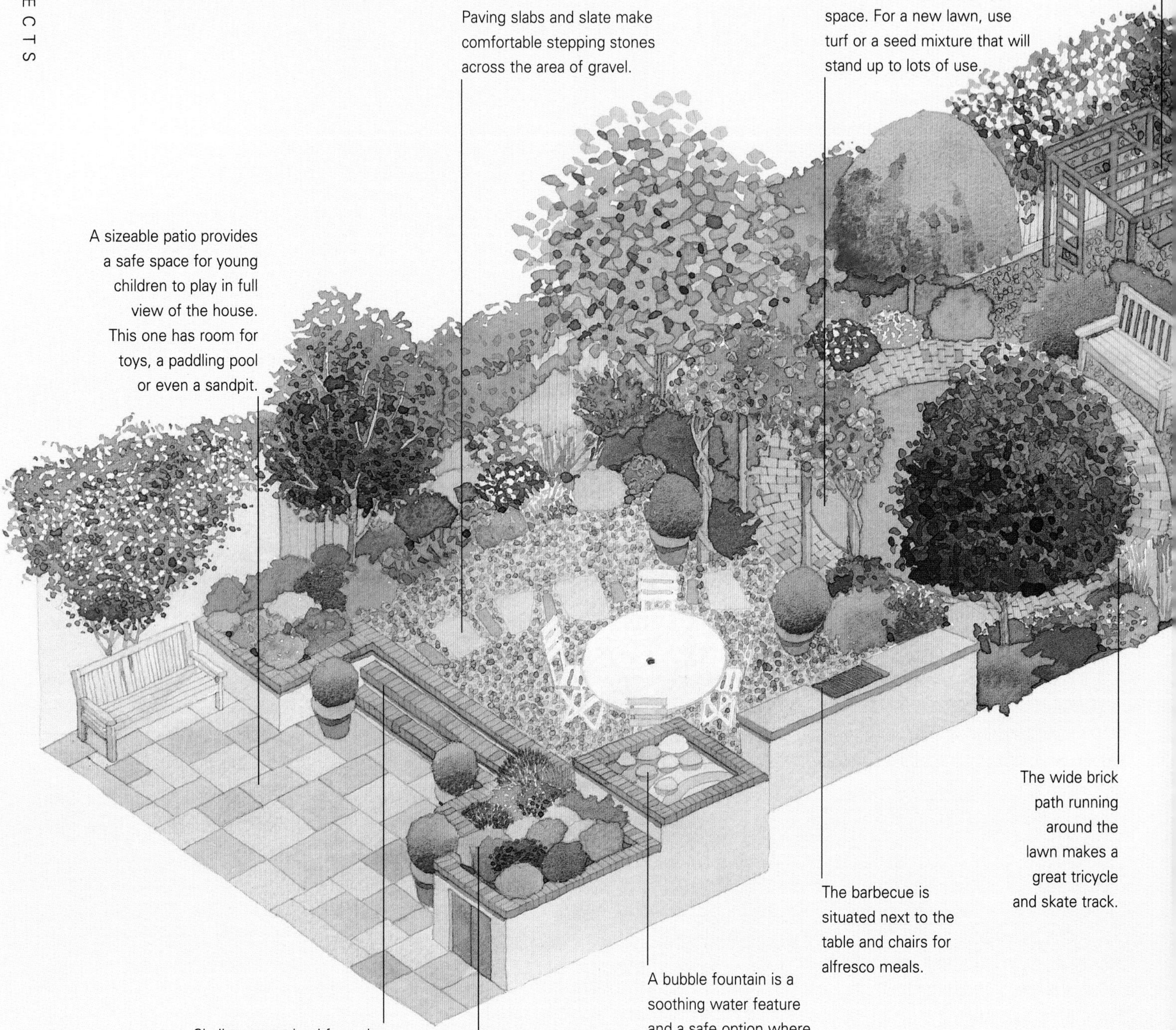

A play area for older children is sited at the end of the garden on a surface of bark chips, and partially screened from view.

A lawn is everyone's play space. For a new lawn, use turf or a seed mixture that will stand up to lots of use.

Paving slabs and slate make comfortable stepping stones across the area of gravel.

A sizeable patio provides a safe space for young children to play in full view of the house. This one has room for toys, a paddling pool or even a sandpit.

The wide brick path running around the lawn makes a great tricycle and skate track.

The barbecue is situated next to the table and chairs for alfresco meals.

A bubble fountain is a soothing water feature and a safe option where there are young children in the family.

Shallow steps lead from the patio to the eating area, dividing the garden and introducing a deliberate change of level into a sloping site.

Herbs are handy for both kitchen and barbecue.

plant enthusiast's garden

This garden is designed principally for growing plants. It is divided into separate areas with a practical, working space at the end. Good use is made of walls, fences and raised beds to maximise the growing space.

A small nursery area in a tucked-away spot allows annuals and biennials to be raised and patio plants to be rested after flowering.

A fan-trained apple tree is grown up a trellis which screens off the compost bin and shed.

A hedge takes time to establish but it will provide a living backdrop to the garden.

Herbs are accessible for the kitchen.

Make the most of walls and fences by growing scented climbers such as roses and honeysuckle against them.

A greenhouse is invaluable for raising young plants and overwintering tender species.

Space has been made for small vegetable beds, to grow summer salads and soft fruit.

Smaller beds with paths between – either of grass or a hard surface – give better access to the plants.

A raised pond is incorporated into the patio, dividing the steps.

easy-care garden

For those who enjoy being outside but cannot afford to spend much time or energy on gardening, this design provides an attractive, low-maintenance solution for all seasons.

Junipers take the eye upwards at the end of the garden.

A summer house makes decorative storage for garden chairs and tools.

Mixed borders of plants such as shrubs, conifers, herbaceous perennials and ornamental grasses will look good all year with very little work.

Water features such as a small fountain need little upkeep compared to a pond.

A second patio area at the end of the garden makes the most of morning sun.

The paved patio near the house is used for eating and entertaining.

Hard surfaces such as gravel and paving are exceptionally low-maintenance compared to a lawn.

designing a border

Border plants are a wonderful investment, increasing in size and beauty over time. Because there is a vast range to choose from, advance thought and careful selection will produce the best results.

the right conditions

A few plants thrive almost anywhere, but most have preferences as to where they grow. Matching a plant to its preferred site will ensure that it flourishes and remains healthy without undue attention. Plants that enjoy the same conditions often make good-looking combinations. Find out what grows well in your area by doing a bit of local research. Walk around your neighbourhood to see which plants thrive there, visit open gardens and talk to knowledgeable neighbours or staff at nearby nurseries and garden centres.

year-round interest

Borders need to earn their keep, and there can be something of colour and interest in every month of the year. The planning guidelines described here can help you to create a border with year-round structure and form. Take care when choosing the flowering plants: it is all too easy to end up with lots of summer blooms and very little at other times. Start by listing suitable plants for the winter months, when blooms are at their most scarce, then work through autumn, spring and finally summer.

climate and location

As well as assessing conditions such as soil and aspect (see page 120), the climate and location of your garden are important factors in choosing plants. Many plants that happily thrive outdoors in warmer parts of the country would be killed by the winter cold in more northerly areas or on exposed hilltop sites. In coastal places, the sea has a tempering influence on climate and keeps the winter temperatures higher than they are just a few miles inland, but it is vital to select plants that are tolerant of salt-laden winds. There is a big difference between town and country, too, as the warmth and shelter created by tall buildings makes for a warmer, more protected environment than in open, rural areas.

how many, how far apart?

Trees and shrubs must be spaced sufficiently far apart to allow room for their eventual height and spread. Correctly spaced plants will look 'gappy' at first, but will fill out surprisingly quickly; in between you can plant annuals or perennials and grasses that are quite happy to be moved later on.

In small to medium-sized gardens, the largest plants should be planted singly, while small shrubs, perennials and grasses look most effective in groups of three or five. Bulbs look wonderful planted in large quantities, particularly if you limit the number of varieties to create a real impact.

planning guidelines

Whether planning planting schemes for a new garden or just one or two beds or borders, the best starting point is to

One of the most attractive trees for small gardens, *Prunus serrula* has beautiful peeling red-brown bark that is handsome all year round (above).

Beneath deciduous trees are opportunities to plant drifts of shade-lovers such as tiarellas, aquilegias, phlox, ferns and trilliums (right).

Deciduous and evergreen climbers clad the fence backing the border.

Upright juniper gives height to the border.

Low ground-covering plants go at the front.

Plant spring bulbs between perennials for additional early colour.

Spiky phormium brings a strong year-round outline.

Fragrant *Choisya ternata* gives two seasons of flower.

mixed border in early summer

Backed by deciduous and evergreen climbers, this border shows a good proportion of shapely evergreen shrubs infilled by flowering shrubs and herbaceous perennials for all seasons.

1 *Vitis coignetiae*
2 *Trachelospermum jasminoides*
3 *Lonicera* x *americana*
4 *Arbutus unedo*
5 *Berberis* x *stenophylla*
6 *Juniperus communis* 'Hibernica'
7 *Phormium* 'Sundowner'
8 *Viburnum tinus*
9 *Rhododendron* 'Bow Bells'
10 *Pittosporum tobira*
11 *Garrya elliptica*
12 *Choisya ternata*
13 *Miscanthus sinensis* 'Silberfeder'
14 *Hemerocallis* 'Catherine Woodbery'
15 *Osmanthus delavayi*
16 *Geranium* x *magnificum*
17 *Lilium regale*
18 *Bergenia* 'Ballawley'
19 *Iris* 'Jane Phillips'
20 *Hebe* 'Boughton Dome'
21 *Arabis alpina* subsp. *caucasica* 'Variegata'
22 *Juniperus virginiana*
23 *Skimmia japonica* 'Rubella'

sketch out a planting plan on paper, then draw it to scale on graph paper (see page 122). In a large garden you may find it easier to make a separate plan for each border rather than tackling the plot at one go.

If you select your plants in the following sequence, you can build up a framework of permanent planting, which you can then fill in with a succession of seasonal colour.

- **trees** are the most dominant occupants of the garden. Consider how different shapes of tree will fit into your garden, and how many seasons of interest they will provide. Those with green or softly coloured leaves are a safer choice than golds or purples, which can look overpowering when large.
- **evergreen shrubs and conifers** should make up about a third of all the medium to large plants, to give year-round structure and colour, which is particularly important in winter. Choose some that are architectural in form, with large or spiky leaves or a striking shape, as well as some of a gentler habit to provide a backdrop to flowers.
- **deciduous shrubs** offer attractive shapes or colourful or variegated foliage, and often a dramatic flowering season. Those with small, plain green leaves make an effective backdrop to flowers.
- **flowering shrubs** can be selected to bloom at different times of year, to create a succession of interest.
- **herbaceous perennials,** grasses and smaller shrubs can be used as infill, once all the key plants are in place.
- **bulbs** can be planted in the spaces between groups of plants to grow up through carpets of ground cover.
- **seasonal bedding** like annuals, biennials and frost-tender perennials can provide spectacular, long-lasting summer colour. Use them to fill gaps while the permanent planting matures, or to make a display in their own right.

low-maintenance plantin

Few people nowadays have unlimited time to devote to their gardens and, if that is the case, choosing the right plants will go a long way towards creating an attractive space that needs the minimum of upkeep. There are also techniques and practices that can reduce work even further.

easy-care plants

Plants vary enormously in the amount of attention that they need. The greatest and most obvious difference is between seasonal and permanent planting, with annual and frost-tender bedding that has to be planted anew every summer, compared to permanent plants that become bigger and more beautiful as time passes. Lowest on the attention scale are ornamental trees, evergreen shrubs, conifers and ground cover (see below) – these plants are widely used for landscaping schemes for this very reason. Restricting yourself to these alone may result in a rather dull and static planting, so the best solution is to settle for a little more maintenance and a lot of colour. Avoid tall perennials that need staking, such as delphiniums, and invasive species like alchemilla that self-seed around to become a weed problem. Choose from the wide range of deciduous shrubs, herbaceous perennials, grasses and bulbs, most of which need attention only once or twice a year – and be repaid by weeks, even months, of flower and foliage colour.

choosing resistant varieties

No garden is entirely free of disease, but some varieties of plant are more susceptible than others, notably many roses, annuals, vegetables and fruit. Having to spray plants against diseases in order to keep them healthy is not only costly and time-consuming, but environmentally unfriendly too. Where possible, avoid encountering problems in the first place by choosing varieties that have good natural resistance to disease. Plant breeders have developed many new healthy cultivars in recent years. Particularly when choosing susceptible plants such as roses, check an up-to-date catalogue to seek out resistant varieties, or read descriptions on the labels to see whether disease resistance is mentioned before you buy.

Whatever the type of plant, bear in mind that healthy, well-grown specimens are much better able to resist attack than plants which are

using ground cover

Why have bare earth offering an open invitation to weeds when you could have a beautiful, living carpet of flowers and foliage? The secret of success with ground cover is to choose plants that suit the situation.

IN BORDERS BENEATH TREES, SHRUBS AND ROSES choose low-growing plants that are tolerant of shade cast from above and vigorous enough to grow strongly, yet not so rampant as to overwhelm their neighbours, such as:

• bugle (*Ajuga reptans*) • lady's mantle (*Alchemilla mollis*) • epimedium
• pulmonaria • comfrey (*Symphytum* 'Hidcote Blue') • tiarella • lesser periwinkle (*Vinca minor*)

ALONG THE BASE OF HEDGES where the soil tends to become extremely dry, it is essential to choose ultra-tough plants that can cope with these conditions, such as:

• *Arum italicum* 'Marmoratum' • *Cyclamen neapolitanum* • *Euphorbia amygdaloides* var. *robbiae* • *Iris foetidissima*

OPEN BANKS AND LARGE AREAS OF BARE GROUND are the place for rampant and spreading shrubby plants that would be a tremendous nuisance elsewhere, as well as sun-lovers that do not take kindly to being overshadowed, such as:

• *Ceanothus thyrsiflorus* var. *repens* • cotoneasters such as *C. procumbens*
• junipers: prostrate varieties such as *J. squamata* 'Blue Carpet' • ground-cover roses: choose from compact ones like the County Series or vigorous varieties such as the Gamebird Series • greater periwinkle (*Vinca major*)

weak and under stress through lack of food or water, or through being grown in the wrong conditions. Hence the importance of thorough soil preparation (see Autumn), choosing appropriate plants for the designated place in your garden, and providing good care for them in the first few months, or years in the case of woody plants.

using raised beds

Raised beds make superb features by introducing or utilising a change of level. They are, in effect, huge containers, but their bigger size greatly reduces the frequency of watering compared to normal containers. Tending the plants in raised beds can also be easier, as you may not have to bend down.

Providing fantastic structural value in winter, the spiky *Yucca gloriosa* needs minimal maintenance, while the box ball needs only one clip a year (below).

Bronze-leaved *Heuchera micrantha* var. *diversifolia* 'Palace Purple' and campanulas tolerate partial shade and so thrive in their chosen position beneath the japanese maple (above).

Ground-hugging rose 'The Fairy' is low-growing but vigorous. Here, it spreads round the base of a light canopied tree (top).

Evergreen shrubs, including clipped box balls and a yew pyramid (above), provide a foil for deciduous early summer-flowering shrubs such as *Viburnum plicatum* 'Mariesii' and *Cornus alba* 'Variegata', and the perennial horned violet, *Viola cornuta*.

using plant supports

Some plant supports are important decorative features as well as providing a frame for herbaceous climbers such as clematis to scramble over. Making your own gives individuality to the garden.

controlling climbers

Left to their own devices, climbing plants tend to grow into a tangled mess. If they are not planted against a fence or wall, grow them up a specially made structure such as a post or an arch, or use a decorative 'wigwam' or timber obelisk. Such structures allow you to grow climbers within a border; they need to be strong enough to withstand the weight of the plants in full leaf.

True climbers – self-supporting plants with twining stems or tendrils – will use a structure only if they are able to grip it. Trellis, canes or ironwork should be no thicker than 1cm (½in) across; any wider and the plant will need to be tied to the support, using plastic ties, soft string or raffia. If tying is a chore, use a tall wire spiral and let the plant grow through it.

obelisks, spirals and cones

These vertical structures provide eye-catching focal points as you wait for the plants to grow, and allow plenty of light to reach the plant while providing stability and support. They are made from wood or canes, metal strips or tubing or, for a more rustic effect, hazel or willow. Sizes range from 45cm (18in) up to 2.5m (8ft).

stakes, frames and rings

Many plants become top-heavy when they are about to flower, so benefit from being supported. Plastic or plastic-coated wire frames, often linked together, are designed to stay hidden but keep border perennials upright when in flower, if they are put in place early enough. Some have interlocking horizontal arms, others a circle of plastic mesh, supported on legs, allowing the plant to grow through. Ranging from 30cm–1m (1–3ft) in height, many can be raised to match the height of plants as they grow.

rustic wigwams

Made from willow or hazel stems, 'wigwams' are ideal for annual climbers, such as sweet peas. Hazel wands may last 6–10 years, but willow stems (withies) last only about half that time. Winter or early spring is a good time to make your own wigwam, before planting in mid-spring.

- Take about 15 thick stems, each about 6ft (2m) long, and soak them for a couple of hours in cold water to make them more flexible. Mark out a circle about 1m (3ft) in diameter on the soil and space eight of the stems upright around the circle, pushing one end at least 15cm (6in) deep. Check that tops are roughly the same height and draw them together, then bind securely with string or wire, as a temporary tie.
- Weave one long, thin, flexible stem between the uprights, horizontally, about 30cm (12in) from the ground, then weave three or four more close to it. Leave a space above and weave through a further four to five flexible stems until you have three or four 'tiers'.
- At the top, use a final stem to secure the ends of the uprights; remove the temporary tie. If you wish, fill in the spaces by weaving the thinnest shoots through the whole wigwam to add strength and stability, enable plants to cling better, and make it decorative.

Wire spirals (left) are simply pushed into the ground so that climbers can use them for support.

This home-made willow 'wigwam' is a well-crafted and individual garden feature (below). Any support with plants growing up through it should be as open as possible, because the natural tendency for plants is to reach towards the light through the structure's top and sides.

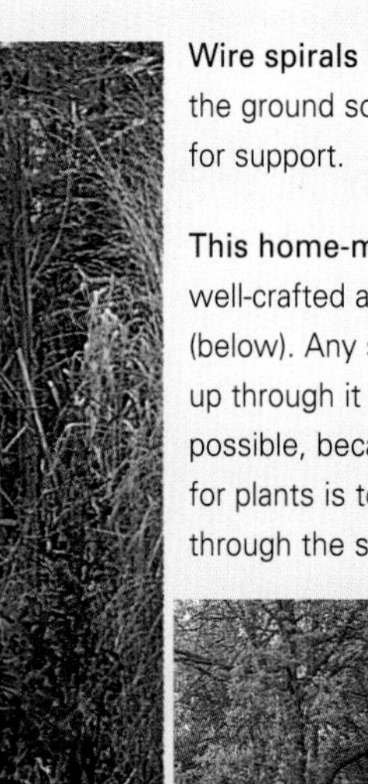

A tall metal cone adds height to a border and looks almost as handsome bare in winter as when clothed by climbing plants (left).

building a trellis obelisk

YOU WILL NEED • 4 leg timbers each 5 x 5cm (2 x 2in) x 2m (6ft) long • 4 cross rail timbers each 2.5 x 5cm (1 x 2in) x 60cm (2ft) long • for the trellis: 4 sheets of expanding wooden trellis or wood battens 2.5 x 1cm (1 x ½in), bought in 2m (6ft) lengths • pencil • cordless drill (or hand drill) • 3 and 5mm drill bits and a screwdriver bit • screwdriver and wood screws: 8 x 4cm (1½in) long and 2 x 8cm (3in) long • saw • wood glue • clamp • nails or panel pins, 2.5cm (1in) long • water-based garden spray paint (optional)

1 With the pencil, mark a point 60cm (2ft) from one end of each leg timber as a guide for the cross rails.

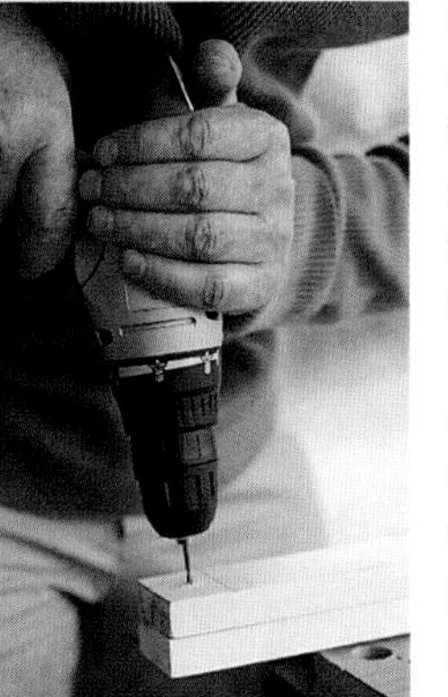

2 On the cross rails, mark the width of the leg timber at both ends and drill a hole in the centre of the marked area.

3 Fasten one cross rail across two of the legs at the marked point with 4cm (1½in) screws; repeat with the other two legs.

4 Ease the tops of each pair of joined legs together so that the ends cross over and mark both overlaps with a pencil. Use the saw to cut away the overlapping sections, so that the top end of each leg is tapered.

5 Glue and clamp, then screw these tops together with 8cm (3in) screws, forming a triangle. Repeat with the second pair of legs to form a second triangle.

6 Fix the two remaining cross rails in position. Drill and screw the two triangles together at the top to form the obelisk.

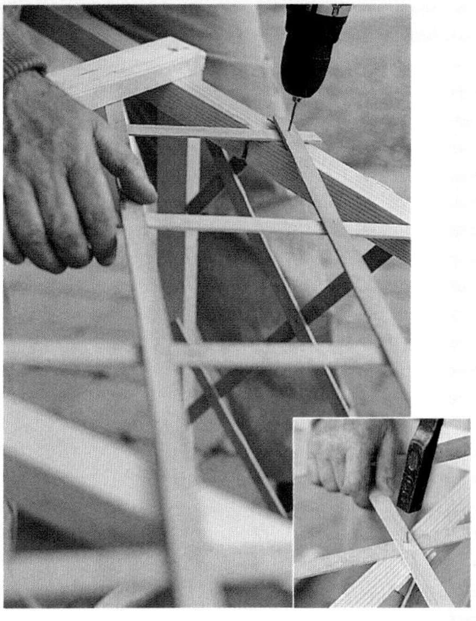

7 On one side of the obelisk, fix a section of expanding trellis to the underside of the cross rail, then pull it out sufficiently to fill in the side area. Secure the trellis to the sides of the leg timbers using small nails or pins; drill the trellis before nailing to prevent the wood from splitting. Using a saw, trim off any surplus wood before repeating the process on the other three sides.

8 Once the structure is complete, it can be sprayed with garden paint. Allow to dry before placing it in position in the garden.

garden buildings

Because of their size, plain sheds or ornamental garden buildings are likely to have considerable visual impact. When choosing one, consider not just its function and its siting, but also its style and colour – do you want it to blend in, or stand out as a feature in its own right?

siting and positioning

Before you buy a garden shed, think carefully about its intended use – it can range in purpose from a simple storage space for house and garden tools to garaging for larger items such as mowers and hedge trimmers, barbecues, play equipment and garden furniture. It may have windows and double as a potting shed with shelving for pots and trays, or as a summer house for relaxation.

A garden shed needs to be readily accessible but sited where it is out of the way. 'Dead' corners and dry spots under trees where little will grow are ideal. Such a building can also be positioned to provide shelter from prevailing winds, while still allowing maximum light into the garden. If the site is very exposed, however, using a shed as a windbreak may lead to turbulence on the sheltered side.

size, structure and design

Once you have decided what you will use the building for, you will know how large it needs to be; try to keep it in scale with the garden. Decide whether you need solid walls or a window to allow in natural light while you work. It is vital that a shed is weatherproof: most ready-made or DIY-kit shed roofs are protected by a covering of at least one layer of heavy-duty bitumised felt which will need replacing every five years or so. A 'flat' roof should have at least a slight slope to it, to allow rainwater to run off.

materials and foundations

Most sheds are made of softwood, because of its cost and ready availability. Providing it has been pressure-treated with a preservative prior to construction, the timber should last 15–25 years, depending on its thickness and quality. Preservative should be applied every other year – a preservative colour stain will resolve colour and weatherproofing in one.

Flat-packed sheds come with all the items needed for their construction (screws, bolts, pins etc.) and will have a pre-felted roof, or felt supplied as strips; they may or may not come with interior fittings such as shelves.

Every garden building needs a firm foundation to keep it level and stable and to distribute the weight evenly. A shed with a wooden floor could stand

In a small garden, where a shed is impossible to hide, painting it will turn it into a feature. Here its presence is emphasised by the symmetrically placed cordylines growing in containers and standing sentinel (below).

evergreen plants for screening

Many of the following are not reliably hardy and need a sheltered position and winter protection unless your garden climate is mild.

CLIMBERS • *Clematis armandii, C. cirrhosa* and *C. canariensis* • *Lonicera henryi* • *Pileostegia viburnoides* • *Trachelospermum asiaticum* and *T. jasminoides*

WALL SHRUBS • *Azara dentata* • *Ceanothus arboreus* • *Fremontodendron californicum* • *Garrya elliptica* • *Itea ilicifolia* • *Osmanthus heterophyllus* • *Pyracantha* • *Rhamnus alaternus* 'Argenteovariegata'

on a levelled base of shingle supported by squared timbers, or on a base of concrete or paving slabs.

screening

You may wish to screen a functional storage or potting shed, or help it blend in with its surroundings. Grow plants up a trellis screen in front of the shed or fastened to the building, or strategically plant a hedge or screen to obscure its outline – but keep access clear.

Screening a shed with perennial plants softens its appearance, but only during the growing season (above right).

Wires have been fixed to this newly erected shed so that evergreen and deciduous climbers can grow up to screen it (right).

When fitting out the inside of a shed, use wall hooks and shelves to keep maximum floor space free for large items such as a lawn mower (below right).

In larger gardens, it should be possible to site a shed well out of the way (below).

choosing a greenhouse

For enthusiastic gardeners, a greenhouse is an extension of the garden, enabling you to enlarge your range of plants. Within its protected environment the length of the growing season is longer and, if heated, tender plants and others at sensitive stages of their life cycle can be nurtured.

size and style

Greenhouses vary considerably, from modest lean-to and freestanding models to fully customised and palatial Victorian styles. Your choice will be limited only by price and by the size of your garden, but it is wise to go for the biggest you can afford and fit in. A useful minimum size worth considering is 1.8m (6ft) wide x 2.5m (8ft) long, but smaller models can still be a boon in restricted gardens. Bear in mind, however, that a central pathway takes up at least 60cm (2ft), whatever the size of greenhouse.

Greenhouses come with vertical walls or with sloping or curved sides, allowing in more light, which is of critical importance for winter crops. A lean-to model is a popular option for a sunny house or garage wall, especially in small gardens. It has the advantage of being warmer than a free-standing model as residual heat is stored in the wall, which should ideally be painted white to improve light levels inside. There are also hexagonal and other multi-sided greenhouses designed for small spaces.

materials

A greenhouse should let in as much natural light as possible to benefit the plants inside. However, the glass or glazing panels must be supported by a strong structure, which can vary in thickness, depending on the material.

metal frames

Aluminium greenhouses are virtually maintenance free as they are almost totally resistant to corrosion. The surface does become pitted and covered by a whitish deposit in the early years, but thereafter it remains almost totally unaffected by climate. Painted aluminium is an attractive, though slightly more expensive option. The glazing bars are slim so there is less obstruction to light than in wooden models. Various systems have been developed to hold the glass, including a continuous glazing-bar cap which traps the glass in position, and narrow rubber strips and spring clips that secure it. All are designed to give a complete seal against draughts and drips. Most aluminium greenhouses come with a galvanised steel base for extra strength.

wooden frames

The longest-lasting greenhouses are constructed from hardwoods, which are

A hexagonal greenhouse, positioned where it receives full sun (left), is a useful and decorative addition to a small garden.

Wooden-framed greenhouses may be glazed right down to the ground (opposite), or they can be set on low brick walls for increased plant protection (above).

Basic aluminium-framed greenhouses (above right) are comparatively cheap and are the preferred choice for many gardeners.

polytunnels

The cheapest but least permanent form of greenhouse is a polytunnel. This consists of a framework of large hoops, slotted into foundation tubes, and covered with heavy-duty plastic sheeting tucked into the soil along the sides. It is advisable to fit door units at either end for ventilation. Polytunnels give plants fairly limited protection compared with a greenhouse. Condensation is frequently a problem and insulation is poor, although there are thermal anti-fog coverings available that go some way to reducing these problems.

highly rot-resistant and very strong, so glazing bars can be quite thin. They are, however, very expensive, and their use has declined in recent years.

Softwoods are widely used, but although they have great strength they do need constant maintenance, without which they quickly rot. Not only must they come treated with preservative, but this must be re-applied regularly for extra protection. Western red cedar is popular because it is somewhat more rot-resistant, but as it lacks the strength of other woods, models have thicker glazing bars and a more solid overall construction. Many modern wooden greenhouses have grooves cut in the glazing bars so you can slide and clip the glass panes in position, rather than having to fix them with nails and putty.

glazing

For centuries glass has been the traditional material for cladding greenhouses. It admits more light and retains heat for longer than any other material. Horticultural glass is 3mm (⅛in) thick and quite heavy; each 60 x 60cm (2 x 2ft) sheet of glass weighs about 3.5kg (8lb). Toughened glass is available at extra cost. You can check the quality and light transmission of a sheet of glass by looking at it edge on: the greener the colour, the poorer the light transmission.

In recent years rigid plastics have increased in popularity as an alternative to glass. They do more or less the same job, but can be curved. Corrugated or flat glass-reinforced polyesters are the best substitute for glass, with 90 per cent or more light transmission. However, they are more expensive than glass and attract atmospheric dirt because of the static electricity they build up. Polycarbonate is cheaper, with lower light transmission but improved heat retention if twin or triple-walled.

installing a greenhouse

To get the best out of your greenhouse, decide first on the right position and then establish firm foundations of the correct size well in advance of construction. If you are erecting the structure yourself, choose a fine day when you and your helper are not pressed for time.

the best position

A greenhouse needs to be sited in an open position, away from overhanging trees, and where it gets the greatest amount of sunlight, particularly in the darkest winter months. Have the ridge of the roof running east to west. This will allow the maximum amount of light to enter, while casting the smallest amount of shadow, especially when the sun is low in the sky. If you want mains electricity installed, it will probably be more convenient to site the greenhouse fairly close to the house or mains supply.

good foundations

Greenhouse foundations and bases vary, depending on the type of greenhouse and the manufacturer's specifications. It is important that the foundations are strong enough to support the weight of the structure and that they are level. Often the base comes as part of the kit and is fixed to anchor pins buried in the ground (see opposite); it should be capable of anchoring the structure in windy conditions and preventing it from lifting. Other greenhouse models will need a concrete or brick plinth.

If the lower part of the greenhouse sides are to be built of brick, you need to construct permanent foundations as for a patio (see Late Summer). If you want to accommodate soil borders within the structure, the foundations must correspond exactly to the greenhouse measurements given by the manufacturer. If in any doubt, discuss the requirements with the supplier. At this stage you could also lay down concrete or paving slabs to make the permanent central path, which should be no less than 60cm (2ft) wide.

An alternative to having soil beds is to construct an entire solid floor of slabs or concrete over a hardcore foundation, in which case the base should extend beyond the greenhouse on all sides to spread the weight and help to reduce settlement later. Or the floor to either side of the path can be covered with a layer of gravel over a weed-proof membrane.

Although many suppliers offer a construction service, it is not difficult for two people to erect a small greenhouse. Read the instructions before you start. Begin by unpacking the sections and check that all items are present and correct. Each section will come as a numbered bundle: lay these out in order of construction.

A metal-framed, fully glazed greenhouse is reasonably easy to install. It is important to site it in an open position, with the ridge running east to west for maximum light.

erecting a greenhouse

YOU WILL NEED • ready-to-assemble greenhouse • spirit level • ready-mix concrete • ratchet or spanner

1 **Lay out the base section** and bolt together on a firm, level area where the greenhouse will stand. Make sure the base is square, then sink the metal posts into prepared concrete-filled holes to anchor it.

2 **Identify and lay out** the two ends of the greenhouse framework on the ground before bolting them together.

3 **Next, lay out and assemble** the sides of the greenhouse framework, and bolt them together loosely. Lift the back and one side of the greenhouse onto the base and hold them in position while you or your helper bolts them together, making sure that the corner is square.

4 **Bolt the second side** and the front of the greenhouse onto the sections already erected, one person holding each section steady while the other fixes the bolts. Then fasten the sides and ends onto the base.

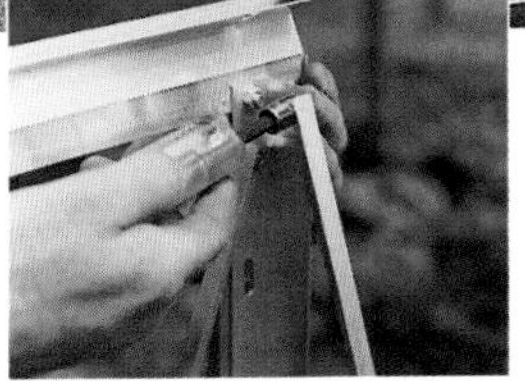

5 **Fix the ridge bar** of the roof into place and slot all the roof bars into position.

GOOD FIT TIP Loosely bolt the sections of the greenhouse together and tighten them only after the glass has been fitted. Since most glass is cut to right angles, it can be used to make the structure fit square around it.

6 **Now that the structure** has been erected, slide the rubber glazing strips into position along the glazing bars to cushion the glass. (A small amount of washing-up liquid applied to the glazing bars helps the strips to slip into place.)

7 **Start glazing** the structure with the glass or plastic sheets, starting with the roof. It is easier and safer to work on the roof before the sides are glazed. Fasten the glass to the glazing bars using the W-shaped wire glazing clips supplied.

8 **Finally, assemble and glaze** the door, checking that it will open and close smoothly. Once this is done you can tighten all the bolts.

equipping a greenhouse

The basic equipment needed to get your greenhouse up and running is some shelves and staging, and you will have to decide whether to heat your greenhouse as well as make sure that the ventilation is adequate.

soil borders and containers

You can grow your plants either at ground level, directly in soil borders, or in containers, or raised on staging, where it is often easier to work and to check on your plants. Soil borders are suitable for growing some plants such as winter salads, tomatoes and melons, but you have much less control over the growing environment than when using containers or growing bags. The main problem with growing in border soil is the build up of soil-borne pests and diseases. To keep the soil healthy it should be revitalised annually with organic matter and every few years replaced to a depth of around 60cm (2ft).

staging

Greenhouse staging, or raised shelving, can be made of aluminium, concrete, brick, steel or wood. Strong supports are essential, as they must bear the considerable weight of plants, compost, and possibly wet sand or gravel. The surfaces or shelves can be solid or open.

- **solid tops** These come in wood or sheet metal. Sheet metal trays with a 2–3cm (1in) rim can be filled with sand or gravel to help watering in summer, as pots can take up moisture from the trays by capillary action.
- **open tops** These may be wooden slats or a form of wire mesh. Their advantage over solid tops is that they allow better air circulation around the plants.

Growing bags held in trays (left) are a good way to grow tomatoes at ground level.

Metal staging, supplied with some ready-to-assemble greenhouses, provides a working area that can be filled with gravel (right).

Two-tier wooden staging gives plenty of room for cuttings and seedlings (below).

ventilation

Greenhouses usually have at least one vent, but you will probably want to supplement this. The best combination is to have ventilators in the sides and the roof to create a 'chimney' effect, as cool air enters through the side vents and is expelled through the roof vents as it warms. A change of air equivalent to two or three times the volume of the greenhouse each hour is ideal, and the

total area of vents should equal one-sixth of the greenhouse floor.

If you are out for much of the day it is worth installing automatic vents, which open and close as temperatures rise and fall. You can also buy louvred panels for fitting in side walls. Leaving the door open on warm days provides extra ventilation. In very hot weather you could also install an electric extractor fan to move air through the greenhouse. These can also cool air in summer by passing it over wet pads.

The basic ventilator is a roof panel on a hinged arm that is operated by hand and held on a stay (above).

In winter you will need to line the glass walls with sheets of bubble plastic for extra insulation (left).

heated or unheated?

A wide range of plants can be grown in an unheated greenhouse, but most of the growing will take place between the beginning of March and the end of October. You may need to provide some protection over winter, but this will not necessarily be enough in extreme conditions, when plants inside can be frost-damaged. A compromise can be achieved by growing plants mainly in an unheated greenhouse, but providing some heat as frost protection through the winter or very early spring.

It is easy to heat a greenhouse, but it can be costly. Check that the greenhouse is:

- **well maintained** in order to exclude draughts and heat leak.
- **well insulated** during winter months by lining the walls with bubble plastic. At night lowering shading blinds helps to retain heat, but raise them every morning.
- **divided into sections,** so plants that require high winter temperatures are grouped together in one well-insulated area that is heated, leaving the other area unheated for hardier plants.

If you plan to install heating, decide on the kinds of plants you wish to grow and the temperature regime they prefer (see below). Buy a maximum-minimum thermometer to monitor temperatures.

- **frost-free conditions** mean a minimum temperature of 5°C (40°F).
- **a temperate house** heated to 10°C (50°F) allows many plants to grow through winter, but costs twice as much to heat as a frost-free house.
- **a tropical regime** of 15°C (60°F) is preferred by most houseplants, but can be five times as expensive to heat as maintaining a frost-free house.

heating methods

- **electric heaters** are very efficient and many have thermostatic control, which reduces their running costs. Fan heaters are fast-acting and also circulate the air. Tubular heaters are cheaper and equally portable. A mains supply is essential and should be installed by a qualified electrician. Never run an electric heater off an extension lead from the house.
- **gas heaters** require good ventilation. Propane gas heaters are portable but need checking regularly. Have at least one full cylinder in store. There are models that run off natural gas, but a qualified gas fitter must install them.
- **paraffin heaters** are cheap but discharge fumes, which can harm some plants, and also water vapour, so good ventilation is important. They also need regular refilling and maintenance. They are most useful in small greenhouses.

heated propagators

These are electrically heated closed cases with bottom heat used to germinate seedlings or root cuttings. They should have a thermostat to monitor the temperature within this enclosed environment. You can create your own by installing a heating mat or cables on solid staging and covering with a small portable frame or cloche.

Try to select a propagator that conforms to the dimensions of a set number of seed trays, as this will reduce heat loss and wasted space.

making a vegetable plot

It is possible to include a few favourite vegetables almost anywhere in the garden, but the time may come when you want to grow a more ambitious selection of crops in a dedicated kitchen garden or vegetable plot. At this stage, some thought and planning will pay dividends.

the right site

Choosing the best place to grow vegetables is important, as it can make the difference between success and failure. Factors to consider include:

- **shelter** Cold winds seriously affect cropping, with even light winds reducing yields by 20 per cent or more, especially in winter. Fences and hedges filter winds and limit their impact, and both can be used to protect vegetables and fruit crops, adding to the total productivity of your garden. Walls can be a mixed blessing. They are valuable for supporting trained fruit, but solid barriers can produce strong wind turbulence within the garden and trap frost. Make sure that boundary or internal walls are not affecting the proposed site adversely.
- **sun and shade** Most crops need plenty of sunlight, particularly winter crops, if they are to yield well. Light shade can be welcome in summer to protect leafy vegetables like lettuce and kohl rabi from drying out, but heavy shade from buildings or trees is best avoided.
- **good drainage** Heavy waterlogged soil causes all kinds of problems for vegetables. If puddles lie on the surface for any length of time after prolonged rain, you might have to dig the site deeply to improve drainage (see Autumn), or consider raising the soil level in beds or ridges to increase the depth of well-drained earth.
- **soil** No soil is perfect, but most can be improved over time. Incorporating large amounts of organic material, such as garden compost and rotted manure, adds body to light soils and opens up heavy clays. With regular cultivating and mulching, your soil and crops will steadily improve in quality.
- **size** Even a small area can be productive, but plot size will influence your choice of plants to grow. If you have a small plot, choose vegetables that can grow close together. Include tall varieties that use vertical space, like beans, and crop the ground intensively by close-spacing the plants.

Winter in this kitchen garden (below) reveals the skeletons of fan-trained and tree fruit. The low box hedges edging the half-empty vegetable beds have chicken wire at their base to deter rabbits.

a practical design

In drawing up a plan for your vegetable plot, do your best to incorporate the permanent features detailed below. Some of these will make your day-to-day gardening easier, while others, like paths, form a key part of the layout.

permanent features

- **one or two compost bins** allow you to dispose of annual weeds and vegetable waste, and to recycle their fertility back into the garden.
- **space to stack** manure, leaf-mould and other bulky materials for digging into and improving the soil.
- **water** – you don't want to carry this far, so consider installing a tap and standpipe, or a tank to collect rainwater.
- **a coldframe** (see page 152).
- **borders** or other space for herbs and perennial vegetables, such as asparagus and globe artichokes.
- **fruits are permanent** and should be considered early in the planning stage.
- **paths** provide essential access, both for cultivation and for harvesting, particularly on a wet day. Depending on the size of your plot, you will need at least one all-weather path, ideally wide enough to manoeuvre a wheelbarrow. Narrower paths between beds can be of beaten earth or made from more durable materials.
- **edges to beds** such as treated timber boards, bricks or a low hedge of perennial herbs, keep the paths clean.

making a traditional vegetable plot

YOU WILL NEED • spade • rake • string and pegs • measuring tape • 16 treated timber boards 8–10cm (3–4in) wide by 2.5cm (1in) thick • 16 battens 30cm (12in) long • sledgehammer • screwdriver and screws • cocoa shells and grit, or bark

1 **Dig the whole site,** removing as many weeds as possible, especially the roots of perennial species. Rake the area level.

2 **Using the string and pegs,** mark out the plot as a square. Divide this into quarters by marking out two central paths 50cm (20in) wide, crossing at right angles in the centre.

3 **Edge the beds** with the treated boards. Drive the battens firmly into the ground at the corners of the beds and screw the boards to these.

4 **Surface the paths** with a layer of cocoa shells and grit or shredded bark. For a permanent surface, such as brick or slabs, dig out some of the soil and spread this on the beds before laying the paving material.

5 **Allocate the beds** as 1, 2, 3 or 4 for crop rotation (see page 142) and prepare as follows: **bed 1**, fork in rotted manure for peas and beans; **bed 2**, fork in garden compost and fertiliser for potatoes or green manure; **bed 3**, rake in fertiliser for root crops; **bed 4**, fork in compost and fertiliser for brassicas.

6 **Rake the beds level,** and plant any edging crops of perennial herbs, flowers or low hedges. You are now ready to plan plantings for each bed.

making a vegetable plot/2

crop rotation

Growing vegetables in a new position each year is an important precaution against building up soil pests and diseases, and depleting soil nutrients. The traditional method is to divide the ground into three or four plots or beds, then move groups of vegetables with similar needs and disorders from one bed to the next in annual sequence. The three main groups are legumes (peas and beans), brassicas (the cabbage family), and root crops, including onions, with potatoes and squashes in a fourth bed. Fit in salad leaves and sweetcorn wherever there is space. Additions of rotted manure or garden compost are made to each bed when digging and preparing it for planting, depending on the type of crop grown in it (see below). Fertiliser, where required, is applied just before planting the crop. In small gardens, where only a few vegetables are grown, simply avoid growing a particular group or individual crop in the same place for two consecutive years.

rotation groups

	YEAR 1	YEAR 2	YEAR 3	YEAR 4
BED ONE	legumes (add well-rotted manure)	brassicas (add compost and fertiliser)	roots and onions (add fertiliser)	potatoes (add manure or compost and fertiliser)
BED TWO	potatoes (add manure or compost and fertiliser)	legumes (add well-rotted manure)	brassicas (add compost and fertiliser)	roots and onions (add fertiliser)
BED THREE	roots and onions (add fertiliser)	potatoes (add manure or compost and fertiliser)	legumes (add well-rotted manure)	brassicas (add compost and fertiliser)
BED FOUR	brassicas (add compost and fertiliser)	roots and onions (add fertiliser)	potatoes (add manure or compost and fertiliser)	legumes (add well-rotted manure)

Crop rotation is clearly at work in this vegetable garden, with box-edged square beds dedicated to different groups of crops that have varying requirements in terms of soil and fertilisers. The all-weather brick paths are wide enough for a wheelbarrow. Cloches are used to protect young plants until they become established.

style and layout

There are alternative layouts to the traditional one shown on page 141, which make efficient use of the space. And a vegetable garden need not always be strictly functional, as many crops are ornamental as well as edible.

- **traditional kitchen gardens** were quartered by crossing paths, a system that allowed for efficient crop rotation and a large number of bed edges to plant with herbs, fruit or flowers for cutting.
- **raised or narrow beds,** up to 1.2m (4ft) wide, are very productive; they make the most of small spaces and organic matter and are useful in planning crop rotations too. Several can be arranged to form a kitchen garden, or you can include them as an integral part of a flower border.
- **potagers** are plots that exploit the decorative potential of vegetables by arranging them like bedding plants, balancing their shapes and colours in a pattern of formally shaped beds.
- **a cottage garden patchwork** can be made by organising small square beds in a flexible layout for any size or shape of site, perhaps combined with flowers.

no-dig beds

The deep bed, or no-dig, system of cultivation is based on the concept that routine cultivation damages the soil structure and can lead to a reduction in the population of worms and other beneficial organisms within the soil. Instead of digging the soil to work in organic matter, the organic matter is spread over the surface and left for worms and other organisms to gradually draw it down into the upper layers, improving fertility in the area penetrated by most plant roots. Worm activity not only breaks down organic matter but improves the soil's aeration, drainage and water-holding capacity.

Narrow beds, edged by boards, are one way to grow vegetables in a small space. The soil level drops slightly as the organic matter rots down.

The no-dig system is ideal for dealing with heavy clay soils, which are difficult to work and are easily compacted. By protecting the surface with organic matter structural damage is avoided, while below worms open up the soil's close structure and improve its drainage.

preparation

A once-only, very thorough cultivation is essential to the success of the no-dig system. Double digging, incorporating large quantities of organic matter, enriches the soil and improves texture (see page 61 and Autumn). But from this point on, any cultivation and walking on beds must be avoided to prevent disturbance or compaction, and to allow a natural soil structure to develop. For this reason you need to be able to reach to the middle of the bed comfortably from either side, which limits the width to about 1.2m (4ft).

maintenance of no-dig beds

After the initial preparation is done you should mulch annually (see left). After harvesting leafy vegetables, leave the roots in the soil to decay naturally, trim vegetables near to where they were growing, and lay any leaf litter or waste on vacant areas of the bed to rot down.

maintaining a no-dig bed

1 **Mulch the surface every year** with well-rotted organic matter to a depth of about 10cm (4in) to keep soil fertile. This deep mulching will reduce moisture loss, suppress the germination of weed seeds and keep the soil warmer, extending the growing season. Always work from a path.

2 **When you want to plant,** scrape back the mulch to expose the soil surface and replace it afterwards, keeping it clear of young stems. The timber edging helps to retain the mulch layer within the bed until it rots down.

making a vegetable plot/3

choosing your crops

To some extent, deciding what to grow is a matter of trial and error, but it is a good idea to start with vegetables that are favourites with your family and also those that are expensive, or hard to find, in the shops.

- **list your favourite vegetables** and decide what not to grow. Good quality maincrop potatoes and cabbages may be available locally, whereas salad leaves, sweetcorn or early baby carrots taste better picked fresh.
- **match your list** to the available space, and the time and energy you can devote to their cultivation. Recognise the difference between vegetables that sprint to maturity, allowing you to grow something else afterwards, and slow crops such as brussels sprouts that need a long growing season (see pages 146–7).
- **use your space** to best effect. Do you want to harvest a wide variety of produce for as long as possible, or simply raise large amounts of a few varieties for storing or self-indulgence?
- **find out** what does well locally. As your soil and skills improve, your range of produce will increase, but some crops may not suit your ground or local climate.
- **keep a garden diary.** Note your most successful crops and varieties, with their sowing or planting dates, to help you plan for the next year.

raising from seed

The cheapest and possibly the most rewarding way to grow vegetables is to raise them from seed, but this depends on having a greenhouse (see page 134) or at least a coldframe (see page 148), to start plants off in the warmth. Growing from seed also gives you a wider choice of vegetables and allows you to select more unusual varieties.

Small plug plants of lettuce, beetroot and brassicas are ready to pot on or plant out.

buying plug plants

Where space is at a premium, it is a good idea to visit a garden centre and buy plug plants or small trays of seedlings. This allows you to buy just as many plants as you have space to grow, without the trouble of raising them from seed. You can buy a wide range of crops in this form, both direct and through mail-order and internet outlets.

Plug plants and seedlings are also an invaluable way of raising vegetables if you do not have a greenhouse or even a coldframe, and prefer not to fill your windowsills with propagating cases and pots of seedlings for the first few months of every year. Instead, let the professionals germinate the seeds and grow on the young plants in controlled conditions. You can then take over in spring, when growing conditions are more favourable.

Mesclun (right) is a mixture of spicy salad leaves best freshly picked. Since it is not readily available in shops, it is an ideal crop to grow yourself.

Turnips are a brassica; they take up relatively little space and the tops can be eaten as greens (below).

cropping continuity

The challenge of vegetable growing is having a range of crops available all year round. There are various ways in which you can make the most of your vegetable plot and keep it healthy.

• **successional sowing** Usually it is the quick-maturing crops like spinach, beetroot, radishes and lettuce that are most likely to produce gluts and gaps, but this can be avoided if you sow small amounts of seed at regular intervals. Timing can be difficult to gauge, but a good guide is to sow a new batch of seed when the first true leaves (those forming after the seed leaves) start to emerge on the previous sowing. In this way you avoid 'bolting' lettuces, woody roots or bitter spinach leaves.

• **intercropping** This means using the space between slow-growing crops as a seedbed for vegetables that will later need transplanting or are quick maturing. Radishes, rocket, lettuce, turnips and beetroot (pulled young) are all suitable for growing between crops such as winter cabbages, brussels sprouts or parsnips, spaced a little further apart than usual.

• **catch crops** Take advantage of vacant soil by growing a 'catch', or quick-maturing, crop. For example, rapidly maturing lettuce, spinach or peas could precede a tender crop of runner beans, tomatoes, sweetcorn or courgettes, none of which can be planted in the ground until the risk of frost is over. The catch crop is harvested before the tender crop is planted, or at least before it gets established.

maximising your space

Make full use of available ground by spacing plants equally in each direction rather than in rows. This planting 'on the square' (or in staggered rows) works well in a bed system, where equally spaced plants grow evenly and weeds are quickly crowded out. You can also space plants closer than recommended to produce 'baby' vegetables, a method particularly suited to root crops.

vegetables in small gardens

If you have a really tiny garden that cannot encompass dedicated vegetable beds, it is still possible to grow a few vegetables. Here are some ideas, but try to experiment too.

• **flower borders** A number of vegetables have handsome foliage, which will look attractive among the flowers. There are varieties of chard with rainbow-coloured stems in yellow, orange, pink and ruby red, while beetroots have dark red-veined leaves and stems. Carrot foliage is soft and ferny, and in winter there are few plants that can match the majestic curly kale. Spinach beet and frilly loose-leaved lettuces are always worth growing as cut-and-come-again crops. Sweetcorn is another possibility, planted in a group in a sunny spot. Runner or climbing french beans trained up vertical canes at the back of a border, or along a boundary, give both privacy and produce during summer months. Don't expect the yields to be quite as high as they would be in a dedicated vegetable plot, however.

• **containers** Many vegetables are easy to grow in large containers, tomatoes and salad crops especially, but also peas, beans, courgettes and squashes. Early potatoes are particularly successful when grown in a deep, barrel-like container. Fill it about a third full of soil-based compost, space out the sprouted seed tubers and cover with more compost. As the foliage appears, earth it up with more compost until the container is full. To harvest, just scrape away the compost and lift a helping at a time, then cover up the remaining potatoes to grow on.

• **window boxes** Choose shallow-rooted crops for a window box, although carrot varieties with ball-like roots and radishes should also succeed. Peppers and cherry tomatoes crop well in a sunny aspect, so long as they are well fed and watered. Bush tomato varieties like 'Tumbler' need no training and will even grow successfully in a hanging basket. Lettuces and salad leaves do best on a windowsill shaded from the midday summer sun.

Quick-maturing spring onions and lettuces are grown here as an intercrop between rows of slower-growing maincrop carrots.

vegetables in containers

Vegetables grown in containers must be watered regularly (daily in hot weather) and fed every 7–14 days with an appropriate fertiliser if they are to do well.

• **feed fruiting crops** like tomatoes, beans, courgettes, peppers, aubergines and cucumbers with a tomato fertiliser, which is high in phosphate and potash, to develop flowers and seeds.

• **leafy vegetables,** such as spinach, ruby chard, cut-and-come-again salad crops and lettuces, need a high-nitrogen feed to promote leafy growth.

making a vegetable plot/4

implementing crop rotations

To rotate crops efficiently you need to know which vegetables fall into which group, and this is not always obvious. For example, turnips and swedes grow alongside cabbages because they are also brassicas, whereas potatoes, though they grow underground, need more in the way of organic matter than root vegetables like carrots or onions, and so are more easily treated on their own.

The vegetables here are listed under their crop rotation group, where relevant. Perennial vegetables need a permanent home, so should be grown in a separate bed, while tender fruiting crops, though annuals, need plenty of space and are therefore also grown in a bed of their own. To make the best use of space, fit in quick-maturing salads and spinach as a catch crop or an intercrop (see page 145), to provide a continuous succession of fresh pickings.

SEED PACKET TIP Read the seed packet:

- before buying – it will tell you if the variety is appropriate for the season
- before sowing – it gives precise growing instructions for the best results.

spacing

The spacings given are final, maximum spacings based on vegetables growing in rows. The between-plants distance is given first, followed by the distance between rows. If you prefer to grow plants equidistant from one another, follow the between-plant spacings.

feeding

Most plants grow well without additional feeding as long as the soil has been well-prepared and is mulched regularly with organic matter. With vegetables, however, an application of fertiliser in advance of planting makes a real difference to the quantity and quality of your harvest. Extra feeding during growth is not essential for crops growing in open ground, but vital for those in containers.

ROOTS & ONIONS

Root vegetables, such as carrots, onions and parsnips, do not need a great deal of space, but they prefer a deep soil to allow good root development and do not do well on shallow soils. Rake in a balanced fertiliser before planting or sowing.

bulb onions Raise onions from seed or from plant sets, which is easier.
sow February–March **plant sets** February–March or September–October
spacing 10–15 x 30cm (4–6 x 12in)

garlic Plant individual cloves in autumn. for the biggest bulbs. Grows well in pots.
plant February or October
spacing 20 x 20cm (8 x 8in)

leeks There are varieties for autumn and winter use, so check the packet.
sow February–March **plant** June–August
spacing 15 x 30cm (6 x 12in)

shallots Traditionally planted on Christmas Day.
plant December–March
maximum spacing 15 x 25cm (6 x 10in)

spring or salad onions Successional sowing, or as an intercrop.
sow March–June
spacing 2–3 x 25cm (1 x 10in)

beetroot Easy to grow. For successional sowing, or as an intercrop for baby beets.
sow March–July
spacing 5–8 x 30cm (2–3 x 12in)

carrots Sow early varieties as successional sowings or as an intercrop to be pulled young. Sow Nantes types early and late in the season. 'Sytan' is resistant to carrot fly. Stony ground may create forked roots.
sow March–July
spacing 5–10 x 15cm (2–4 x 6in)

celeriac Tolerates light shade.
sow April **plant** June
spacing 30 x 40cm (12 x 16in)

parsnips Stony ground may split roots.
sow March–May
maximum spacing 8–15 x 30cm (3–6 x 12in)

LEGUMES

These follow root crops or potatoes in rotation. Add well-rotted manure when preparing the soil in Autumn. Before sowing or planting, rake in a balanced fertiliser. After harvesting, leave the roots in the ground or dig them in for the benefit of a following brassica or other leafy crop.

broad beans Tall varieties need support.
sow November or April–May
maximum spacing 25 x 30cm (10 x 12in)

dwarf beans These need no support but crop less heavily than climbing varieties.
sow April–July
spacing 20 x 60cm (8 x 24in)

french & runner beans Canes, arranged in single or double rows or as wigwams, are essential for support. Raise these tender plants in pots under cover for an early start, or direct sow in late May.
sow April–May
maximum spacing 15 x 60cm (6 x 24in)

peas & mangetout Make successional sowings about 5–10cm (2–4in) apart in a broad row and as an early catch crop. Put in place netting or twiggy branches to support the growing plants.
sow earlies March–April; maincrop April–July
maximum spacing 8 x 90cm (4 x 36in)

POTATOES

Potatoes need a deep soil. They can follow brassicas in a rotation and are best grown on their own. Dig in garden compost when preparing the soil and rake in a general-purpose fertiliser a couple of weeks before planting. They can also be grown under black plastic sheeting tucked in round the edge of the bed. Plant tubers 10–15cm (4–6in) deep through a cross cut in the plastic. To harvest, lift the plastic, remove as many tubers as you want and replace the plastic.
plant earlies March–May; maincrop April–May
spacing earlies 30 x 50cm (12 x 20in); maincrop 38 x 75cm (15 x 30in)

BRASSICAS

Brassicas follow legumes to benefit from the residual nitrogen. Dig in compost when preparing the soil and rake in a balanced fertiliser before planting. Dress acid and neutral soils with lime to reduce the risk of club root disease. Leafy brassicas benefit from a high-nitrogen feed in summer.

LIMING TIP Apply lime well in advance of planting, and at least a month after any organic matter has been added, to avoid a chemical reaction taking place that would result in loss of nitrogen from the soil.

broccoli Pick regularly for long harvest.
sow March–April **plant** June–July
maximum spacing 60 x 60cm (2 x 2ft)

brussels sprouts Easy to grow, but tall varieties need support, especially in windy gardens in winter.
sow March–April **plant** May–June
maximum spacing 60 x 60cm (2 x 2ft)

cabbages Easy to grow, especially winter varieties. Choose a variety appropriate for the season. Winter cabbages need the widest spacing.
sow March–September **plant** September–July
spacing 30–50 x 30–50cm (12–20 x 12–20in)

cauliflowers A challenging crop. Raise or buy young plants in pots so that there is no check to growth when transplanting, and never let them dry out. Choose a variety appropriate for the season.
sow/plant April–May
spacing 50–75 x 60–75cm (20–30 x 24–30in)

kale Decorative and easy to grow. Pick shoots regularly for long harvesting.
sow April–August
spacing 45 x 60cm (18 x 24in)

kohl rabi Tolerates light shade. Successional sowing.
sow April–August
spacing 20 x 30cm (8 x 12in)

radishes For successional sowing or an early catch crop or intercrop.
sow March–September
spacing 2–3 x 15cm (1 x 6in)

swedes Easy to grow.
sow April–June
spacing 25 x 40cm (10 x 16in)

turnips Easy to grow. For successional sowing, or pull as baby turnips for an early or late catch crop and intercrop.
sow April–August
maximum spacing 15 x 25cm (6 x 10in)

PERENNIAL VEGETABLES

Because these vegetables grow in the same place for many years, they must be planted in well prepared soil enriched with plenty of rotted manure or garden compost and given a general-purpose feed every year.

asparagus Have patience and wait two years after planting before cutting any spears. In the third year, begin to cut for 4–6 weeks and in subsequent years up to 8 weeks. Earthing up emerging shoots gives a longer blanched stem. After harvesting, apply fertiliser and in autumn mulch with rotted manure after ferns are cut down.
plant March–April
spacing 30 x 45cm (12 x 18in)

globe artichokes These need time to establish before you crop them heavily. The second year after planting limit yourself to one head per plant, the next year cut two or three. In subsequent years you can pick the smaller side heads after picking the main buds. Apply a balanced fertiliser in early spring and in autumn mulch with rotted manure and compost.
plant February–April
spacing 1 x 1m (3 x 3ft)

jerusalem artichokes Tubers can be lifted in the first year. Apply fertiliser in spring and mulch with organic matter in autumn. Will tolerate light shade.
plant February–May
spacing 30 x 60cm (12 x 24in)

LETTUCE & SPINACH

Fit these in wherever there is space, with brassicas or in a bed devoted to salad crops.

lettuce It is most important to sow the appropriate variety for the time of year. Mix with spinach and other salad leaves for a cut-and-come-again seedling crop. Good for successional sowing and intercropping.
sow all year round according to variety
maximum spacing 25 x 30cm (8 x 12in)

spinach & chard Choose a variety appropriate to the season or grow spinach beet, which will crop throughout the year.
sow true spinach in small batches for succession, or as an early catch crop; summer spinach March–May; winter spinach August–October; chard April–August
spacing 15–20 x 30cm (6–8 x 12in)

TENDER FRUITING CROPS

These need plenty of space and are best grown in a bed of their own. Like legumes they need well-manured ground so they can follow roots in a crop rotation.

outdoor cucumbers Train plants up wigwams or other supports. You may need to pollinate the flowers to ensure a crop. Also grow well in growing bags.
sow April–May **plant** May–June
maximum spacing 60 x 60cm (2 x 2ft)

outdoor tomatoes Support tall-growing, or cordon, varieties with canes or other means and remove sideshoots regularly. Pinch out the growing tips two leaves above the third or fourth fruit truss; the fifth or sixth truss in the case of cherry tomatoes. Allow bush varieties to sprawl and do not remove fruit-bearing sideshoots. Outdoor tomatoes also do well in growing bags.
sow April–May **plant** May–June
spacing 75 x 75cm (30 x 30cm)

squash, courgettes, marrows & pumpkin Plant out on mounds of soil, to ensure good drainage, or even on top of your compost heap. You may need to pollinate the flowers to ensure fruits form.
sow April–May **plant** May–June
spacing Give each plant about 1m² (1sq yd); pumpkins and large-fruiting winter squash need 1.5m² (1½sq yd). Alternatively, plant them two to a growing bag.

sweetcorn Plants are wind pollinated so plant in a block, rather than in rows.
sow April–May **plant** May–June
spacing 35 x 35cm (14 x 14in)

cloches & coldframes

In cooler climates, or where the weather is unpredictable, cloches and coldframes allow you to extend the season and protect vulnerable plants. Whether you regard them as accessories or substitutes for a greenhouse, they have their own unique merits.

the value of plant protection

Cloches and coldframes are invaluable in the attempt to protect plants from extreme weather conditions. They also enable you to extend the growing season by several weeks so that you can grow more crops for longer with less risk from the elements.

They will shield plants from frost, fog, cold winds, persistent rain and, if shaded, from scorching sunshine. By trapping the sun's energy, they gather and retain warmth in spring and autumn, the seasons when they are most useful, and allow tender plants and seedlings to continue growing or cropping throughout the winter. They can also be used to keep plants dry at critical times of the year: alpines, bulbs and winter lettuce, for example, can all be sensitive to lingering dampness.

The use of cloches and coldframes relieves pressure on limited greenhouse space. Overall, they provide a considerable measure of control over the unpredictability that can make unprotected gardening a gamble in some climates and seasons.

some advantages of cloches and coldframes

Compared to a greenhouse,

- **they are cheap and versatile** and damage is easily repaired.
- **they occupy less space** than a greenhouse, warm up more quickly and are easier to insulate.
- **cloches are portable,** to some extent frames too, and can be moved round the garden as needed.
- **they act as a half-way house,** hardening off plants in their journey from greenhouse to the open air.
- **cloches and movable frames** can be used to warm the soil before planting and to protect transplants while they get established.
- **they can be opened** or removed completely to admit rain or fresh air in hot weather.
- **pests and diseases** are unlikely to invade and multiply, and are more easily dealt with if they do.

glazing materials

Maximum light and adequate warmth are essential for healthy plant growth and, as with greenhouses, the choice of glazing material can affect conditions in the protected environment.

- **glass** admits more light and retains heat better than other materials, but it is heavy (possibly an advantage for cloches in windy gardens), and potentially dangerous if broken, especially where children and pets are concerned. It is possible to fit toughened glass for safety; otherwise 3mm (⅛in) horticultural glass is adequate.
- **flat or corrugated glass-reinforced polyester** is the best substitute for glass among the rigid plastics.
- **polycarbonate** is cheaper, with lower light transmission but good heat retention if twin or triple-walled.
- **acrylic** is a clearer glazing material, but very brittle and easily cracked.
- **flexible plastic sheets,** widely used for tunnel cloches and lightweight frames, has good light transmission but a limited life, even when treated with an ultra-violet inhibitor to delay yellowing. There is also an increased risk of condensation, which can be a problem with disease-susceptible plants in winter, and heat is rapidly lost at night.

using with a greenhouse

- **coldframes** are the equivalent of a cool or unheated greenhouse, and can be used for growing and storing plants that do not need such cosseted

In severe weather, a line of glass barn cloches, constructed with special wire clips, have been joined together and closed at the ends to form a continuous insulated row over young broad bean plants (top right).

A coldframe on open ground is insulated with straw to give extra protection for young vegetable plants in winter (above).

Tent cloches, made using two sheets of glass joined with wire and a wooden spacer, are the simplest form of movable protection. Here, they shelter young lettuce seedlings (right).

conditions, or for those being prepared for the open air after being started in heat. Coldframes with a soil base can be used for sowing and growing out-of-season plants like salads and flowers that would take up excessive space in a greenhouse border. Since it is also possible to heat a coldframe (see page 153), using the frame as an extension to the greenhouse can relieve congestion within it.

• **cloches** are mainly for open ground use, although they can provide extra protection for crops growing in the border of an unheated greenhouse. Their role is to help plants on the final stage of their journey from the greenhouse or coldframe to the open air, and their greatest value lies in protecting young plants during the first few days after being transplanted or moved outdoors.

Cloches also have an important role, independent of the greenhouse, as temporary, movable protection. Use them to warm the soil before sowing, to cover early outdoor sowings, to provide warmth for tender summer crops and to extend the growing time for crops in autumn.

a year in a coldframe

JANUARY • force rhubarb, kale and witloof chicory
• sow sweet peas in pots
• sow early lettuce

FEBRUARY • sow carrots and radishes
• sow onions, leeks, brassicas for transplanting
• transplant lettuces into the soil

MARCH • plant early potatoes in the soil or in boxes or buckets
• sow dwarf french beans
• root chrysanthemum cuttings

APRIL • sow runner beans and sweetcorn for transplanting
• sow half-hardy annuals
• harden off hardy annuals

MAY • harden off tender flowers and vegetables
• plant ridge cucumbers, melons and self-blanching celery

JUNE • sow biennials and perennials
• train melons and cucumbers
• fork over the soil and add compost after clearing crops grown in it

JULY • sow parsley for winter
• root soft and semi-ripe cuttings

AUGUST • root semi-ripe cuttings and strawberry runners
• house cuttings from pelargoniums and other tender perennials
• dry garlic and shallots

SEPTEMBER • plunge early forced bulbs
• sow hardy annuals
• ripen onions

OCTOBER • plant lettuce
• transplant annual herbs for winter use
• store chrysanthemum roots

NOVEMBER • harvest salads and herbs
• overwinter brassica seedlings

DECEMBER • sow carrots, turnips and radishes in heated frames
• start forcing rhubarb

types of cloche

Cloches are the simplest of glazed structures for protecting plants, and come in all shapes and sizes. From the original bell jar and ornate lantern cloche to functional plastic tunnelling, they all do a useful job in protecting growing plants from the weather.

simple cloches

The earliest kinds of cloche, still available today, were made from two panes of glass joined in the form of a tent to cover sowings and low plants. For taller plants, the barn cloche uses two more panes to raise the basic tent on low walls (see page 148). The glass panes are joined with wires, or metal or plastic clips, or you can improvise with clothes pegs or short canes. Although heavy and breakable, well-made glass cloches are stable in windy positions.

Plastic cloches have now largely superseded glass models. Some use rigid or semi-rigid plastic in the form of tents, squares or short tunnels to cover small areas. Others use plastic sheeting supported on wire hoops to make a low tunnel, 60cm–2m (2–6ft) wide, to cover rows of plants and seedlings.

Plastic sheeting stretched over wire hoops forms a continuous open-ended cloche. The plastic can be tied at the end for greater insulation in winter (top).

Decorative as well as functional, this Victorian lantern cloche forms a cosy environment for overwintering plants (above).

Bell jars and a lantern cloche protect individual plants while they are establishing (left). The cloche lid is angled to allow some ventilation.

Young lettuces are protected under a row of flat-topped cloches (right). Clay pots on top help to prevent them from lifting in windy weather.

other kinds of cloche

• **bell jar** This is the original cloche (*cloche* is French for a bell), formerly glass but increasingly made from plastic. It is used to cover individual plants.

• **flat-topped cloche** Similar to the glass barn cloche, this is a wide, heavy type with a central horizontal panel, adjustable for watering and ventilation. A modified plastic version with slots or small perforations is known as the self-watering cloche.

• **dome cloche** A moulded plastic enclosure, this has a handle and open ends, so several can be arranged in a row.

• **lantern cloche** A square, free-standing cloche, this has a lid like a pitched roof. Victorian models were made of leaded glass panels, but modern replicas are available in plastic.

• **floating cloche** The hoops deployed for continuous plastic tunnels can be used to support fleece over plants to give them temporary protection from light frost as well as from various winged insect pests.

• **improvised cloches** Many kinds of individual cloche made from waxed paper or bottomless clear plastic bottles are used for protecting single plants.

using cloches in strip cropping

This is the most efficient method of using cloches. Plan the crops you wish to grow, so that their starting times are staggered. Set the cloches over the first row until they are no longer needed, then move them to cover new sowings or plantings in the adjacent row. Continue in this way across the plot, or move the cloches back to the first row to cover the next crop. Here is an example of how cloches might be used throughout the year in a kitchen garden.

OCTOBER–APRIL

• cover autumn-sown lettuces, intercropped with peas, in row 1.

APRIL–JUNE

• as lettuces and peas mature, move cloches to cover transplanted bush tomatoes in row 2.

JUNE–SEPTEMBER

• transfer cloches back to row 1, now replanted with melons, and keep plants covered until harvest.

SEPTEMBER–OCTOBER

• move cloches to row 2, to ripen late tomato fruits.

managing cloches

Covering and warming seeds and plants promotes more rapid growth and intensive production, so cultivate the ground well, increase fertility, and rake the surface level and free from stones so that the base of the cloche makes good contact with the ground. This also helps to reduce the risk of breaking glass cloches.

• **most cloches are open-ended** so that they can be joined together to cover a row of plants. If then left open, however, they will become wind tunnels, defeating the object of using them and often injuring plants. Close rigid cloches with end panels of glass or plastic held in place with bricks or other means. Tie the loose ends of polythene tunnels to stakes or bury them securely in the ground.

• **warm the soil** by setting cloches in place two weeks before sowing or planting (see right).

• **check underneath regularly** during the growing season to see what is happening. The soil dries out faster, the weeds grow rapidly, and pests and diseases may not be visible from outside, especially through plastic cloches.

• **when watering is necessary,** it can often be done lightly and steadily over the top of narrow cloches, allowing the water to run down and soak the edges, where it will be accessible to the plant roots. Wider cloches will need to be moved or opened before watering the plants, or you could run a seep hose down the centre.

• **keep the cloches clean,** and shade them in a hot bright spring or autumn by covering them with fleece, fine netting or old sheets.

• **ventilate in warm weather** by lifting the side of polythene tunnels, especially if plants such as strawberries need pollinating. With rigid cloches, remove one and move the others slightly to make gaps in between, or lift up one side onto small stones.

CLOCHES TIP When hoeing, thinning or weeding under a row of cloches, remove the first two and take them to the far end of the row. You can then move a pair at a time along the row as you cultivate in stages.

warming the soil

Setting out cloches a week or two before sowing or planting warms the soil and ensures rapid germination and establishment. The same principle can be used in a cold or wet spring, to dry and warm the ground before preparing a seedbed, and also to keep it in good condition afterwards until sowing is possible. In early winter, cover root crops like parsnips and swedes before a hard frost so you can lift supplies when the rest of the ground is frozen.

making a coldframe

A coldframe is a low four-sided structure, with a glazed sloping lid, or 'light', that sheds water. If you do not have room for a greenhouse, fit in at least one frame to extend the scope of your gardening in every season.

making a coldframe

YOU WILL NEED

• saw • 2.4 x 1.2m (8 x 4ft) sheet 1cm (½in) thick treated exterior plywood • pencil • measuring tape • straight edge • 21m (70ft) of 5 x 2cm (2 x ¾in) treated battening • waterproof wood glue • hammer • 4cm (1½in) galvanised nails • drill • screwdriver • 6cm (2½in) countersunk screws • 4 x 5cm (2in) angle brackets and screws • paintbrush • microporous wood stain (white) • 1 pair 10cm (4in) brass butt hinges and screws • 1.2 x 1.25m (48 x 50in) rigid plastic panel, or about 1.5m² (5sq ft) polythene sheeting • weatherproof adhesive tape or staple gun • wood preservative or exterior wood stain

1 **Saw the plywood** sheet lengthways in two. On one half mark out the two sides, each 1.2m (4ft) long, 50cm (20in) high at the back and 38cm (15in) at the front. On the other half, mark out the back, 1.2m (4ft) by 50cm (20in), and the front, 1.2m (4ft) by 38cm (15in). Cut out all four panels.

2 **Frame the inside** of each panel by cutting, glueing and nailing four battens around the perimeter.

3 **Join the front panel** to the sides. Drill five equally spaced holes 2–3cm (1in) in from the edges, and screw it in place. Repeat for the back panel. Measure both diagonals to check that the frame is square; they should be equal.

4 **Cut and assemble** four lengths of battening on edge for the lid frame. Butt-join them with glue and screws, then reinforce the joints with angle brackets screwed inside at each corner.

5 **Paint the inside** of the frame with white wood stain to improve light levels.

6 **Strengthen the lid** with a central batten from front to back, fixed by glue and screwed in place. Cut four battens as glazing bars and space these equidistant from one another, two in each half of the lid. Glue and screw in position.

7 **Screw the lid** to the back edge of the frame using the brass hinges.

8 **Glaze the lid with clear rigid plastic panels**, drilled and screwed onto the top of the lid, and seal their edges with weatherproof tape. Alternatively, use a sheet of thick polythene stretched over the lid and stapled in place underneath.

9 **Treat the outside of the frame** with wood preservative or paint with exterior wood stain, but leave for a few days before using it for plants. Make a notched pole to act as a lid stay.

using coldframes

Frames can have solid walls of wood, metal or brick for good insulation, or glazed walls in a galvanised aluminium or steel framework to admit most light. For access and ventilation, the opening lid can be hinged and held open with a slotted pole or casement stay; some types also have sliding side panels.

Frames can stand on a solid surface of concrete, bricks or paving slabs, which is useful for pots and trays. Alternatively, they can have a base of sand, gravel or ashes laid over a weed-proof membrane to create a firm surface; this can double as a plunge bed for pots of bulbs, alpines and houseplants during their summer break outdoors, to keep roots cool as well as reduce watering. If the bed is made of good, coarsely sifted soil, used potting compost or the contents of old growing bags, you can use a coldframe for sowing or rooting cuttings.

siting a coldframe

Brick and timber coldframes are, by their nature, permanent fixtures and should be sited in a sheltered position, away from prevailing winds and overhanging trees, protected by a wall, fence or windbreak. Face the slope south or south-west to catch as much winter sunlight as possible; a second frame in a lightly shaded position can prove valuable in summer to avoid scorching delicate plants.

A small, light frame can be moved round the garden as needed. In spring, when plants are constantly being moved indoors and out to acclimatise, a site near the greenhouse is practical. Later you can stand it in the open garden, over early sowings for example, like a large cloche. In winter, move the frame nearer to the house to protect pots of herbs and salads, handy for the kitchen.

heating frames

This is worth considering if you raise a lot of cuttings that benefit from bottom heat, or if you intend growing plants during winter and very early spring. Traditional coldframes were built of brick and set against the side of a greenhouse, with openings in the back to admit warmth from it. A modern option is to install a soil-heating cable in a sand foundation inside the frame, coupled with a watertight connection to the mains electricity supply in the house or greenhouse. To provide temporary heat without electricity you can use a small paraffin heater.

A small paraffin heater heats a coldframe.

managing a coldframe

- **ventilate whenever possible,** to avoid a build-up of damp, stagnant air.
- **keep the lights, or lid, clean,** but treat with greenhouse shading paint if you are growing tender plants in summer.
- **make sure the frame will be tall enough** for the plants. Raise it up on bricks, or dig out some of the soil inside.
- **in a cold winter,** insulate frames inside with polystyrene, and cover with sacking or bubble plastic overnight.
- **move a soil-based frame** to a new location every few years as the soil inside becomes exhausted.
- **after sowing, keep the frames closed** until germination occurs, then ventilate whenever the weather allows.

winter index

Page numbers in *italic* refer to the illustrations and captions.

acknowledgments

Photographs were supplied by the following people and organisations. Where relevant, the number of a picture as it appears on the page is given. Abbreviations are used as follows: **t** top, **c** centre, **b** bottom, **l** left, **r** right. CB Chris Burrows, JB Jonathan Buckley, LB Lynne Brotchie, MB Mark Bolton, NB Nicola Browne, HSC Harry Smith Collection, EC Eric Crichton, SC Sarah Cuttle, JD Jacqui Dracup, RD Reader's Digest, VF Vaughan Fleming, GPL Garden Picture Library, JG John Glover, JH Jerry Harpur, MH Marcus Harpur, NH Neil Holmes, SH Sunniva Harte, AL Andrew Lawson, ML Michelle Lamontagne, MM Marianne Majerus, S&OM S & O Mathews, CN Clive Nichols, MLS Mayer Le Scanff, MN Mike Newton, JP Jerry Pavia, HR Howard Rice, JS J Sira, RS Ron Sutherland, SSP Sea Spring Photos, BT Brigitte Thomas, MT Maddie Thornhill, JW Jo Whitworth, MW Mark Winwood,

Front cover GPL/JG **Back cover tl** MW, **tcl** JW, **tcr** SC, **tr** GPL/CB, **bl** RD, **br** RD **1** MB **2-3** S&OM **4-5** SC **8-9** GPL/HR **10 tl** GPL/JS, **r** GPL/MLS, **bl** JB (Design: H Yemm) **11 t** MH, **c & bl** AL, **br** JH **12 t** GPL/CN, **b** JH (Lord Carrington, Manor House, Bledlow) **13 tl** MB (S White), **tr** GPL/HR (J Drake), **c** GPL/S Wooster, **br** JB (Upper Mill Cottage, Kent), **bl** S&OM **14 tl** GPL/Z McCalmont, **tr** GPL/R Hyam, **br** CN (Wollerton Old Hall Shropshire), **bl** GPL/CN (Design: A Noel) **15 tl** JH (Park Farm, Essex), **tr** GPL/MB, **b** JH (Design: B Daly & A Chapman) **16 tl** GPL/HR, **tr** GPL/NH, **br** GPL/HR, **bl** NB **17 tl** GPL/HR, **tr** GPL/M Heuff, **br** GPL/NH, **bl** GPL/R Evans **18 l** GPL/K Charlton, **tr** GPL/R Estall, **br** S&OM **19 tl** MB (S White), **tr** AL, **b** GPL/M O'Hara **20 tl** GPL/HR, **tc** GPL/G Strong, **tr** MH, **br** JH (S Borun, California, USA), **bl** GPL/JG **21 tl** GPL/J Wade, **c** GPL/JG, **r** GPL/LB, **br** GPL/J Bouchier, **bl** JH (Design: G Pickard) **22 l** GPL/R Hyam (Old Rectory, Burghfield), **tr** JB (Upper Mill Cottage, Kent), **b** S&OM **23 tl** GPL/HR (Cambridge Botanic Gardens), **tr** GPL/BT, **br** GPL/HR, **bl** S&OM **24-5** SC **26 l** S&OM, **c & r** MW **27** MW **28 l** MW, **r** MT **29** MW **30-31** SC **32 l** SC, **r** GPL/HR **33 t** MW, **b** SC **34 l** GPL/JG, **r** MW **35** MW **36** MW **37** MW except **tl** SC **38** MW **39** MW except **tl** HSC **40** MW **41** MW except **br** GPL/M O'Hara **42** RD **43 t** SC, **b** MW **44** SC except **tr** GPL/BT **45** MW **46** MW **47** MW except **ct & tr** SC **48 t** CN, **b** SC **49** MW except **t** MB **50** MW **50-51** S&OM **51** SC except **br** MW **52** MW except **bl** GPL/JG **53** JH (Design: K Akers, Essex) **54 l** CN (Design: L Hampden), **r** MW **55** SC except **t** GPL/LB **56** GPL/HR **57** MW except **tl** GPL/HR **58 l** S&OM, **r** MW **59** MW **60 t** MT, **b** S&OM **61** MW **62 l** GPL/J Wade, **c** MW, **br** SC **63 tl** MW, **tr** MT, **b** MN **64 l** MW, **tr** MT, **b** SC **65** MW except **tr** GPL/C Boursnell **66** SC **67** MW **68** MW **69 t** GPL/MLS, **b** SC **70 tl & bl** MW, **r** SC **71** MW except **bl** SC **72-73** JW **74-75 (1, 2, 7, 8, 9)** RD, **(3)** GPL/NH, **(4, 6, 11)** JW, **(5)** GPL/JP, **(10)** GPL/MB, **(12)** S&OM **76 (1)** Courtesy of Thompson & Morgan, **(2, 3, 4, 5)** HSC **77 (1, 4)** GPL/NH, **(2)** RD, **(3)** S&OM, **(5)** GPL/JG, **(6)** GPL/CB **78-79 (1)** GPL/JS, **(2, 4)** HSC, **(3)** GPL/SH, **(5, 8, 9, 11, 12)** RD, **(6)** PH, **(7)** GPL/JG, **(10)** SC **80 (1)** GPL/CB, **(2, 6)** MB, **(3, 4, 5, 8)** RD, **(7)** GPL/JG **81 (1, 2)** GPL/JS, **(3)** HSC, **(4)** GPL/BT, **(5)** GPL/P Bonduell, **(6)** RD **82-83 (1, 4, 7, 11)** RD, **(2, 3, 12)** HSC, **(5)** GPL/JG, **(6)** GPL/D Willery, **(8, 9)** MW, **(10)** JW **84-85 (1)** MB, **(2)** HSC, **(3)** GPL/VF, **(4, 12)** S&OM, **(5)** GPL/NH, **(6, 7, 9, 11)** JW, **(8)** GPL/C Fairweather **86-87 (1)** RD, **(2, 3, 4, 8)** JW, **(5, 6)** HSC, **(7, 9)** GPL/HR, **(10)** J Willsmore, **(11)** GPL/BC, **(12)** SC **88-89 (1)** HSC, **(2)** GPL/JG, **(3, 7, 11)** RD, **(4)** GPL/ML, **(5)** GPL/VF, **(6)** JW, **(8)** S&OM, **(9)** CN, **(10)** GPL/CN **90-91 (1, 9, 10, 11)** RD, **(2, 4, 5)** JW, **(6)** JD, **(7)** CN, **(8)** S&OM **92-93 (1, 2, 6, 7, 9)** RD, **(3, 10)** JW, **(4)** SC, **(5)** S&OM, **(8)** GPL/JG, **(11)** HSC **94-95 (1)** S&OM, **(2, 3, 4, 5, 6, 7, 8, 9)** RD, **(10)** MB, **(11, 12)** GPL/JS **96-97 (1, 8)** GPL/HR, **(2)** GPL/CN, **(3, 7, 12)** HSC, **(4, 6, 9, 10, 11)** RD, **(5)** GPL/JS **98-99 (1)** GPL/Joanne Pavia, **(2, 4, 8, 9, 11)** RD, **(3, 6, 12)** HSC, **(5)** MB, **(7)** S&OM, **(10)** GPL/JS **100 (1)** J Willsmore, **(2)** GPL/SH, **(3)** RD, **(4)** JW, **(5, 7, 8)** RD, **(6)** GPL/NH **101 (1)** GPL/NH, **(2)** S&OM **(3)** RD, **(4, 6, 7)** JW, **(5)** GPL/JG **102-103 (1, 2, 6, 11)** HSC, **(3)** GPL/SH, **(4, 7, 8, 10, 12)** RD, **(5)** GPL/ML, **(9)** GPL/JG **104-105** MT except **(8, 10)** MN **106-107 (1)** GPL/SH, **(2, 8)** MN, **(3, 4, 6, 9, 11)** MT, **(5, 10)** SSP, **(7)** GPL/P Bonduell **108-109 (1, 8, 9, 12)** RD, **(2)** GPl/JS, **(3, 10)** GPL/HR, **(4, 6)** GPL/BC, **(5)** GPL/JG, **(7, 11)** HSC **110-111 (1)** GPL/ML, **(2)** GPL/JS, **(3, 10, 11)** HSC, **(4)** GPL/HR, **(5)** GPL/LB, **(6, 7, 9, 12)** RD, **(8)** GPL/SH **112-113 (1)** GPL/SH, **(2, 6, 8, 10, 11)** RD, **(3)** SC, **(4, 5)** HSC, **(7)** GPL/C Carter, **(9)** GPL/B Carter, **(12)** AL **114 l** GPL/JG, **r** JW **115** JW **116 l** RD, **r** GPL/JS **117 l** RD, **c** GPL/CB, **r** SC **118-119** SC **120** AL **121** JH (M Duchem, London) **126 l** CH, **r** AL **128-129** CN (Osler Road, Oxford) **129 t** AL, **br** GPL/JP, **c** GPL/J Sorrell **130 l** MB, **c** GPL/MB, **r** JB (Design: H Yemm; Ketley's, East Sussex) **131** MW **132** AL (Design: P Hobhouse) **132-133** GPL/M Heuff (Priona Gardens, Holland) **133 tr** GPL/HR, **c** SC,**br** GPL/ML **134** GPL/R Estall **135 t** GPL/HR, **br** JH (Malley Terry), **bl** AL **136** GPL/J Wade **137 (1, 3, 4, 5)** SC, **(2)** D Murphy, **(6, 7, 8)** MW **138 tl & r** SC, **bl** GPL/JG **139** SC **140** GPL/CN (Chenies Manor Garden, Bucks) **141** SC **142** S&OM **143 t** GPL/M Howes, **b** SC **144 t** SC, **br** MT, **bl** MN **145** GPL/MB **146 r** GPL/M Howes **146 l** MT **147** GPL/C Carter **148-149** GPL/M Howes **149 t** GPL/B Carter, **b** GPL/MB **150 t** GPL/M Howes, **br & c** GPL/HR, **bl** GPL/G Dann **152** SC **153** SC except **r** MW

Illustrations on pages 122-3, 124-5 and 127 by Ian Sidaway.

Front cover: Frosted berries on *Cotoneaster*. **Back cover**, clockwise from top left: raising the crown of a tree; *Viburnum bodnantense* 'Dawn'; planting young vegetables in a deep bed; *Crocus laevigatus* 'Fontenayi'; *Jasminum nudiflorum*; *Galanthus* 'S. Arnott'

Amazon Publishing would like to thank Adrian Hall Garden Centres, and Eden Greenhouses for supplying the greenhouse on page 137.
Thanks also to the following individuals who allowed us to use their gardens for photography: Andi and Meg Clevely, Alison Shackleton.
We are grateful to David Murphy for help with the projects.

Winter is part of a series of gardening books called the **All-Season Guide to Gardening**. It was created for Reader's Digest by Amazon Publishing Limited.

Series Editor Carole McGlynn
Art Director Ruth Prentice
Editors Barbara Haynes, Jackie Matthews, Alison Freegard; also Norma MacMillan
Design Jo Grey, Mary Staples
Photographic art direction Ruth Prentice
Special photography Sarah Cuttle, Mark Winwood
Writers Steve Bradley, Andi Clevely, Sue Fisher, David Joyce, Mike Lawrence, Anne Swithinbank
Picture research Clare Limpus, Mel Watson, Sarah Wilson
Consultants Jonathan Edwards, Mike Lawrence
DTP Felix Gannon
Editorial Assistant Elizabeth Woodland

FOR READER'S DIGEST GENERAL BOOKS
Project Editor Christine Noble
Pre-press Accounts Manager Penny Grose
Editorial Director Julian Browne
Art Director Nick Clark
Product Production Manager Claudette Bramble
Production Controller Katherine Bunn

We are committed to both the quality of our products and the service we provide to our customers. We value your comments, so please feel free to contact us on **08705 113366**, or via our website at **www.readersdigest.co.uk**
If you have any comments about the content of our books, you can email us at **gbeditorial@readersdigest.co.uk**

Origination Colour Systems Limited, London
Printed and bound in Europe by Arvato Iberia

ISBN 0 276 42712 2
BOOK CODE 621-005-04
CONCEPT CODE UK0087